D1196339

Byzantine Theology

BYZANTINE THEOLOGY

Historical Trends and Doctrinal Themes

JOHN MEYENDORFF

Fordham University Press
New York

Printed in the United States of America

Contents

PREFACE TO THE SECOND EDITION

The publication of a new edition of this book has given the author an opportunity to correct minor inaccuracies and to add several bibliographical references. It is clear, however, that in a field which is constantly being enriched with new publications, a general survey like this one cannot be fully comprehensive, even if the author feels himself greatly indebted to the findings of many of his colleagues, whose names do not appear in the Bibliography.

The largely positive response which met *Byzantine Theology* seems to indicate that the attempt at combining the historical and the systematic methods of approach to the subject was basically justified. There was, however, a risk of misunderstanding the use of any adjective in the title, and particularly the adjective "Byzantine," to define "theology." The adjective appears today in a variety of different contexts, and the limit of what is properly "Byzantine" is difficult to determine. On the other hand, the Byzantine theologians themselves did not conceive of their own religious tradition as being culturally or doctrinally limited. They used Scripture and the early Christian Fathers as a constant reference, and, at the same time, claimed to be the spokesmen of true Christian doctrine, as distinct from the non-Chalcedonian East and the Latin West. Furthermore, the modern Orthodox Church identifies herself, in a very particular way, with that "Byzantine" tradition (without excluding the potentiality of other expressions or developments of the same Christian truth), because she sees it as having been historically consistent with the Apostolic faith itself. Under such conditions, an historical survey—and, particularly, an attempt at a systematic account of Byzantine theology—could easily be interpreted either as confessionally biased or, on the contrary, as deliberately rejecting the claim of the Byzantines themselves and of modern Orthodox theology, in the name of historical objectivity.

The author can certainly understand the critics who, in expressing their views about the book, have reflected one or the other of these mutually exclusive interpretations. He is firmly convinced that it is both possible and necessary to study Byzantium and Byzantine theology, not only as carriers of religious orthodoxy, but also as historical phenomena of mixed cultural content. Theological orthodoxy itself cannot be fully defined and conceptually expressed without careful and critical historical research, which serves to overthrow idols and to avoid misconceptions. On the other hand, this same research, if it is really objective, shows the existence of a remarkable and theologically consistent tradition, which includes the Greek Fathers of the fourth century, the christology of Cyril of Alexandria, and the synthesis of Maximus the Confessor and of Gregory Palamas. In the author's opinion, this consistent tradition represents the *mainstream* of theological thought in Byzantium and coincides with the very content of Orthodox religious experience.

I fully realize that the existence of the "mainstream" is challenged by some historians. Some would claim, for example, that the group of anti-Palamite theologians of the fourteenth century were, in fact, the true representatives of the earlier patristic thought, which was being betrayed by Palamas. The debate on this point was started earlier in this century by Martin Jugie and was recently resumed by several authors, including particularly Gerhard Podskalsky. The issue has a number of historical, philosophical, and, certainly, confessional implications; it must be pursued further.

The debate itself shows that Byzantine theology involved crucial issues of Christian thinking and experience, which continue to be at the center of theological thinking today. Thus, a purely historical approach inevitably leads to a debate on substance.

The author would like to repeat here his acknowledgments from the original edition of this work. He is particularly indebted to the late Edwin A. Quain, s.j., formerly Editorial Associate of Fordham University Press, who was not sparing of his time, energy, and extraordinary competence in improving the text, and also to the Rev. Walter J. Burghardt, s.j., Editor of *Theological Studies*, for reading the manuscript and making several useful suggestions. He also owes thanks to Professor Jaroslav Pelikan, Dean of the Graduate School, Yale University, for allowing him pre-publication access to and use of his monumental *The Christian Tradition*.

J. M.

The Character and the Sources of Theology in Byzantium

> Centuries of struggle and super-human effort will be required to go beyond Hellenism, by liberating it from its natural attachments and its ethnic and cultural limitations, before it will finally become a universal form of Christian truth.
>
> VLADIMIR LOSSKY,
> *Vision of God,* 58.

> Ancient culture proved to be plastic enough to admit of an inner "transfiguration." . . . Christians proved that it was possible to re-orient the cultural process, without lapsing into a pre-cultural state, to reshape the cultural fabric in a new spirit. The same process which has been variously described as a "Hellenization of Christianity" can be construed rather as a "Christianization of Hellenism."
>
> GEORGES FLOROVSKY,
> "Faith and Culture," *St. Vladimir's Quarterly,* 4, 1–2 [1955–1956], 40.

EMPEROR CONSTANTINE (324–337) ended the period of confrontation between Christianity and the Roman Empire. He also abandoned the ancient capital, and moved the center of political and cultural life of what was then seen as the "civilized world" to the site of an ancient Greek city on the rivers of the Bosporus—Byzantium. It was officially called Constantinople, the "New Rome," and remained the capital of an Empire still called "Roman" for over eleven centuries, until its fall to the Turks in 1453.

Especially after the disappearance of the ancient Christian centers in Egypt, Palestine, and Syria, Constantinople became the unquestionable center of Eastern Christianity. Its bishop assumed the title of "ecumenical patriarch." In the Balkans, in the great Eastern European plain, in the Caucasus, its missionaries converted immense territories to the Christian faith. In fact, the "New Rome" became the cradle of civilization for the Middle East and Eastern Europe, just as the "old Rome" has been for the Latin West.

The aim of this book is to describe the categories of theological thought as they were shaped in the framework of Byzantine Christian civilization, its philosophy of life, its liturgy, and its art, and as they persist in contemporary Eastern Orthodoxy. The central theme, or intuition, of Byzantine theology is that man's nature is not a static, "closed," autonomous entity, but a dynamic reality, determined in its very existence by its relationship to God. This relationship is seen as a process of ascent and as communion —man, created in the image of God, is called to achieve freely a "divine similitude"; his relationship to God is both a givenness and a task, an immediate experience and an expectation of even greater vision to be accomplished in a free effort of love. The dynamism of Byzantine anthropology can easily be contrasted with the static categories of "nature" and "grace" which dominated the thought of post-Augustinian Western Christianity; it can prove itself to be an essential frame of reference in the contemporary theological search for a new understanding of man.

As a culture and civilization, Byzantium died long ago; yet the quality of its impact on the historical development of human society is still open to question. Since the time of Gibbon, historians have cited social immobilism, lack of creativity in the fields of science and technology, and a sacralized view of the state as its major defects. But it is the contention of this book that Byzantium made its real and *permanent* contribution to the history of mankind in the field of religious thought. The continuous attraction of Byzantine art and the remarkable survival of Eastern Christianity throughout the most dramatic of social changes are the best available signs that Byzantium did indeed discover something fundamentally *true* about man's nature and its relationship to God.

To express this "theocentric" view of man—so akin to the contemporary attempts to build a "theocentric anthropology"—Byzantine theologians used the concepts of Greek philosophy, particularly the notion of *theōsis,* or "deification." In the last century, Adolf Harnack passed severe judgments on the "Hellenized Christianity" of the Greek Fathers, but he is unlikely to be followed by many today. The unavoidable necessity of reformulating and rethinking the Christian faith in the light of changing cultural patterns is widely recognized, and the effort of the Greek Fathers to formulate Christianity in the categories of Hellenism can only be viewed as legitimate. Actually, Byzantine theology, as Lossky realized, was nothing but a continuous effort and struggle to express the tradition of the Church in the living categories of Greek thought, so that Hellenism might be converted to Christ.

It is legitimate to ask whether this effort was successful, but it is impossible to deny that it was justified in its basic intent. This book attempts to describe the major historical trends of Byzantine theology, always relating them to its main theme, and, in a second part, to show, in a more systematic form, that the results of Byzantine theological thought can also be envisaged as a synthesis. It is not our intention simply to describe the idea of "deification" and its development in Greek patristic thought (numerous technical studies are available on that subject), but to analyze the entire historical development of theological ideas in Byzantium concerning God–man relationships. Whether one deals with Trinitarian or Christological dogma, or whether one examines ecclesiology and sacramental doctrine, the main stream of Byzantine theology uncovers the same vision of man, called to "know" God, to "participate" in His life, to be "saved," not simply through an extrinsic action of God's, or through the rational cognition of propositional truths, but by "becoming God." And this *theōsis* of man is radically different in Byzantine theology from the Neoplatonic return to an impersonal One: it is a new expression of the neo-testamental life "in Christ" and in the "communion of the Holy Spirit."

1. CHRONOLOGICAL LIMITS

There are decisive reasons for viewing as specifically Byzantine the period which followed the Council of Chalcedon (451) and the barbarian invasion of Italy. The council resulted in the Monophysite schism, which severed Constantinople from Alexandria and Antioch (the ancient Eastern centers of theological creativity) and from the entire non-Greek East. Latins and Greeks, meanwhile, although they still belonged to the same Catholic imperial Church, began to develop an increasing sense of estrangement from one another, as divergent trends in Christology, ecclesiology, and pneumatology appear very clearly in the context of the unparalleled cultural and intellectual superiority of Constantinople.

Historical circumstances thus placed Byzantium in an exclusive, preeminent, and, to some degree, self-sufficient, position, from which it was to develop a theological tradition, both synthetic and creative.

For several centuries, Byzantium would be vitally concerned with pulling together the parts of a disintegrating Christian world: by maintaining its Christological commitment to the Council of Chalcedon and to the Tome of Leo, it would keep bridges toward the West intact, in spite of all the tensions; and by remaining rigidly faithful to the Alexandrian Christology of Athanasius and Cyril, it would also try—unfortunately without success —to keep all doors open to the Monophysites.

These Christological commitments and debates imply a concept of the relationship between God and man, a theology of "participation" which would, through the creative synthesis of Maximus the Confessor, serve as a framework for the entire development of Byzantine Christian thought until the fall of Constantinople to the Turks. Thus, between the patristic age and later-Byzantine theology, there exists an essential continuity—as the present study will attempt to show—spanning almost exactly a millennium of Christian history in the East, from the Council of Chalcedon to the fall of Constantinople.

This continuity does not express itself, however, in any formal authority or pattern which would have been acceptable during that entire period. It lies rather in a consistent theological way of thought, in a consistent understanding of man's destiny in relation to God and to the world. "God became man," Athanasius writes, "so that man may become God." This fundamental statement of Alexandrian theology, which was to dominate the entire theological discussion about "deification," prompted many problems. Pantheism, escapism from history, and Platonizing spiritualism are the obvious dangers, and, though orthodox Chalcedonian theology generally remains aware of them, it implies the positive concept of man as a being called to overcome constantly his own created limitations. Man's real nature is considered not as "autonomous" but as destined to share divine life which had been made accessible in Christ. In this concept, man's role in the created world can be fulfilled only if he keeps intact the "image" of God which was part of his very humanity from the beginning.

From the Christological controversies of the fifth century to the debates on the "essence" and "energy" of God in the fourteenth, all the major crises of Byzantine theological thought can be reduced to one or the other aspect of this basic Christian issue. Authors as different as Leontius of Jerusalem and Gregory Palamas, Maximus the Confessor and Symeon the New Theologian, Photius and Nicholas Cabasilas, can here be found in basic agreement. It is this consensus which distinguishes Byzantine theology, taken as a whole, from the post-Augustinian and Scholastic West, and makes possible the attempt, which we undertake in the second part of our study, at a systematic presentation of Byzantine Christian thought.

2. A LIVING TRADITION

This presentation is rendered difficult, however, by the very character of Byzantine church life, as it is reflected in the theological literature. In the Byzantine period, as in the patristic, neither the councils nor the theologians show particular interest in positive theological systems. With a few exceptions, such as the Chalcedonian definition, the conciliar statements themselves assume a negative form; they condemn distortions of the Christian Truth, rather than elaborate its positive content—which is taken for granted as the living Tradition and as a wholesome Truth standing beyond and above doctrinal formulae. By far the greatest part of the theological literature is either exegetical or polemical, and in both cases the Christian faith is assumed as a given reality, upon which one comments, or which one defends, but which one does not try to formulate exhaustively. Even John of Damascus, sometimes referred to as the "Aquinas of the East" because he composed a systematic *Exposition of the Orthodox Faith* (*De fide orthodoxa*), produced only a short textbook, not a theological system;

if his thought lacks anything, it is precisely that original philosophic creativity which a new system would presuppose.

The lack of concern for systematization, however, does not mean a lack of interest in the true content of the faith or an inability to produce exact theological definitions. On the contrary. No civilization has ever lived through more discussions on the adequacy, or inadequacy, of words reflecting religious truths. The *homoousion* as distinct from the *homoiousion,* "of two natures" or "in two natures"; two wills or one will; *latreia* of icons or *proskynesis* of images; the created or uncreated character of the divine "energies"; procession "from the Son" or "through the Son"—these were issues debated by Byzantine Christians for centuries. It would seem, then, that the Greek Christian spirit consisted precisely in optimistically believing that human language is fundamentally adequate to express religious truth and that salvation depends upon the exact expression used to convey the meaning of the Gospel. Yet these same Greek Christians firmly confessed the incapacity of conceptual language to express the *whole* truth, and the incapability of the human mind to attain the essence of God. There was in Byzantium, therefore, an antinomy in the very approach to theology: God has really revealed Himself in Christ Jesus, and the knowledge of His Truth is essential to salvation, but God is also above the human intellect and cannot be fully expressed in human words.

In Byzantium, theology was never a monopoly of professionals or of a "teaching church." During the entire Byzantine period, no church council went unchallenged, and attempts by several emperors to regulate their subjects' consciences by decree were checked not so much by a consistently independent hierarchy as by the tacit opposition of the entire body of the Church. This lack of a clearly and juridically defined criterion of orthodoxy implied that the responsibility for the truth was shared by all. The majority of the laity, of course, followed the most pre-eminent bishops, whose magisterial responsibility was never denied, or monastic leaders, who often played a central role in doctrinal disputes; but the simple faithful also knew how to decide for themselves, especially when the episcopate was divided. It is sufficient to recall here the witness of Gregory of Nazianzus, complaining about salesmen discussing the concept of "consubstantial" in the market place.

Yet imperial interventions in theological debates, which today appear as intolerable intrusions of the secular power into the sacred precincts of the Church, were considered quite normal at a time when the emperor was required by law to be "glorified in his divine zeal and versed in the doctrine of the Holy Trinity." [1] Though no one was ready to grant the emperor the privilege of infallibility, still no one objected to the principle of his expressing theological views which *de facto* acquired greater, and sometimes decisive, weight because they were pronounced by the *Autokrator.*

Caesaropapism, however, never became an accepted principle in Byzantium. Innumerable heroes of the faith were constantly exalted precisely because they had opposed heretical emperors; hymns sung in church praised Basil for having disobeyed Valens, Maximus for his martyrdom under Constans, and numerous monks for having opposed the iconoclastic emperors of the eighth century. These liturgical praises alone were sufficient to safeguard the principle that the emperor was to preserve, not to define, the Christian faith.

Throughout Byzantine history, it was actually the monks who were the real witnesses of the Church's internal independence. That the Byzantine Church was primarily monastic is reflected in the character of Greek theology. It is no wonder that emperors who endeavored to strengthen iconoclasm had first to sponsor an anti-monastic movement in the Church, for monasticism was, of necessity, hostile to the caesaropapistic system for which some emperors showed a predisposition.

Numbering thousands in Constantinople itself, in the major cities, and in practically every corner of the Byzantine world, the monks consistently opposed doctrinal compromises; they defended a rigorous orthodoxy, but at times they could also place their zeal at the service of Monophysitism or of Origenism. From the sixth century on, candidates for the episcopacy were chosen almost exclusively from the ranks of the monks; thus Byzantine spirituality and much of the Byzantine liturgy were shaped by monks. That Byzantine Christianity lacked what today would be called a "theology of the secular" is largely the result of the predominant position of monasticism. Yet this very predominance prevented the Christian Church from becoming totally identified with the empire, which constantly tended to sacralize itself and to assimilate the divine plan of salvation to its own temporal interests. The numerical, spiritual, and intellectual strength of Byzantine monasticism was the decisive factor which preserved in the Church the fundamental eschatological dimension of the Christian faith.

The last major preliminary observation to be made concerning the specific character of Byzantine theology is the importance of the liturgy in the Byzantine religious outlook. In Eastern Christendom, the Eucharistic liturgy, more than anything else, is identified with the reality of the Church itself, for it manifests both the humiliation of God in assuming mortal flesh, and the mysterious presence among men of the eschatological kingdom. It points at these central realities of the faith not through concepts but through symbols and signs intelligible to the entire worshipping congregation. This centrality of the Eucharist is actually the real key to the Byzantine understanding of the Church, both hierarchical and corporate; the Church is universal, but truly realized only in the local Eucharistic assembly, at which a group of sinful men and women becomes fully the "people of God." This Eucharist-centered concept of the Church led the Byzantines to embellish and adorn the sacrament with an elaborate and sometimes cumbersome ceremonial, and with an extremely rich hymnography, in daily, weekly, paschal, and yearly cycles. Besides the sacramental ecclesiology implied by the Eucharist itself, these hymnographical cycles constitute a real source of theology. For centuries the Byzantines not only heard theological lessons and wrote and read theological treatises; they also sang and contemplated daily the Christian mystery in a liturgy, whose wealth of expression cannot be found elsewhere in the Christian world. Even after the fall of Byzantium, when Eastern Christians were deprived of schools, books, and all intellectual leadership, the liturgy remained the chief teacher and guide of Orthodoxy. Translated into the various vernacular languages of the Byzantine world —Slavic, Georgian, Arabic, and dozens of others—the liturgy was also a powerful expression of unity in faith and sacramental life.

3. SCRIPTURE, EXEGESIS, CRITERIA

The Christian East took a longer time than the West in settling on an agreed canon of Scripture. The principal hesitations concerned the books of the Old Testament which are not contained in the Hebrew Canon ("shorter" canon) and the Book of Revelation in the New Testament. Fourth-century conciliar and patristic authorities in the East differ in their attitude concerning the exact authority of Wisdom, Ecclesiasticus, Esther, Judith, and Tobit. Athanasius in his famous *Paschal Letter* 39 excludes them from Scripture proper, but considers them useful for catechumens, an opinion which he shares with Cyril of Jerusalem. Canon 60 of the Council of Laodicea—whether authentic or not—also reflects the tradition of a "shorter" canon. But the Quinisext Council (692) endorses the authority of Apostolic Canon 85, which admits some books of the "longer" canon, including even 3 Maccabees, but omits Wisdom, Tobit, and Judith. John of Damascus († ca. 753), however, considers Wisdom and Ecclesiasticus as "admirable," yet fails to include them in the canon.[2] Therefore, in spite of the fact that Byzantine patristic and ecclesiastical tradition almost exclusively uses the Septuagint as the standard Biblical text, and that parts of the "longer" canon—especially Wisdom—are of frequent liturgical use, Byzantine theologians remain faithful to a "Hebrew" criterion for Old Testament literature, which excludes texts originally composed in Greek. Modern Orthodox theology is consistent with this unresolved polarity when it distinguishes between "canonical" and "deuterocanonical" literature of the Old Testament, applying the first term only to the books of the "shorter" canon.

Among the writings of the New Testament, the Book of Revelation was accepted into the canon only with reluctance. It is omitted from the canon in the lists of the Council of Laodicea (canon 60), in Apostolic Canon 85, and by Cyril of Jerusalem.[3] The commentators of the School of Antioch also ignore it, reflecting the view prevailing in the Church of Syria. In the

Byzantine liturgical rite, which was dependent upon Syria and Palestine, Revelation is the only book of the New Testament which is never used for liturgical reading. The position of the School of Alexandria, however, expressed in particular by Athanasius and followed, in the eighth century, by John of Damascus, was finally endorsed by the Byzantine Church. After the sixth century, no one expressed any doubt about the canonicity of Revelation.

The written form of the apostolic message was always understood by the Byzantines in the framework of "apostolic tradition"—the wider, living, and uninterrupted continuity of the apostolic Church. The famous sentence of Basil of Caesarea († 379) on Scripture and Tradition can be considered to reflect the consensus of later Byzantine theologians: "We do not content ourselves with what was reported in *Acts* and in the *Epistles* [the term *ho apostolos,* translated here as "Acts and Epistles," designates the liturgical book containing all the New Testament writings, except the four Gospels and Revelation] and in the Gospels; but, both before and after reading them, we add other doctrines, received from oral teaching, and carrying much weight in the mystery [of the faith]." [4] The "other doctrines" which Basil mentions are, essentially, the liturgical and sacramental traditions which, together with the more conceptual consensus found in the continuity of Greek patristic theology, always served in Byzantium as a living framework for the understanding of Scripture.

In exegetical methods as in their theory of knowledge, the Byzantines accepted the patristic criterion set in the fourth and fifth centuries. By harmonizing the fundamental ideas of the Cappadocian Fathers on the Trinity with the Christological thought of the fifth, sixth, and seventh centuries, John of Damascus could compose his *De fide orthodoxa,* which would serve as a theological textbook during the following period. Other, less imaginative authors composed even more simple florilegia of patristic quotations, or "panoplies" refuting all heresies. Much of Byzantine theological literature is of a strictly anthological nature. Still, a living theology also developed, especially in monastic circles.

In any attempt to review the major doctrinal themes of Byzantine theology, constant reference to the Fathers of the classical period is unavoidable, for they served as the major traditional authorities for the Byzantines. Yet in acknowledging that in the Church every Christian, and the saint in particular, possesses the privilege and opportunity of seeing and experiencing the truth, the same Byzantines presupposed a concept of Revelation which was substantially different from that held in the West. Because the concept of *theologia* in Byzantium, as with the Cappadocian Fathers, was inseparable from *theoria* ("contemplation"), theology could not be—as it was in the West—a rational deduction from "revealed" premises, i.e., from Scripture or from the statements of an ecclesiastical magisterium; rather, it was a vision experienced by the saints, whose authenticity was, of course, to be checked against the witness of Scripture and Tradition. Not that a rational deductive process was completely eliminated from theological thought; but it represented for the Byzantines the lowest and least reliable level of theology. The true theologian was the one who saw and experienced the content of his theology; and this experience was considered to belong not to the intellect alone (although the intellect was not excluded from its perception), but to the "eyes of the Spirit," which place the whole man—intellect, emotions, and even senses—in contact with divine existence. This was the initial content of the debate between Gregory Palamas and Barlaam the Calabrian, which started the theological controversies of the fourteenth century (1337–1340).

Revelation, therefore, was limited neither to the written documents of Scripture nor to conciliar definitions, but was directly accessible, as a living truth, to a human experience of God's presence in His Church. This possibility of an immediate contact with God has been seen by some historians of Eastern Christian thought as a form of Messalianism, a term which, since the fourth century, has designated an anti-hierarchical and anti-sacramental monastic sect repeatedly condemned by the councils. But the mainstream of Eastern Christian gnosiology, which indeed affirms the possibility of direct experience of God, is precisely founded upon a sacramental, and therefore hierarchically structured, ecclesiology, which gives a Christological and pneumatological basis to personal experience and presupposes that Christian theology must always be consistent with the apostolic and patristic witness.

This experiential character of revelation has a direct bearing on the notion of "development": Byzantine theologians generally took it for granted that new revelations could never be added to the unique witness of the apostles. Precisely because their understanding of the Truth was not conceptual, the theologians could not admit either that Truth was expressed by the New Testament writings in a verbally and conceptually exhaustive manner, or that the experience of the Fathers and of the saints could enrich the *content* of the apostolic faith. Nothing new could be learned about Christ and salvation beyond what the apostles "have heard, have seen with their eyes, have looked upon and touched with their hands, concerning the word of life" (1 Jn 1:1). The experience of the saints would be fundamentally identical with that of the apostles: the notions of "development" or "growth" could be applied only to the human appropriation of divine Truth, not to Truth itself, and, of course, to the conceptual elaboration of Church doctrine, or to the refutation of heresies.

In Jesus Christ, therefore, the fullness of Truth was revealed once and for all. To this revelation the apostolic message bears witness, through written word or oral tradition; but, in their God-given freedom, men can experience it to various degrees and in various forms. The world to which this witness is announced continually raises new challenges and new problems. The very complexity of the human being; the reluctance of the Byzantine Christian mind to reduce theology to one particular form of human appropriation—the intellectual; the character of the New Testament message, concerned not with abstract truths, but with a Person; the absence in the Byzantine Church of a permanent, infallible criterion of truth: all these elements contributed, in Byzantium, to an understanding of Christianity as a living experience, for whose integrity and authenticity the sacramental structure of the Church is certainly responsible, but whose living content is carried on, from generation to generation, by the entire community of the Church.

These same elements also determined that the evolution of theology in the Byzantine Church could only have been a slow and organic process, requiring a tacit agreement of the entire body of the hierarchy and the faithful. No significant changes of theology or of Church polity could ever be imposed by Church authority alone; and when such attempts were made, they resulted either in failure or in prolonged resistance—or even in schism.

Thus, the experiential nature of theology produced a theological conservatism (not a subjectivism, as one might expect if one misunderstands experience for individualistic mysticism) because the experience of the saints—and all Christians are called to be saints—was always understood as necessarily identical with that of the apostles and the Fathers. Actually, the unity of the Church in time and in space was conceived as experiential unity in the one Christ, to whom the apostles witnessed in the past and whom all generations will contemplate again when He comes in power on the last day.

But if there is no development in the *content* of the faith—i.e., in the person of Christ, always identical with Himself—but only in its formulations and in its relatedness to the changing world, what was the significance for the Byzantines of doctrinal definitions and conciliar statements? Their very text gives the answer: all the ecumenical councils, beginning with Ephesus (431)—the first whose minutes are preserved—emphasize explicitly that doctrinal definitions are not ends in themselves, and that the council fathers—reluctantly—proceed to define issues of doctrine only to exclude the wrong interpretations proposed by heretics. The most famous of the conciliar definitions, that of the Council of Chalcedon, is also most explicit in this regard. The conciliar decree begins with a solemn reaffirmation of the creeds of Nicaea and of Nicaea–Constantinople, and proceeds to declare, in reference to the latter:

This wise and salutary formula of divine grace *sufficed for the perfect knowledge and confirmation of religion*; for it teaches the perfect doctrine concerning Father, Son, and Holy Spirit, and sets forth the Incarnation of the Lord to those who faithfully receive it. But, *inasmuch as persons undertaking to nullify the preaching of the truth* have through their individual heresies given rise to empty babblings . . . this present holy, great, and ecumenical council, desiring to exclude every device against the Truth, and *teaching that which is unchanged from the beginning,* has at the very outset decreed that the faith of the 318 fathers [of Nicaea] shall be preserved inviolate.[5]

The definition on the two natures of Christ, which follows that preamble, is thus considered simply as a means to protect what had already been said at Nicaea. It actually starts again with the standard formula "Following the holy fathers. . . ." Identical formulae are used by all the Byzantine councils in the succeeding period.

The really important implication of this attitude concerns the very notion of Truth, which is conceived, by the Byzantines, not as a concept which can be expressed adequately in words or developed rationally, but as God Himself—personally present and met in the Church in His very personal identity. Not Scripture, not conciliar definitions, not theology can express Him fully; each can only point to some aspects of His existence, or exclude wrong interpretations of His being or acts. No human language, however, is *fully* adequate to Truth itself, nor can it exhaust it. Consequently, Scripture and the Church's magisterium cannot be considered as the only "sources" of theology. Orthodox theology cannot fail to check its consistency with them, of course, but the true theologian is free to express his own immediate encounter with the Truth. This is the authentic message maintained most explicitly by the Byzantine "mystical" tradition of Maximus the Confessor, Symeon the New Theologian, and Gregory Palamas.

4. THEOLOGY, POSITIVE AND NEGATIVE

The whole of Byzantine theology—and particularly its "experiential" character—would be completely misunderstood if one forgets its other pole of reference: apophatic, or negative, theology.

Usually associated with the name of the mysterious sixth-century author of the *Areopagitica,* the form of apophaticism which will dominate Byzantine thought is, in fact, already fully developed in the fourth century in the writings of the Cappadocian Fathers against Eunomios. Rejecting the Eunomian view that the human mind can reach the very essence of God, they affirm the absolute transcendence of God and exclude any possibility of identifying Him with any human concept. By saying what God *is not,* the theologian is really speaking the Truth, for no human word or thought is capable of comprehending what God *is*. The ascent of the human soul to God is thus described by Gregory of Nyssa as a process of elimination which, however, never truly reaches a positive end:

> [The soul] rises afresh and in the spirit passes through the intelligible and hypercosmic world . . . ; it passes through the assembly of celestial beings, looking to see if its Beloved is among them. In its quest it passes through the whole angelic world and when it does not find the One it seeks among the blessed ones it encounters, it says to itself: "Can any of these at least comprehend the One whom I love?" But they hold their tongues at this question, and by their silence make him realize that the One whom he seeks is inaccessible even to them. Then, having by the action of the Spirit passed through the whole of the hypercosmic city, having failed to recognize the One he desires among intelligible and incorporeal beings, and abandoning all that he finds, he recognizes the One he is seeking as the only One he does not comprehend.[6]

The process of elimination is, therefore, a necessary stage in the knowledge of God. It is an intellectual process, but also a spiritual purification (*katharsis*) which discards all forms of identifying God with that which is not God—i.e., all idolatry. But the paradox is that, by itself, the process does not allow man to know God, except as the Unknowable and Incomprehensible, even if the experience of this transcendence is itself a positive Christian experience. On this point, orthodox patristic tradition is clearly distinct from both the Gnostic and the Neoplatonic traditions, represented in Christianity by Clement of Alexandria and by Origen. Neoplatonic thought had affirmed the inaccessibility of God to the human mind, but viewed this inaccessibility as the result of the fallen character of the soul and, in particular, of its union with a material body. When the mind returns to its original and natural state—where God wants it to be—it is indeed united, according to Origen, with the divine essence itself: its ascent reaches a definite end in perfection, knowledge, and blessedness. But at this point Origen's God ceases to be the absolute Other, the God of Abraham, of Isaac, and of Jacob, and becomes the god of the philosophers. And for this reason Gregory of Nyssa, who otherwise tasted so much of the charms of Origenism, affirms that God is inaccessible even to celestial beings.

The Greek Fathers affirm in their apophatic theology, not only that God is above human language and reason because of man's fallen inadequacy, but that He is inaccessible *in Himself*. Human knowledge concerns only "beings," i.e., the level of created existence. On this level, therefore, it can be said that "God does not exist." For the pseudo-Dionysius, God is "non-being" (*mē on*). This is the theme of the famous Chapter 5 of Dionysius' *Mystical Theology*.[7] The Plotinian concepts of the "monad" which Origen had applied to God [8] are for pseudo-Dionysius quite irrelevant to a description of God's existence. God, he writes, is "neither the One, nor Unity." [9]

Byzantine theologians were fully aware of the fact that "negative" theology was known to Neoplatonic thought as an intellectual method of approaching the mystery of God, and that it did not necessarily imply that God was absolutely unknowable in Himself. Barlaam the Calabrian made the point clear when he wrote:

> If you want to know whether the Greeks understood that the superessential and anonymous Good transcends intelligence, science, and all other achievement, read the works of the Pythagoreans—Pantaenetos, Brotinos, Philolaos, Charmidas, and Philoxenos—which are devoted to that subject; there you will find the same expressions as the great Dionysius employs in his *Mystical Theology*. . . . Plato too understood divine transcendence.[10]

And Gregory Palamas in fact agrees with Barlaam when he recognizes that monotheism and the concept of God as a philosophical Absolute were accepted by the pagans, and that "apophatic theology necessarily follows from this."[11] But the formal, intellectual "apophatism" of the Greek philosophers differs from the Biblical notion of transcendence, for transcendence leads to a positive meeting with the Unknown, as the Living God, to a "contemplation greater than knowledge."[12] Christian theology is based on this notion.

A possibility of experiencing God through means other than intellectual knowledge, emotion, or the senses stands behind the Greek patristic understanding of the Christian faith and theology. This means simply an opening of God, His existence outside of His own nature, His actions or "energies" through which He *voluntarily* reveals Himself to man, as well as a peculiar property of man, which permits him to reach outside of the created level. The meeting of God's love and "energy" and of man's capability of transcending himself is what makes an encounter possible, a "contemplation greater than knowledge" to which the Fathers refer as the "eyes of faith," "the Spirit," or, eventually, "deification."

Theology, therefore, may and should be based on Scripture, on the doctrinal decisions of the Church's magisterium, or on the witness of the saints. But to be a true theology, it must be able to reach beyond the letter of Scripture, beyond the formulae used in definitions, beyond the language employed by the saints to communicate their experience. For only then will it be able to discern the unity of Revelation, a unity which is not simply an intellectual coherence and consistency, but a living reality experienced in the continuity of the one Church throughout the ages: the Holy Spirit is the only guarantor and guardian of this continuity; no external criterion which would be required for man's created perception or intellection would be sufficient.

Thus Byzantium never knew any conflict, not even a polarization between theology and what the West calls "mysticism." Indeed, the whole of

Eastern Christian theology has often been called "mystical." The term is truly correct, provided one remember that in Byzantium "mystical" knowledge does not imply emotional individualism, but quite the opposite: a continuous communion with the Spirit who dwells in the whole Church. It implies as well the constant recognition of the inadequacies of the human intellect and of human language to express the fullness of truth, and the constant balancing of positive theological affirmations about God with the corrective of apophatic theology. Finally, it presupposes an "I–Thou" relationship with God—i.e., not knowledge only, but love.

Commenting upon Ecclesiastes 3:7—"a time to keep silence, and a time to speak"—Gregory of Nyssa suggests to the theologian that

> In speaking of God, when there is question of His essence, then is *the time to keep silence*. When, however, it is a question of His operation, a knowledge of which can come down even to us, that is *the time to speak* of His omnipotence by telling of His works and explaining His deeds, and to use words to this extent. In matters which go beyond this, however, the creature must not exceed the bounds of its nature, but must be content to know itself. For, indeed, in my view, if the creature never comes to know itself, never understands the essence of the soul or the nature of the body, the cause of being . . . , if the creature does not know itself, how can it ever explain things which are beyond it? Of such things it is the *time to keep silence*; here silence is surely better. There is, however, a *time to speak* of those things by which we can in our lives make progress in virtue.[13]

The character and method of Byzantine theology are determined, therefore, by the problem of the relationship between God and the world, between creator and creation, and involve an anthropology, which finds its ultimate key in Christology. This unavoidable sequence will determine the subjects of the following chapters.

NOTES

1. *Epanagogē tou nomou*, 9th C., III, 8, ed. C. E. Zachariae von Lingenthal, in J. Zepos, P. Zepos, *Jus Graecoromanum, 2* (Athens, 1931), p. 242.

2. John of Damascus, *De fide orthodoxa*, IV, 17; PG 94:1180BC.

3. Cyril of Jerusalem, *Hom. cat.*, 4, 36; PG 33:500BC.

4. Basil of Caesarea, *On the Holy Spirit*, 27; ed. B. Pruche, *Sources Chrétiennes* 17 (Paris, 1945), p. 234.

5. Chalcedon, *Definitio fidei, Conciliorum oecumenicorum decreta* (Bologna: Istituto per le Scienze Religiose, 1973), p. 84.

6. Gregory of Nyssa, *In Cant. or. VI*; ed. W. Jaeger (Leiden: Brill, 1960), 6:182; PG 44:893B.

7. PG 3:1045D–1048B.

8. Origen, *De princ.*, I, 1, 6. Ed. B. Koetschau, GCS, 22.

9. Pseudo-Dionysius, *Mystical Theology*; PG 3:1048A.

10. Barlaam the Calabrian, *Second Letter to Palamas,* ed. G. Schiro, *Barlaam Calabro: epistole* (Palermo, 1954), pp. 298–299.

11. Gregory Palamas, *Triads,* II, 3, 67; ed. J. Meyendorff (Louvain: Spicilegium Sacrum Lovaniense, 1959), p. 527.

12. *Ibid.,* 53; p. 493.

13. Gregory of Nyssa, *Commentary on Ec.,* sermon 7; PG 44:732D; ed. W. Jaeger (Leiden: Brill, 1962) 5:415–416; trans. H. Musurillo in *From Glory to Glory: Texts from Gregory of Nyssa's Mystical Writings* (New York: Scribner, 1961), p. 129.

I

Historical
Trends

1

Byzantine Theology After Chalcedon

CONSTANTINOPLE, the great cultural melting pot, the "New Rome" and capital of the empire, did not produce any really outstanding theologian in the fifth and sixth centuries; but the city witnessed the great theological debates of the day, since their conclusion often depended upon imperial sanction. Bishops, monks, exegetes, and philosophers, coming to the capital to seek favor and support, created around the episcopal see of the imperial city—from which the government's theological advisers were usually drawn—a convergence of ideas and a predisposition to syncretic, compromise solutions. The bishops of Constantinople and their staffs, however, were still able to defend explicit theological convictions, even against the imperial will, as the lonely pro-Chalcedonian stand adopted by the patriarchs Euphemius (489–495) and Macedonius II (495–511), under the reign of the Monophysite emperor Anastasius, bears witness. Thus, a theology which can be termed specifically "Byzantine," in contrast to the earlier currents of Eastern Christian thought centered mainly in Egypt and Syria, comes into being during the post-Chalcedonian period. It would receive official sanction under Justinian (527–565) and expression in the balanced synthesis of Maximus the Confessor († 662).

It would seem that no individual figure played a decisive role in the formation of this theology, and one is equally hard-pressed to locate any school or other intellectual center in the capital where theological thought was creatively elaborated. Though it seems reasonable to assume that a theological school for the training of higher ecclesiastical personnel was connected with the patriarchate, sources about its character or the level of its teaching are wanting. A center of theological learning is attested at the famous monastery of the *Akoimetai* (the "Non-Sleepers"), and others certainly existed elsewhere, but very little is specifically known about them. Theologians who were active during the fifth and sixth centuries often received their training in distant parts of the empire, such as Syria or Palestine. The Lavra of St. Sabbas near Jerusalem, for example, was the scene of violent debates between competing Origenist factions.

The imperial, secular University of Constantinople, founded by Constantine and reorganized by a decree of Theodosius II (408–450), did not include theology among its subjects; yet it certainly served as a channel for the perpetuation of ancient Greek philosophical ideas. The university remained bilingual (Greek and Latin) until the seventh century and, until the reign of Justinian, included pagans among its professors. But the drastic measures taken by Justinian, in excluding both pagans and non-Orthodox Christians from the teaching profession and in closing the pagan University of Athens, must have emphasized that the role of secular studies in Christian Byzantium was purely ancillary. Even if a small circle of intellectuals perpetuated the philosophical traditions of the ancient Greeks, the official position of both Church and state now considered philosophy as at best a tool for expressing Revelation, but it never admitted that philosophy was entitled to shape the very content of theological ideas. In practice, one might readily admit that Aristotelian logic be taught in the schools, but one would be consistently distrustful of Platonism because of its metaphysical implications. Yet Platonism would subsist, mainly through patristic literature, and especially through the Origenist tradition; but it would never be formally acknowledged as a valid expression of religious ideas.

Conservative in form and intent, Byzantine theology in the age of Justinian continually referred to tradition as its main source. The Christological debates of the period, in particular, consisted chiefly of a battle between exegetes of Scripture, about philosophical terms adopted by Christian theology in the third and fourth centuries, and about patristic texts making use of these terms. Liturgical hymnology, which began to flourish at this time, incorporated the results of the controversies and often became a form of credal confession. The various elements of Byzantine theological traditionalism dominant in the fifth and sixth centuries constituted the basis of further creativity in the later periods, and require very special attention.

1. EXEGETICAL TRADITIONS

It is necessary for those who preside over the churches . . . to teach all the clergy and the people . . . , collecting out of divine Scripture the thoughts and judgments of truth, but not exceeding the limits now fixed, nor varying from the tradition of the God-fearing Fathers. But if any issue arises concerning Scripture, it should not be interpreted other than as the luminaries and teachers of the Church have expounded it in their writings; let them [the bishops] become distinguished for their knowledge of patristic writings rather than for composing treatises out of their own heads.

This text of Canon 19 of the Council *in Trullo* (692) reflects the traditionalist and conservative character of the Byzantine approach to theology and to exegesis in particular, and explains the presence, in all monastic and private libraries of Byzantium, of innumerable copies of patristic *catenae,* "chains" of authoritative interpretations of particular Biblical texts, expressing, or claiming to express, the continuity of exegetical tradition.

Even though the *consensus patrum* reached by this method was in some instances partial and artificial, the standard Church teaching came to rely on it, especially when it was sanctified by liturgical and hymnographical usage. The Bible was always understood not simply as a source of revealed doctrinal propositions, or as a description of historical facts, but as a witness to a living Truth which had become dynamically present in the sacramental community of the New Testament Church. The veneration of the Virgin, Mother of God, for example, was associated once and for all with a typological interpretation of the Old Testament temple cult: the one who carried God in her womb was the true "temple," the true "tabernacle," the "candlestick," and God's final "abode." Thus, a Byzantine who, on the eve of a Marian feast, listened in church to a reading from the Book of Proverbs about "Wisdom building her house" (Pr 9:1ff.) naturally, and almost exclusively, thought of the "Word becoming flesh"—i.e., finding His abode in the Virgin. The identification of the Old Testament Wisdom with the Johannine Logos had been taken for granted since the time of Origen, and no one would have thought of challenging it. As early as the fourth century, when much of the Arian debate centered on the famous text "The Lord created me at the beginning of his works" (Pr 8:22), it was quite naturally interpreted by the Arians in favor of their position. Athanasius, and other members of the Nicaean party, declined to challenge the identification between Logos and Wisdom, preferring to find references to other texts supporting the uncreated character of the Logos–Wisdom. No one questioned the established exegetical consensus on the identification itself.

Much of the accepted Byzantine exegetical method had its origin in Alexandrian tradition and its allegorism. St. Paul, in describing the story of Abraham's two sons as an allegory of the two covenants (Ga 4:23), gave Christian sanction to a non-literal method of interpreting Scripture, known as *midrash,* which had developed among Palestinian rabbis in pre-Christian times. Thus, in pushing the allegorical method of interpreting Scripture to its very extremes, the Alexandrian Hellenistic milieu, common to Philo, Clement, and Origen, could refer to the illustrious precedent of St. Paul himself. Allegory was, first of all, consonant with the Hellenic, and especially the Platonic, concern for eternal things as opposed to historical facts. The Greek intellectual's main difficulty in accepting Christianity often lay in the absence of direct speculation on the Unchangeable, since his philosophical training had led him to associate changeability with unreality. The allegorical method, however, allowed the possibility of interpreting all concrete, changeable facts as symbols of unchangeable realities. History itself was thus losing its centrality and, in extreme cases, was simply denied.

But consonance with Hellenism was not the only element which contributed to the widespread use of allegory in exegesis. The method provided an easy weapon against Gnosticism, the main challenge to Christianity in the second century. The major Gnostic systems—especially those of Valentinus and Marcion—opposed the Demiurge, the Yahweh of Judaism, to the true God manifested in the New Testament. Christian apologists used allegory to "redeem" the Old Testament and counteracted the Gnostic dualism with the idea that the Old and the New Testaments have one and the same "spiritual" meaning and reflect a continuous Revelation of the same true God.

Origen also made use of this concept of the "spiritual meaning" in his notion of Tradition. The Spirit which had inspired the Biblical writers was also present in the "spiritual men" of the Christian Church. The saint alone, therefore, could decipher the authentic meaning of Scripture.

> The Scriptures [Origen writes] were composed through the Spirit of God and they have not only that meaning which is obvious, but also another which is hidden from the majority of readers. For the contents of Scripture are the outward forms of certain mysteries and the images of divine things. On this point the entire Church is unanimous, that while the whole Law is spiritual, the inspired meaning is not recognized by all, but only by those who are gifted with the grace of the Holy Spirit in the word of wisdom and knowledge.[1]

Although it raises the important problem of authority in exegesis, this passage certainly expresses a view largely taken for granted in medieval Byzantine Christendom, and explains the concern for a *consensus patrum,* expressed in a formal way in the canon of the Council *in Trullo* quoted at the beginning of this section.

In addition to Alexandrian allegorism, the Byzantine tradition of exegesis incorporated the more sober influence of the School of Antioch. The opposition between Alexandria and Antioch—which found a well-known and violent expression in the Christological debates of the fifth century—should not be exaggerated on the level of exegesis. The chief minds of the Antiochian school—Diodore of Tarsus (*ca.* 330–*ca.* 390), Theodore of Mopsuestia (*ca.* 350–428), and Theodoret of Cyrus (*ca.* 393–*ca.* 466)—did not deny the possibility of a spiritual meaning in Biblical texts; yet they reacted strongly against the elimination of the literal, historical meaning and against an arbitrary allegorism based on Platonic philosophical presuppositions foreign to the Bible. Thus, the notion of *theoria* ("contemplation"), which implies the possibility of discovering a spiritual meaning behind the letter of the text, was not rejected, but the emphasis was placed upon what actually happened or was said historically, as well as upon the moral or theological implications of the text.

The theological authority of the School of Antioch was shattered by the condemnation of Nestorius, a pupil of Theodore of Mopsuestia, at Ephesus in 431, and by the anathemas against the Three Chapters (Theodore of Mopsuestia, and the anti-Cyrillian writings of Theodoret of Cyrus and Ibas of Edessa) pronounced by the Second Council of Constantinople in 553. After 553, the scriptural commentaries of Theodore, one of the greatest exegetes of early Christianity, could be preserved only clandestinely in Syriac or Armenian translations, while the Greek original survived only in fragments scattered in the *catenae*. But the tradition of Antiochian exegesis survived in the exegetical works of Theodoret, which were never prohibited, and even more so in the writings of Theodore's friend John Chrysostom, by far the most popular of all Greek ecclesiastical writers. His definition of typology, as opposed to allegory, as "a prophecy expressed in terms of facts" [2] and his concern for history served as safeguards against the spiritualizing excesses of the Alexandrian tradition in late-Byzantine exegetical literature, while still leaving room for *theoria*, i.e., fundamentally a Christ-oriented typological interpretation of the Old Testament.

2. PHILOSOPHICAL TRENDS

The philosophical trends in post-Chalcedonian Byzantium were determined by three major factors: (1) the patristic tradition and its implications—the transfer, for example, of the Cappadocian Trinitarian terminology to the problem of the hypostatic union of the two natures in Christ; (2) the ever-reviving Origenism with its implied challenge to the Biblical doctrine of creation and to Biblical anthropology; (3) the continuing influence of non-Christian Neoplatonism upon intellectuals (Justinian's closing of the University of Athens put a physical end to a center of thought and learning, only recently adorned by the last major figure of pagan Greek philosophy, Proclus [410–485]). In all three cases the basic issue implied was the relation between ancient Greek thought and Christian Revelation.

Some modern historians continue to pass very divergent judgments on the philosophy of the Greek Fathers. In his well-known *Histoire de la philosophie,* Emile Bréhier writes: "In the first five centuries of Christianity, there was nothing which could properly be called Christian philosophy and which would imply a scale of intellectual values either original or different from that of the pagan thinkers." [3] According to Bréhier, Christianity and Hellenic philosophy are not opposed to each other as two intellectual systems, for Christianity is based on revealed facts, not on philosophical ideas. The Greek Fathers, in accepting these facts, adopted everything in Greek philosophy which was compatible with Christian Revelation. No new philosophy could result from such an artificial juxtaposition. A seemingly opposite view, more in line with the classical appraisal of Adolf Harnack, has been expressed by H. A. Wolfson whose book on *The Philosophy of the*

Church Fathers presents the thought of the Fathers as "a recasting of Christian beliefs in the form of a philosophy [which] thereby produc[ed] also a Christian version of Greek philosophy." [4] Finally, the monumental work of Claude Tresmontant *La Métaphysique du Christianisme et la naissance de la philosophie chrétienne* (Paris: Editions du Seuil, 1961) strongly maintains the historical existence of a Christian philosophy which the Fathers consistently defended against the Hellenic synthesis. This philosophy implies basic affirmations on creation, on unity and multiplicity, on knowledge, freedom, and so on, incompatible with Hellenism, and is fundamentally Biblical. "From the point of view of metaphysics," he writes, "Christian orthodoxy is defined by its fidelity to the metaphysical principles found in Biblical theology." [5] Therefore, if the Greek Fathers were orthodox, they were not, properly speaking, "Greek." Actually, in modern historical and theological writing, there is no term more ambiguous than "Hellenism." Thus, Georges Florovsky makes a persistent plea for "Christian Hellenism," meaning by the term the tradition of the Eastern Fathers as opposed to Western medieval thought,[6] but he agrees fundamentally with Tresmontant on the total incompatibility between Greek philosophical thought and the Bible, especially on such basic issues as creation and freedom.[7]

Therefore, Tresmontant's and Florovsky's conclusions appear to be fundamentally correct, and the usual slogans and clichés which too often serve to characterize patristic and Byzantine thought as exalted "Christian Hellenism," or as the "Hellenization of Christianity," or as Eastern "Platonism" as opposed to Western "Aristotelianism" should be avoided.

A more constructive method of approaching the issue and of establishing a balanced judgment consists in a preliminary distinction between the *systems* of ancient Greek philosophy—the Platonic, the Aristotelian, or the Neoplatonic—and individual concepts or terms. The use of Greek concepts and terminology was an unavoidable means of communication and a necessary step in making the Christian Gospel relevant to the world in which it appeared and in which it had to expand. But the Trinitarian terminology of the Cappadocian Fathers, and its later application to Christology in the Chalcedonian and post-Chalcedonian periods, clearly show that such concepts as *ousia, hypostasis,* or *physis* acquire an entirely new meaning when used out of the context of the Platonic or Aristotelian systems in which they were born. Three *hypostases* united in one "essence" (*ousia*), or two "natures" (*physeis*) united in one *hypostasis,* cannot be a part of either the Platonic or Aristotelian systems of thought, and imply new personalistic (and therefore non-Hellenic) metaphysical presuppositions. Still the Trinitarian and Christological synthesis of the Cappadocian Fathers would have dealt with a different set of problems and would have resulted in different concepts if the background of the Cappadocians and the audience to which they addressed themselves had not been Greek. Thus, Greek patristic thought remained open to Greek philosophical problematics, but avoided being imprisoned in Hellenic philosophical *systems*. From Gregory of Nazianzus in the fourth century to Gregory Palamas in the fourteenth, the representatives of the Orthodox tradition all express their conviction that heresies are based upon the uncritical absorption of pagan Greek philosophy into Christian thought.

Among the major figures of early Christian literature, only Origen, Nemesius of Emesa, and pseudo-Dionysius present systems of thought which can truly be defined as Christian versions of Greek philosophy. Others, including even such system-builders as Gregory of Nyssa and Maximus the Confessor, in spite of their obvious philosophical mentality, stand too fundamentally in opposition to pagan Hellenism on the basic issues of creation and freedom to qualify as Greek philosophers. Origen and pseudo-Dionysius suffered quite a distinct posthumous fate which will be discussed later, but the influence of Nemesius and of his Platonic anthropological "system" was so limited in Byzantium, in contrast to its widespread impact on Western medieval thought, that the Latin translation of his work *Peri physeōs anthrōpou* (*De natura hominis*) was attributed to Gregory of Nyssa.[8]

Thus, as most historians of Byzantine theology will admit, the problem of the relationship between philosophy and the facts of Christian experience remained at the center of the theological thought of Byzantium, and no safe and permanent balance between them has ever been found. But is such a balance really possible if "this world" and its "wisdom" are really in permanent tension with the realities of the kingdom of God?

3. THE PROBLEM OF ORIGENISM

Recent research has cast a completely new light on the history of Origenism in the fifth and sixth centuries. The publication of the works of Evagrius Ponticus, in particular, has clarified the issues which divided rival monastic parties in Egypt, in Palestine, and in other areas of Eastern Christendom.

While the Trinitarian problematics of Origen served as one of the starting points for the Arian controversies of the fourth century, his views on creation, the Fall, man, and God–man relations fascinated the first Greek intellectuals to the point of inducing them to join the monastic movement. In his system, monastic asceticism and spirituality find a justification, but contradict the basic presuppositions of Biblical Christianity. As a result, Origen and his disciple Evagrius were condemned in 400 by Theophilus of Alexandria and in 553 at Constantinople II. But even these condemnations did not preclude the lasting influence of their systems, which served as background for the integrated Christian philosophy of Maximus the Confessor. Origenism thus remained at the center of the theological thought of post-Chalcedonian Eastern Christianity, and its influence on spirituality and theological terminology did not end with the condemnation of the Origenistic *system* in 553, but continued at least until the iconoclastic crisis of the eighth century.

Origen was undoubtedly the most successful of the early apologists of Christianity. His system made the Christian religion acceptable to Neoplatonists, but the acceptance of Christianity on Origenistic terms does not necessarily imply the rejection of the basic Neoplatonic concepts of God and of the world. If the Cappadocian Fathers, for example, after reading Origen in their student years, were finally led to orthodox Christianity, others, such as their friend and contemporary Evagrius Ponticus, developed Origenism in quite a different direction.

In his famous *De principiis*, Origen first postulates creation as an *eternal* act of God. God has always been the all-powerful Creator, and "we cannot even call God almighty if there are none over whom He can exercise His power." [9] But since Origen is very careful to refute the Aristotelian doctrine of the eternity of matter, he maintains that the ever-existing created world is a world of "intellects," not of matter. The basic Platonizing spiritualism implied here will always appeal to monastic circles looking for a metaphysical justification of asceticism. The next step in Origen's thought is to consider that the "intellectual" world, which includes "all rational natures—that is, the Father, the Son, and the Holy Spirit, the Angels, the Powers, the Dominions, and other Virtues, as well as man himself in the dignity of his soul—are one unique substance." [10] Later patristic tradition will oppose to this idea the notion of the absolute transcendence of God expressed in apophatic theology, but for Origen the monistic structure encompassing God and the "intellects" in one single substance is broken only by the Fall. Misusing their "freedom," the intellects committed the sin of revolting against God. Some sinned heavily, and became demons; others sinned less, and became angels; others still less, and became archangels. Thus each received a condition proportionate to its own sin. The remaining souls committed sins neither heavy enough to rank with the demons nor light enough to become angels, and so it was that God created the present world, linking the soul with a body as a punishment. [11] The present visible world, which includes man—understood as an intellect transformed through sin into a body—is the result of the Fall; man's ultimate destiny is dematerialization and a return to a union with God's substance.

Evagrius Ponticus significantly developed this Origenistic system by applying it to Christology. According to Evagrius, Jesus Christ was not the Logos taking flesh, but only an "intellect" who had not committed the original sin and, thus, was not involved in the catastrophe of materialization. He assumed a body in order to show the way toward a restoration of man's original union with God.[12] Around this teaching of Evagrius', serious conflicts, which lasted until the reign of Justinian, arose between feuding monastic parties. At the center of these disturbances, the Lavra of St. Sabbas in Palestine, some monks claimed to be "equal to Christ" (*isochristoi*), since in them, through prayer and contemplation, the original relationship with God, which also existed in Christ, had been restored. This extreme and obviously heretical form of Origenism was condemned first by imperial decree, then by the ecumenical council of 553. The writings of Origen and Evagrius were destroyed, to be preserved only partially in Latin or Syriac translations, or protected by pseudonyms. Ancient Hellenism had to give way once again to the basic principles of Biblical Christianity.

4. PSEUDO-DIONYSIUS

The condemnation of Origen and Evagrius did not mean, however, the total disappearance of the Platonic world-view from Byzantine Christianity. The Hellenic concept of the world as "order" and "hierarchy," the strict Platonic division between the "intelligible" and the "sensible" worlds, and the Neoplatonic grouping of beings into "triads" reappear in the famous writings of a mysterious early-sixth-century author who wrote under the pseudonym of Dionysius the Areopagite. The quasi-apostolic authority of this unknown author went unchallenged in both East and West throughout the Middle Ages.

Historians of Eastern Christian thought usually emphasize the role of Dionysius—together with that of Gregory of Nyssa and of Maximus the Confessor—in expounding apophatic theology. According to Vladimir Lossky, Dionysius, far from being "a Platonist with a tinge of Christianity," is the very opposite: "a Christian thinker disguised as a Neoplatonist, a theologian very much aware of his task, which was to conquer the ground held by Neoplatonism by becoming a master of its philosophical method." [13] And, indeed, several elements of Dionysius' thought appear as successful Christian counterparts both to Neoplatonic and to Origenistic positions. Dionysius specifically rejects Origen's notion of the knowledge of God "by essence," since there cannot be "knowledge" of God. For knowledge can apply only to "beings," and God is above being and superior to all opposition between being and non-being. With God, there can be a "union," however: the supreme end of human existence; but this union is "ignorance" rather than knowledge, for it presupposes detachment from all activity of the senses or of the intellect, since the intellect is applicable only to created existence. God, therefore, is absolutely transcendent and above existence, and—as long as one remains in the categories of existence—can be described only in negative terms.[14] God does, however, make Himself known outside of His transcendent nature: "God is manifested by His 'powers' in all beings, is multiplied without abandoning His unity." [15] Thus, the concepts of beauty, being, goodness, and the like, reflect God, but not His essence, only His "powers" and "energies" [16]—which are not, however, a diminished form of deity, or mere emanations, but themselves fully God, in whom created beings can participate in the proportion and analogy proper to each. Thus, the God of Dionysius is again the living God of the Bible and not the One of Plotinus, and, in this respect, Dionysius will provide the basis for further positive developments of Christian thought.

One must remember, however, that Dionysius' theology proper—i.e., his doctrine of God and of the relationship between God and the world—is not wholly original (in fact, its essential elements appear in the writings of the Cappadocian Fathers), and that, through his hierarchical view of the universe, Dionysius exercised a highly ambiguous influence, especially in the fields of ecclesiology and sacramental theology.

If, for Origen, the hierarchy of created beings—angels, men, demons—is the result of the Fall, for Dionysius it is an immovable and divine order through which one reaches "assimilation and union with God." [17] The three "triads"—or nine orders—of the celestial hierarchy and the two "triads" of the ecclesiastical hierarchy are essentiallly a system of mediations. Each order participates in God "according to its capacity," but this participation is granted through the order immediately superior.[18] The most obvious consequences of that system occur in the field of ecclesiology; for Dionysius, the ecclesiastical hierarchy, which includes the triads "bishops (hierarchs)–priests–deacons" and "monks–laymen–catechumens (sinners)," is nothing but an earthly reflection of the celestial orders; each ecclesiastical order, therefore, is a *personal state,* not a function in the community. "A hierarch," Dionysius writes, "is a deified and divine man, instructed in holy knowledge." [19] And since the hierarch is primarily a gnostic, or an initiator, there is fundamentally no difference between his role and that of a charismatic. The same applies, of course, to the other orders.[20]

And, since Dionysius also holds very strictly to the Platonic divisions between the intellectual and material orders, the material being only a reflection and a symbol of the intellectual, his doctrine of the sacraments is both purely symbolic and individualistic; the function of the Eucharist, for example, is only to symbolize the union of the intellect with God and Christ.[21]

Our conclusion to these brief comments on Dionysius must be, therefore, that in areas where he transcends Neoplatonism—the area of the *theologia*— he is a real Christian, without, however, being truly original; but that his doctrine of the hierarchies, even if it represents a genuine attempt to integrate the Neoplatonic world-view into the Christian framework, is an obvious failure, the consequences of which have led to much confusion, especially in the fields of liturgy and of ecclesiological formulations. One wonders, too, if the Western Scholastic doctrine of the sacerdotal "character" and, to a lesser extent, the confusion, frequent in the Byzantine East, between the role of the ecclesiastical hierarchy and that of "holy men" do not go back ultimately to Dionysius.

5. LITURGY

The appearance of the Dionysian writings coincides chronologically with a turning point in the history of Christian liturgy. When Justinian closed the last pagan temples and schools, Christianity became unquestionably the religion of the masses of the empire. The Christian liturgy, originally conceived as the cult of small persecuted communities, now came to be celebrated in immense cathedrals—such as the magnificent "Great Church," Hagia Sophia in Constantinople, one of the glories of Justinian's reign—with thousands of worshippers in attendance. This completely new situation could not help but influence both the practice and the theology of the liturgy. The Eucharist, for example, could no longer really retain the external character of a community meal. The great mass of the people in attendance consisted of nominal Christians who could hardly meet the standard required of regular communicants. Starting with John Chrysostom, the clergy began to preach that preparation, fasting, and self-examination were the necessary prerequisites of communion, and emphasized the mysterious, eschatological elements of the sacrament. The eighth and ninth centuries witnessed such additions as the iconostasis-screen between the sanctuary and the congregation, and the use of the communion spoon, a means to avoid putting the sacramental elements into the hands of laymen. All these developments were aimed at protecting the mystery, but they resulted in separating the clergy from the faithful and in giving to the liturgy the aspect of a performance, rather than of a common action of the entire people of God.

The writings of pseudo-Dionysius contributed to the same trend. The author's ideas about God's grace descending upon the lower ranks of the hierarchy through the personal mediation of the hierarchs did much to shape new Byzantine liturgical forms, which he considered only as symbols revealing the mysteries to the eyes of the faithful. Appearances and disappearances of the celebrant, veiling and unveiling of the elements, opening and closing of the doors, and various gestures connected with the sacraments often originated in the rigid system of the hierarchical activity as described by Dionysius, and found ready acceptance in a Church otherwise concerned with preserving the mysterious character of the cult from profanation by the masses now filling the temples.

Fortunately Dionysian theology has had practically no effect upon such central texts as the baptismal prayer and the Eucharistic canons. It served principally to develop and explain the extremely rich fringes with which Byzantium now adorned the central sacramental actions of the Christian faith, without modifying its very heart, and thus leaving the door open to authentic liturgical and sacramental theology which would still inspire the mainstream of Byzantine spirituality.

Another very important liturgical development of the fifth and sixth centuries was the large-scale adoption of hymnography of a Hellenistic nature. In the early Christian communities, the Church hymnal was comprised of the psalter and some other poetic excerpts from Scripture, with relatively few newer hymns. In the fifth and sixth centuries, however, with the insistence on more liturgical solemnity (often copied from court ceremonial) in the great urban churches, and the unavoidable Hellenization of the Church, the influx of new poetry was inevitable.

This influx met strong opposition in monastic circles, which considered it improper to replace Biblical texts of the liturgy with human poetic compositions, but the resistance was not a lasting one. In fact, in the eighth and ninth centuries, the monks took the lead in hymnographical creativity.

But as early as the sixth century, the religious poetry of Romanos the Melode was regarded as revolutionary in Constantinople. The models of his poetry and music were generally localized in Syria where poetic religious compositions had already been popularized by Ephraem († 373).

Born in Emesus, Romanos came to Constantinople under Anastasius (491–518) and soon attained great fame by composing his *kontakia*. Generally based upon a Biblical theme, or exalting a Biblical personality, the *kontakion* is essentially a metrical homily, recited or chanted by a cantor and accompanied by the entire congregation singing a simple refrain. It follows a uniform pattern beginning with a short prelude and followed by a series of poetic strophae.

Romanos' poetry generally relies on imagery and drama, and contains little or no theology; the Christological debates of the period, for example, are not at all reflected in his *kontakia*. Written in simple popular Greek, they must have played a tremendous role in bringing the themes of Biblical history to the masses; they undoubtedly strengthened profoundly that understanding of Christianity centered on the liturgy which became so characteristic of the Byzantines.

Some of Romanos' *kontakia* remain in the liturgical books in an abridged form, and the pattern which he established was reproduced, almost exactly, in the famous *Akathistos hymnos,* one of the most popular pieces of Byzantine hymnography. Although, as we shall see later, subsequent hymnographical patterns, formed in the monasteries, were quite different from those of Romanos, the work of the great melode of the sixth century played a central role in shaping Byzantine Christianity, as distinct from the Latin, the Syrian, the Egyptian, and the Armenian.

The cultural framework of Byzantine theology after Chalcedon was increasingly limited to the Greek-speaking world. The wealth of the various non-Greek traditions of early Christianity—especially the Syrian and the Latin—was less and less taken into account by the theologians of the imperial capital. One should remember, however, that, until the emergence of the twelfth-century revival of theology in the West, Constantinople remained the unquestioned intellectual center of Christendom, with very little competition. One understands therefore that it developed a sense of increasing, though regrettable, self-sufficiency.

NOTES

1. Origen, *De principiis*, Praefatio 8; ed. B. Koetschau, GCS 22 (1913), 14.6–13; trans. G. W. Butterworth, *On the First Principles* (London: SPCK, 1936), p. 5.

2. John Chrysostom, *De paenitentia*, hom. 6, 4; PG 49:320.

3. Émile Bréhier, *Histoire de la philosophie* (Paris: Presses Universitaires de France, 1931), II, 494.

4. H. A. Wolfson, *The Philosophy of the Church Fathers* (Cambridge: Harvard University Press, 1956), I, vi.

5. Claude Tresmontant, *La Métaphysique du christianisme et la naissance de la philosophie chrétienne* (Paris: du Seuil, 1961), p. 23.

6. Georges Florovsky, "The Eastern Orthodox Church and the Ecumenical Movement," *Theology Today* 7 (April 1950), 74–76.

7. Georges Florovsky, "The Idea of Creation in Christian Philosophy," *Eastern Church Quarterly* 8 (1949), 53–77.

8. See Étienne Gilson, *La philosophie au Moyen-Âge* (2nd ed., Paris: Payot, 1952), pp. 72–77.

9. Origen, *De principiis*, I, 2, 10; ed. Koetschau, p. 42; trans. Butterworth, p. 23.

10. Quoted by Jerome in *Ep.* 124, *ad Avit.*, 15.

11. See anathemas of the Council of Constantinople (553) as given in F. Diekamp, *Die origenistischen Streitigkeiten im sechsten Jahrhundert und das fünfte allgemeine Concil* (Münster, 1898), pp. 90–96.

12. The essential texts are found in A. Guillaumont, *Les "Kephalaia Gnostica" d'Évagre le Pontique et l'histoire de l'origénisme chez les Grecs et les Syriens* (Paris: du Seuil, 1962), esp. pp. 156–160.

13. Vladimir Lossky, *Vision of God* (London: Faith Press, 1963), pp. 99–100.

14. Pseudo-Dionysius, *Mystical Theology*, V; PG 3:1045D–1048A.

15. Lossky, *Vision*, p. 102.

16. See, chiefly, pseudo-Dionysius, *On the Divine Names*, II; PG 3:636ff.

17. Pseudo-Dionysius, *On the Celestial Hierarchy*, III, 2; PG 3:165A.

18. See R. Roques, *L'univers dionysien: Structure hiérarchique du monde selon le pseudo-Denys* (Paris: Aubier, 1954), p. 98ff.

19. Pseudo-Dionysius, *On the Ecclesiastical Hierarchy*, I, 3; PG 3:373c.

20. See the analysis of Roques, *L'univers dionysien*, pp. 172ff.

21. *Ibid.*, pp. 267, 269.

2

The Christological Issue

THROUGHOUT THE MILLENNIUM between the Council of Chalcedon and the fall of Constantinople, Byzantine theological thought was dominated by the Christological problem as it was defined in the dispute between Cyril and Nestorius and in the subsequent discussions and conciliar decrees. It must be remembered, however, that the central issue in these debates was the ultimate fate of *man*.

Western Christological thought, since the early Middle Ages, has been dominated by the Anselmian idea of redemption through "satisfaction"; the idea that Jesus offered to the Father a perfect and sufficient sacrifice, propitiatory for the sins of mankind, has been at the center of Christological speculation, playing a prominent role in modern historical research on the patristic age. The result is that Christology has been conceived as a topic in itself, clearly distinct from pneumatology and anthropology. But if one keeps in mind the Greek patristic notion that the true nature of man means life in God, realized once and for all, through the Holy Spirit, in the hypostatic union of the man Jesus with the Logos and made accessible to all men, through the same Holy Spirit, in the humanity of Christ, in His body, the Church, Christology acquires a new and universal dimension. It cannot be isolated any longer from either the doctrine of the Holy Spirit or the doctrine of man, and it becomes a key for the understanding of the Gospel as a whole.

The issue of "participation in God's life" and of "deification" stands as a necessary background to the clash between Alexandrian and Antiochian Christology in the fifth century. When the great exegetes of Antioch— Diodore of Tarsus, Theodore of Mopsuestia, Nestorius, and even Theodoret of Cyrus—emphasize the full humanity of the historical Jesus, they understand this humanity not merely as distinct from the divinity, but as "autonomous" and personalized. If "deified," Jesus could no longer be truly man; he must simply be the son of Mary if he is to be ignorant, to suffer, and to die. It is precisely this understanding of humanity as autonomous which has attracted the sympathies of modern Western theologians toward the Antiochians, but which provoked the emergence of Nestorianism and the clash with Alexandria. For the concept of "deification" was the very argument with which Athanasius had countered Arius: "God became man, so that man may become God." The great Cappadocian Fathers also shared this argument, and by it they were convinced, as were the vast majority of the Eastern episcopate, of the truth of the Nicaean faith, in spite of their original doubts concerning the term "consubstantial."

Thus, the essential "good news" about the coming of new life—human because it is also divine—was expressed by Cyril of Alexandria and not by the more rational scheme defended by Nestorius. Cyril lacked the vocabulary, however, and the flexibility to satisfy those who feared the Monophysite temptation of seeing in Jesus a God who ceased to be also man. Cyril's formula of "one nature [or, hypostasis] incarnated," in leaving the door open to the Orthodox distinction between the divine nature *per se* and the "divine nature incarnated" and, therefore, recognizing the reality of the "flesh," was still a polemical, anti-Nestorian formula, not a balanced and positive definition of who Christ is. The Chalcedonian definition of 451— two natures united in one hypostasis, yet retaining in full their respective characteristics—was therefore a necessary correction of Cyril's vocabulary. Permanent credit should be given to the Antiochians—especially to Theodoret—and to Leo of Rome for having shown the necessity of this correction, without which Cyrillian Christology could easily be, and actually was, interpreted in a Monophysite sense by Eutyches and his followers.

But the Chalcedonian definition, balanced and positive as it was, lacked the soteriological, charismatic impact which had made the positions of Athanasius and Cyril so appealing. Political and ecclesiastical rivalries, personal ambitions, imperial pressures aimed at imposing Chalcedon by force, abusive interpretations of Cyril in the Monophysite sense, as well as misinterpretations of the council by some Nestorianizing Antiochians who saw in it a disavowal of the great Cyril—all provoked the first major and lasting schism in Christendom.

Understandably, the Byzantine emperors tried to restore the religious unity of the empire. In the second half of the fifth century they made several unhappy attempts to heal the schism by avoiding the issue. But the issue proved to be real, and the passions high. Thus Justinian I (527-565), the last great Roman emperor, after several attempts to achieve unity by imperial decree again turned to conciliar procedure.

In the age of Justinian, four major theological positions can be easily discerned:

1. THE MONOPHYSITES

Although most of the Monophysites were ready to anathematize Eutyches, as well as the idea that Christ's humanity was "confused" with His divinity, they held steadfastly to the theology and terminology of Cyril of Alexandria. Just as the "old Nicaeans" in the fourth century had refused to accept the formula of the three hypostaseis introduced by the Cappadocian Fathers because Athanasius had not used it, so the leaders of fifth- and sixth-century Monophysitism—Dioscoros of Alexandria, Philoxenus of Mabbugh, and the great Severus of Antioch—rejected the Council of Chalcedon and the Christological formula of "one hypostasis in two natures" because Cyril had never used it, and because they interpreted it as a return to Nestorianism. The danger of Eutychianism, they claimed, was not serious enough to justify the Chalcedonian departure from Cyril's terminology. They objected most violently—and this objection may be the really serious difference between their Christology and Chalcedonian orthodoxy—to the idea that the two natures, after the union, "retain in full their proper characteristics."

2. THE STRICT DYOPHYSITES

The strict Dyophysites were Chalcedonians who still rigidly maintained the Antiochian Christology, and who objected to some of Cyril's propositions, such as the Theopaschite formula: "One of the Holy Trinity suffered in the flesh." For them, the subject of suffering is Jesus, the son of Mary, not the divine Logos. But, one may ask, is there not then in Christ a duality of subjects? The existence of this party in the Chalcedonian camp and the influence exercised by its representatives—Theodoret of Cyrus until his death around 466, Gennadios of Constantinople (458–471), his successor Macedonios (495–511), and others—provided the Monophysites with their main arguments for rejecting Chalcedon as a Nestorian council and as a disavowal of Cyril.

3. THE CYRILLIAN CHALCEDONIANS

The Cyrillian Chalcedonians, who were obviously the majority at the council itself, never admitted that there was a contradiction between Cyril and Chalcedon. Neither terminology was considered an end in itself, but only the appropriate way of opposing Nestorianism and Eutychianism respectively. The position of the Cyrillian Chalcedonians, as distinct from the strict Dyophysite position, is symbolized by the acceptance of the Theopaschite Cyrillian formula. The representatives of this tendency—the "Scythian monk" John Maxentios, John the Grammarian, Ephraem of Antioch, Leontius of Jerusalem, Anastasius of Antioch, Eulogius of Alexandria, Theodore of Raithu—dominated Byzantine theology in the sixth century and won the support of Justinian I. Recent historians (among them, Joseph Lebon and Charles Moeller) often designate this tendency as "neo-Chalcedonian," implying that the strict Dyophysite understanding of Chalcedon is the only correct one and that Antiochian Christology is preferable to Cyrillian. The implications of the debate on this point are very broad, in both Christological and anthropological fields, for it questions the very notion of "deification."

4. THE ORIGENISTS

The Origenists, involved in violent controversies but influential at the court in the beginning of Justinian's reign, offered their own solution based upon the quite heretical Christology of Evagrius Ponticus. For them Jesus is not the Logos, but an "intellect" not involved in the original Fall, and thus united hypostatically and essentially with the Logos. The writings of Leontius of Byzantium, the chief representative of Origenist Christology in Constantinople, were included in the pro-Chalcedonian polemical arsenal, however, and his notion of the *enhypostaton* was adopted by Maximus the Confessor and John of Damascus, who, of course, rejected the crypto-Origenistic context in which it originally appeared.

The Fifth Ecumenical Council (553), convoked by Justinian in order to give formal ecclesiastical approval to his attempts at making Chalcedon acceptable to the Monophysites, was a triumph of Cyrillian Chalcedonianism. It approved Justinian's earlier posthumous condemnation of the Three Chapters, and, though Theodore was personally condemned as a heretic and the teacher of Nestorius, Ibas and Theodoret, whom the Council of Chalcedon had officially accepted as orthodox, were spared as persons; their writings directed against Cyril, however, fell under the anathemas of 553. Thus, the authority of Chalcedon was formally preserved, but the strict Dyophysite interpretation of its decisions was formally rejected. The council very strongly reaffirmed the unity of *subject* in Christ (anathemas 2, 3, 4, 5) and, hence, formally legitimized the Theopaschite formula (anathema 10). This formula was henceforth chanted at every liturgy in the hymn "The Only-Begotten Son of God," which has been attributed to Justinian himself. Though anathema 13 gave formal approval to the Twelve Chapters of Cyril against Nestorius, anathema 8 specified that if one should use the Cyrillian formula "one nature incarnated," the word "nature" would stand for hypostasis. Thus, in joining the Orthodox Church, the Monophysites were not required to reject anything of Cyrillian theology, but only to admit that Chalcedon was not a Nestorian council.

Unfortunately, by 553 the schism was too deeply rooted in Egypt and Syria, and the conciliar decision had no practical effect. The decision represents, however, a necessary pre-condition for any future attempts at reunion and an interesting precedent of a reformulation of an article of faith, already defined by a council, for the sake of "separated" brethren who misunderstand the previous formulation.

The Council of 553 also adopted a series of anathemas against Origen and Evagrius Ponticus. The *Gnostic Chapters* of Evagrius help greatly in understanding the meaning of these decisions, which were directed, not as was previously thought against non-existent heresies attributed to Origen, but against an active group of Evagrians, closely connected with the Christological debates of the day. Despite these condemnations, however, some aspects of the thought of Origen, Evagrius, and Leontius of Byzantium continued to exercise an influence on the development of theological thought and of spirituality.

The condemnation of Origenism in 553 was, therefore, a decisive step in Eastern Christian theology, which then committed itself to a Biblical view of creation, of an anthropocentric universe, of man as a coherent psychosomatic whole, of history as a linear orientation toward an ultimate *eschaton,* of God as a personal and living being independent of all metaphysical necessity.

The decision of 553, however, did not close the Christological debate. Actually, each doctrinal definition—at Ephesus, Chalcedon, Constantinople ii—by solving some issues had raised new ones. The schism of the Monophysites remained a political nuisance to the empire and a threat to the Church, which in the East would soon be faced with the Persian Zoroastrian and the Moslem challenges. The reaffirmation of Cyrillian orthodoxy in 553 raised the permanent issue of the two stages in Cyril's personal attitude: his proclamation, against Nestorius, of Christ's unity (especially the Twelve Anathemas), and his later stand, more appreciative of Antiochian fears. Thus, in 430 Cyril did not admit that a distinction could be drawn in Christ's actions between those which were divine and those which were only human, but in his famous letter to John of Antioch in 433, he admits that such a distinction is inevitable.

Monophysites, after Chalcedon, generally preferred the "first Cyril" to the "second." Severus, their great theologian, admitted duality in Christ's being, but for him this duality was a duality "in imagination," while "in actuality" there was only one nature, or being. This position leads directly to Monoenergism: "one is the agent," writes Severus, "and one is the activity." [1] For terminological reasons, however, the Monophysites were generally reluctant to speak of "one will" in Christ because of the possible Nestorian associations. In Antiochian Christology it was possible to say that the two natures were united by one common "will."

The Persian wars of Emperor Heraclius (610–641) again deeply involved the Byzantine government in unionist policies with the Monophysites, especially with the Armenians. Patriarch Sergius (610–638), Heraclius' friend and theological adviser, devised a formula of union, according to which the Monophysites would accept the Chalcedonian formula of the "two natures" with the specification that they were united into one "energy" and one will. The policy reached a measure of success both in Armenia and in Egypt, and local unions were concluded. Monoenergism and Monotheletism, however, met with staunch opposition on the part of some Chalcedonians, led by Sophronius, Patriarch of Jerusalem, and by Maximus the Confessor. In spite of the support given to it by Heraclius and his successors, Monotheletism was finally condemned by the Sixth Ecumenical Council in 680, which restated the Chalcedonian affirmation that in Christ each nature keeps the entirety of its characteristics, and, therefore, there are two "energies" or wills, the divine and the human, in Christ.

Maximus the Confessor (*ca.* 580–662) the architect of this decision, dominates the period intellectually, and, in many respects, may be regarded as the real Father of Byzantine theology. For in his system one finds a Christian philosophical counterpart to Origen's myth of creation, and, as the real foundation of Christian spiritual life, a doctrine of "deification" based on Cyril's soteriology and on Chalcedonian Christology.

Maximus never tried, or had the opportunity, to compose an ordered analysis of his system. His writings include only a large collection of *Ambigua,* a most unsystematic compilation of commentaries on obscure passages from Gregory of Nazianzus or from pseudo-Dionysius, a collection of "Answers to Questions" by Thalassius, several series of Chapters (short sayings on spiritual or theological matters), and a few polemical treatises against the Monothelites. In these *membra disjecta,* however, one discovers a most coherent view of the Christian faith as a whole, formed quite independently of the Monothelite controversy. His attitude against the Monothelites thus acquires even greater strength, precisely because its roots go much deeper than the casual historical circumstances in which it had to be expressed and which led Maximus himself to torture and a martyr's death.

In Origen's system immobility is one of the essential characteristics of true being; it belongs to God, but also to creatures as long as they remain in conformity with God's will. Diversity and movement come from the Fall. For Maximus, however, "movement," or "action," is a fundamental quality of nature. Each creature possesses its own meaning and purpose, which reflect the eternal and divine Logos "through whom all things were made." The logos of every creature is given to it not only as a static element but also as the eternal goal and purpose which it is called to achieve.

At this point Maximus' thought uses the Aristotelian concept of each nature's having its own "energy," or existential manifestation. The Cappadocian Fathers had applied the same principle to their doctrine of the three hypostaseis in God. Gregory of Nyssa, in particular, had to defend himself against the accusation of tritheism; the three hypostaseis are not three Gods because they have one nature, as is evident from the fact that there is only one "energy" of God. Already, then, in Cappadocian thought, the concept of "energy" is linked with that of nature. Maximus could therefore refer to tradition in opposing the Monothelite contention that "energy" reflects the one hypostasis or person or actor, and that therefore Christ could have only one "energy."

In Maximian thought, man occupies quite an exceptional position among the other creatures. He not only carries in himself a logos; he is the *image* of the divine Logos, and the purpose of his nature is to acquire *similitude* with God. In creation as a whole, man's role is to unify all things in God, and thus to overcome the evil powers of separation, division, disintegration, and death. The "natural," God-established "movement," "energy" or will, of man is therefore directed toward communion with God, or "deification," not in isolation from the entire creation, but leading it back to its original state.

One understands at this point why Maximus felt so strongly that both Monoenergism and Monothelitism betray the Chalcedonian affirmation that Christ was fully man. There cannot be a true humanity where there is no natural, authentic human will or "movement."

But if the human will is nothing but a movement of nature, is there a place for human freedom? And how can the Fall and man's revolt against God be explained? These questions, to which Origen gave such great importance, find in Maximus a new answer. Already in Gregory of Nyssa, true human freedom does not consist in autonomous human life, but in the situation which is truly natural to man's communion with God. When man is isolated from God, he finds himself enslaved—to his passions, to himself, and, ultimately, to Satan. Therefore, for Maximus, when man follows his natural will, which presupposes life in God, God's cooperation and communion, he is truly free. But man also possesses another potential, determined not by his nature, but by each human person, or hypostasis, the freedom of choice, of revolt, of movement against nature, and, therefore, of self-destruction. This personal freedom was used by Adam and Eve and, after the Fall, in separation from God, from true knowledge, from all the assurance secured by "natural" existence. It implies hesitation, wandering, and suffering; this is the gnomic will (*gnomē,* opinion), a function of the hypostatic, or personal, life, not of nature.

In Christ, human nature is united with the hypostasis of the Logos and, while remaining fully itself, is liberated from sin, the source of which is the gnomic will. Because it is "en-hypostasized" in the Logos Himself, Christ's humanity is perfect humanity. In the mysterious process which started with His conception in the Virgin's womb, Jesus passed through natural growth, ignorance, suffering, and even death—all of them experiences of the fallen humanity which He had come to save—and He fulfilled through the resurrection the ultimate human destiny. Christ could thus be truly the savior of humanity because in Him there could never be any contradiction between natural will and gnomic will. Through the hypostatic union, His human will, precisely because it always conforms itself to the divine, also performs the "natural movement" of human nature.

The doctrine of "deification" in Maximus is based upon the fundamental patristic presupposition that communion with God does not diminish or destroy humanity, but makes it fully human. In Christ the hypostatic union implies the communication of idioms (*perichōresis tōn idiōmatōn*). The characteristics of divinity and humanity express themselves "in communion with each other" (Chalcedonian definition), and human actions, or "energies," have God Himself as their personal agent. It can be said, therefore, that "God was born," that Mary is the *Theotokos,* and that the "Logos was crucified"—while birth and death remain purely *human* realities. But it can and must also be said that a man rose from the dead and sits at the right hand of the Father, having acquired characteristics which "naturally" belong to God alone: immortality and glory. Through Christ's humanity, deified according to its hypostatic union with the Logos, all members of the Body of Christ have access to "deification" by grace through the operation of the Spirit in Christ's Church.

The essential elements of Maximian Christology provided the permanent terminological and philosophical framework for Byzantine thought and spirituality. They were adopted, together with the Trinitarian doctrine of the great Cappadocian Fathers, in the *Exact Exposition of the Orthodox Faith* of John of Damascus (first half of the eighth century), which served as a standard doctrinal textbook in Byzantium. They also provided the most authoritative frame of reference in most of the doctrinal controversies which arose in the East during the Middle Ages.

The following chapter, which is concerned with iconoclasm, will show that the Christological issue recurred indirectly in the eighth and ninth centuries. But even later, Christological debate was reopened, quite specifically, especially in the Comnenian period, and conciliar decisions on the matter were included in the *Synodikon.*

Around 1087, a Constantinopolitan monk named Nilus, who was involved in theological discussions with the Armenians, was condemned for holding that the humanity of Christ was united with God "by adoption" (*thesei*) only.[2] The Monophysite Armenians were, of course, maintaining the concept of a union "by nature" (*physei*). In opposing them, Nilus had apparently weakened the Orthodox doctrine of "hypostatic" union to the point of making it sound Nestorian. In 1117, the Synod of Constantinople dealt with the similar case of Eustratius, Metropolitan of Nicaea, who, like Nilus, had engaged in polemics with Armenians and had expressed orthodox Christology in terms very similar to those of Theodore of Mopsuestia. The humanity assumed by Christ not only was distinct from His divinity but found itself in a position of "servitude"; it was in a position of "worshipping God," of being "purified," and to it alone belongs the human title of high-priest, a term unsuitable to God. In condemning the opinions of Eustratius, the synod reiterated the decisions of the Fifth Council against the Christology of the Three Chapters.[3]

The very Cyrillian conclusion of the council against Eustratius led to further Christological debates, which this time centered on the meaning of the Eucharistic sacrifice. The deacon Soterichos Panteugenos, Patriarch-Elect of Antioch, affirmed that the sacrifice could not be offered to the Holy Trinity, for this would imply that the one Christ performs two opposing actions, the human action of offering and the divine action of receiving, and would mean a Nestorian separation and personalization of the two natures. Nicholas, Bishop of Methone in the Peloponnese, a major Byzantine theologian of the twelfth century, responded to Soterichos with an elaboration of the notion of hypostasis based on the ideas of Leontius of Byzantium and Maximus the Confessor. The hypostatic union is precisely what permits one to consider God as performing humanly in the act of offering, while remaining God by nature and, therefore, receiving the sacrifice. To Soterichos, Nicholas opposed the conclusion of the prayer of the *Cheroubikon,* whose author, as modern research shows, is none other than Cyril of Alexandria himself, but which is a part of both Byzantine liturgies (attributed respectively to Basil and to John Chrysostom): "For it is Thou who offerest and art offered, who receivest and art Thyself received." Nicholas, whose views were endorsed by the Council of 1156–1157, shows that neither the Eucharist nor the work of Christ in general can be reduced to a juridical notion of sacrifice conceived as an exchange. God does not have to receive anything from us: "We did not go to Him [to make an offering]; rather He condescended toward us and assumed our nature, not as a condition of reconciliation, but in order to meet us openly in the flesh." [4]

This "open meeting in the flesh" received further emphasis in 1170 in connection with the condemnation of Constantine of Kerkyra and his supporter John Eirenikos as crypto-Monophysites. Their point was to refuse to apply John 14:18 ("My Father is greater than I") to the distinction between the divinity and the humanity of Christ. The text, they said, concerned the hypostatic characteristics in the Holy Trinity, fatherhood being by definition "greater" than sonship, while the humanity of Christ, which according to the Council of 553 is distinguishable from the divinity only "in our mind," is deified and wholly "one" with the divinity. It cannot, therefore, be "smaller" than the divinity in any sense. By rejecting this view, the Council of 1170 reaffirmed once again the decisions of Chalcedon and Constantinople II about the divinity of Christ, hypostatically united to a real and active humanity, "created, depictable, and mortal." Than such humanity, divinity is certainly "greater."

The very technical Christological discussions of the twelfth century, in fact, reconsidered all the major issues which had been debated in the fifth, sixth, and seventh centuries. The Byzantine Church remained fundamentally faithful to the notion of what Georges Florovsky once called an "asymmetrical union" of God and man in Christ: while the hypostatic source of life—the goal and pattern—remains divine, man is not diminished or swallowed by the union; he becomes again fully human. This notion is also expressed in the Eucharistic sacrifice, a unique act in which no single action of Christ's is represented in isolation, or reduced to purely human concepts, such as an "exchange," or a "satisfaction." Christ, as the *Synodikon* proclaims every year on the Sunday of Orthodoxy, "reconciled us to Himself by means of *the whole mystery of the economy, and* by Himself and in Himself, reconciled us also to His God and Father, and, of course, to the most holy and life-giving Spirit." [5]

NOTES

1. Quoted by J. Lebon, *Le Monophysitisme sévérien, étude historique, littéraire et théologique sur la résistance monophysite au Concile de Chalcédoine jusqu'à la constitution de l'Église jacobite* (Louvain dissertation, 1909), pp. 445–446.

2. Anna Comnena, *Alexiad*, X, 1; ed. B. Leib (Paris, 1943), II, 187–188; *Synodikon*, ed. J. Gouillard, *Travaux et mémoires* 2 (Paris: Presses Universitaires de France, 1967), pp. 202–206. On possible connections between several Byzantine theological trends and Paulician dualism, see N. G. Gersoyan, "Byzantine Heresy: A Reinterpretation," *Dumbarton Oaks Papers* 25 (1971), 87–113.

3. See P. Joannou, "Der Nominalismus und die menschliche Psychologie Christi: das Semeioma gegen Eustratios von Nikaia (1117)," *Byzantinische Zeitschrift* 47 (1954), 374–378.

4. Nicholas of Methone, *Treatise Against Soterichos*, ed. A. Demetrakopoulos, Bibliotheke Ekklesiastike (repr. Hildesheim: Olms, 1965), pp. 337–338.

5. *Fifth Anathema Against Soterichos* in *Synodikon* ed. Gouillard, p. 75.

3

The Iconoclastic Crisis

THE LONG ICONOCLASTIC STRUGGLE, which recurred frequently in Byzantine theology, was intimately connected with the Christological issue which had divided Eastern Christianity in the fifth, sixth, and seventh centuries.

1. APPEARANCE OF THE MOVEMENT

The emperors of the eighth and ninth centuries initiated and supported the iconoclastic movement, and from the start issues of both a theological and a non-theological nature were inseparably involved in this imperial policy.

From contemporary sources and modern historical research, three elements within the movement seem to emerge:

A. *A Problem of Religious Culture.* From their pagan past, Greek-speaking Christians had inherited a taste for religious imagery. When the early Church condemned such art as idolatrous, the tridimensional form practically disappeared, only to reappear in a new, Christian two-dimensional version. Other Eastern Christians, particularly the Syrians and the Armenians, were much less inclined by their cultural past to the use of images. It is significant, therefore, that the emperors who sponsored iconoclasm were of Armenian or Isaurian origins. Moreover, the non-Greek-speaking East was almost entirely Monophysite by the eighth century and, as we shall see, Monophysitism tacitly or explicitly provided the iconoclasts with the essence of their theological arguments.

B. *Confrontation with Islam.* After the Arab conquest of Palestine, Syria, and Egypt, the Byzantine Empire found itself in constant confrontation militarily and ideologically with Islam. Both Christianity and Islam claimed to be world religions, of which the Byzantine emperor and the Arab caliph were, respectively, the heads. But in the accompanying psychological warfare, Islam constantly claimed to be the latest, and therefore the highest and purest, revelation of the God of Abraham, and repeatedly leveled the accusations of polytheism and idolatry, against the Christian doctrine of the Trinity and the use of icons. It was to the charge of idolatry that the Eastern-born emperors of the eighth century responded. They decided to purify Christianity to enable it better to withstand the challenge of Islam. Thus, there was a measure of Islamic influence on the iconoclastic movement, but the influence was part of the cold war against Islam, not the conscious imitation of it.

c. *The Heritage of Hellenic Spiritualism*. The controversy begun by Emperors Leo iii (717–741) and Constantine v (741–775) seems to have been determined initially by the non-theological factors described above. But the iconoclasts easily found in the Greek Christian tradition itself new arguments not directly connected with condemned Monophysitism or with foreign cultural influences. An iconoclastic trend of thought, which could be traced back to early Christianity, was later connected with Origenism. The early apologists of Christianity took the Old Testament prohibitions against any representation of God just as literally as the Jews had. But in their polemics against Christianity, Neoplatonic writers minimized the importance of idols in Greek paganism and developed a *relative* doctrine of the image as a means of access to the divine prototype and not as a dwelling of the divine himself, and used this argument to show the religious inferiority of Christianity. Porphyry, for example, writes:

> If some Hellenes are light-headed enough to believe that the gods live inside idols, their thought remains much purer than that [of the Christians] who believe that the divinity entered the Virgin Mary's womb, became a foetus, was engendered, and wrapped in clothes, was full of blood, membranes, gall, and even viler things.[1]

Porphyry obviously understood that the belief in an historical incarnation of God was inconsistent with total iconoclasm, for an historical Christ was necessarily visible and depictable. And, indeed, Christian iconography began to flourish as early as the third century. In Origenistic circles, however, influenced as they were by Platonic spiritualism which denied to matter a permanent, God-created existence and for whom the only true reality was "intellectual," iconoclastic tendencies survived. When Constantia, sister of the Emperor Constantine, visited Jerusalem and requested an image of Christ from Eusebius of Caesarea, she received the answer that "the form of a servant," assumed by the Logos in Jesus Christ, was no longer in the realm of reality and that her concern for a material image of Jesus was unworthy of true religion; after His glorification, Christ could be contemplated only "in the mind." [2] There is evidence that the theological advisers of Leo iii, the first iconoclastic emperor, were also Origenists with views most certainly identical to those of Eusebius. Thus a purely "Greek" iconoclasm, philosophically quite different from the Oriental and the Islamic ones, contributed to the success of the movement.

2. ICONOCLASTIC THEOLOGY

It seems that no articulate theology of iconoclasm developed in a written form before the reign of Constantine v Copronymos (741–775). The emperor himself published theological treatises attacking the veneration of icons and gathered in Hieria a council claiming ecumenicity (754). The Acts of this assembly are preserved in the minutes of the Seventh Ecumenical Council, the Second of Nicaea, which formally rejected iconoclasm (787).

It is remarkable that Constantine, in order to justify his position, formally referred to the authority of the first six councils; for him iconoclasm was not a new doctrine, but the logical outcome of the Christological debates of the previous centuries. The painter, the Council of Hieria affirmed, when he makes an image of Christ can paint either His humanity alone, thus separating it from the divinity, or both His humanity and His divinity. In the first case he is a Nestorian; in the second case he assumes that divinity is circumscribed by humanity, which is absurd; or that both are confused, in which case, he is a Monophysite.[3]

These arguments do not lack strength and must have impressed his contemporaries, but they fail to account for the Chalcedonian affirmation that "each nature preserves its own manner of being." Obviously, even if they formally rejected Monophysitism, the iconoclasts supposed that the deification of Christ's humanity suppressed its properly human individual character. They also seem to have ignored the true meaning of the hypostatic union, which implies a real distinction between nature and hypostasis. In being assumed by the hypostasis of the Logos, human nature does not merge with divinity; it retains its full identity.

Another aspect of the iconoclasts' position was their notion of the image, which they always considered to be identical or "consubstantial" with the prototype. The consequence of this approach was that a material image could never achieve this identity and was always inadequate. The only true "image" of Christ which they would admit is the sacramental one of the Eucharist as the "image" and "symbol" of Christ, a notion which was drawn from pseudo-Dionysius.[4]

3. ORTHODOX THEOLOGY OF IMAGES:
JOHN OF DAMASCUS AND THE SEVENTH COUNCIL

Some discussion about images must have taken place in Byzantium as early as the late-seventh century and is reflected in Canon 82 of the Council *in Trullo.* The importance of this text lies in the fact that it locates the issue of religious representation in the Christological context:

> In certain reproductions of venerable images, the precursor is pictured indicating the lamb with his finger. This representation was adopted as a symbol of grace. It was a hidden figure of that true lamb who is Christ our God, shown to us according to the Law. Having thus welcomed these ancient figures and shadows as symbols of the truth transmitted to the Church, *we prefer today grace and truth themselves* as a fulfillment of this law. Therefore, in order to expose to the sight of all, at least with the help of painting, that which is perfect, we decree that henceforth Christ our God must be represented *in His human form,* and not in the form of the ancient lamb.[5]

Thus the image of Christ already implied for the fathers of the Council *in Trullo* a confession of faith in the historical Incarnation, which could not be properly expressed in the symbolic figure of a lamb and which needed an image of Jesus "in His human form."

Before Leo III had issued his formal decrees against the images, Germanus I (715–730) the Patriarch of Constantinople, used the same Christological argument against the incipient iconoclasm of the court:

> In eternal memory of the life in the flesh of our Lord Jesus Christ, of His passion, His saving death, and the redemption of the world which results from them, we have received the tradition of representing Him in His human form—i.e., in His visible theophany—understanding that in this way we exalt the humiliation of God the Word.[6]

Germanus thus became the first witness of Orthodoxy against iconoclasm in Byzantium. After his resignation under imperial pressure, the defense of images was taken over by the lonely and geographically remote voice of John of Damascus.

Living and writing in the relative security assured to the Christian ghettoes of the Middle East by the Arab conquerors, this humble monk of the Monastery of St. Sabbas in Palestine succeeded, by his famous three treatises for the defense of the images, in uniting Orthodox opinion in the Byzantine world. His first treatise begins with the reaffirmation of the Christological argument: "I represent God, the Invisible One, not as invisible, but insofar as He has become visible for us by participation in flesh and blood." [7] John's main emphasis is on the *change* which occurred in the relationship between God and the visible world when He became man. By His own will, God became visible by assuming a material existence and giving to matter a new function and dignity.

> In former times, God, without body or form, could in no way be represented. But today, since God has appeared in the flesh and lived among

men, I can represent what is visible in God [*to horaton tou theou*]. I do
not venerate matter, but I venerate the creator of matter, who became matter for my sake, who assumed life in the flesh, and who, through matter,
accomplished my salvation.[8]

In addition to this central argument, John insists on secondary and less
decisive issues. The Old Testament, for example, was not totally iconoclastic, but used images, especially in temple worship, which Christians are
entitled to interpret as prefigurations of Christ. John also denounced the
iconoclasts' identification of the image with the prototype, the idea that an
icon "is God." On this point the Neoplatonic and Origenist traditions,
which were also used by the iconoclasts, supported the side of the Orthodox;
only the Son and the Spirit are "natural images" of the Father, and therefore consubstantial with Him, but other images of God are essentially
different from their model, and therefore not "idols."

It is this discussion on the nature of the image which provided the basis
for the very important definition of the cult of images adopted by the
Seventh Ecumenical Council in 787. The image, or icon, since it is distinct
from the divine model, can be the object only of a relative veneration or
honor, not of worship which is reserved for God alone.[9] This authoritative
statement by an ecumenical council clearly excludes the worship of images
often attributed to Byzantine Christianity.

The misunderstanding on this point is a very old one and is partly the
result of difficulties in translation. The Greek *proskynēsis* ("veneration")
was already translated as *adoratio* in the Latin version of the Conciliar Acts
used by Charlemagne in his famous *Libri Carolini* which rejected the
council. And, later, even Thomas Aquinas—who, of course, accepted Nicaea
II—admitted a "relative adoration" (*latria*) of the images, a position which
gave the Greeks the opportunity of accusing the Latins of idolatry at the
Council of Hagia Sophia in 1450.[10]

In spite of its very great terminological accuracy in describing the veneration of icons, Nicaea II did not elaborate on the technical points of
Christology raised by the iconoclastic Council of Hieria. The task of refuting this council and of developing the rather general Christological
affirmations of Germanus and John of Damascus belongs to the two major
theological figures of the second iconoclastic period—the reigns of Leo V
(813–820), Michael II (820–829), and Theophilus (829–842)—Theodore
the Studite and Patriarch Nicephorus.

4. ORTHODOX THEOLOGY OF IMAGES:
THEODORE THE STUDITE AND NICEPHORUS

Theodore the Studite (759–826) was one of the major reformers of the
Eastern Christian monastic movement. In 798 he found himself at the head

of the Constantinopolitan monastery of Studios (the name of the founder), which by then had fallen into decay. Under Theodore's leadership the community there rapidly grew to several hundred monks and became the main monastic center of the capital. The Studite Rule (*Hypotypōsis*) in its final form is the work of Theodore's disciples, but it applied his principles of monastic life and became the pattern for large cenobitic communities in the Byzantine and Slavic worlds. Theodore himself is the author of two collections of instructions addressed to his monks (the "small" and the "large" *Catecheses*) in which he develops his concept of monasticism based upon obedience to the abbot, liturgical life, constant work, and personal poverty. These principles were quite different from the eremitical, or "hesychast," tradition and were derived from the rules of Pachomius and Basil. The influence of Theodore upon later developments of Byzantine Christianity is also expressed in his contribution to hymnography; many of the ascetical parts of the *Triodion* (proper for Great Lent) and of the *Parakletike,* or *Oktoechos* (the book of the "eight tones"), are his work or the work of his immediate disciples. His role in conflicts between Church and state will be mentioned in the next chapter.

In numerous letters to contemporaries, in his three *Antirrhetics* against the iconoclasts, and in several minor treatises on the subject, Theodore actively participated in the defense of images.

As we have seen, the principal argument of the Orthodox against the iconoclasts was the reality of Christ's manhood; the debate thus gave Byzantine theologians an opportunity to reaffirm the Antiochian contribution to Chalcedonian Christology, and signaled a welcome return to the historical facts of the New Testament. From the age of Justinian, the humanity of Christ had often been expressed in terms of "human nature," assumed as one whole by the New Adam. Obviously, this Platonizing view of humanity in general was insufficient to justify an image of Jesus Christ as a concrete, historical, human individual. The fear of Nestorianism prevented many Byzantine theologians from seeing a man in Christ, for "a man," implying individual human consciousness, seemed for them to mean a separate human hypostasis. In Theodore's anti-iconoclastic writings this difficulty is overcome by a partial return to Aristotelian categories.

> Christ was certainly not a mere man; neither is it orthodox to say that He assumed *an individual among men* [*ton tina anthrōpon*] but the whole, the totality of the nature. It must be said, however, that this total nature was contemplated in an individual manner—for otherwise how could it have been *seen?*—in a way which made it visible and describable . . . , which allowed it to eat and drink. . . .[11]

Humanity for Theodore "exists only in Peter and Paul," i.e., in concrete human beings, and Jesus was such a being. Otherwise, Thomas' experience of placing his finger into Jesus' wounds would have been impossible.[12] The iconoclasts claimed that Christ, in virtue of the union between divinity and humanity, was indescribable, and therefore that no image of Him was possible; but, for Theodore, "an indescribable Christ would be an incorporeal Christ; . . . Isaiah [8:3] described him as a male being, and only the forms of the body can make man and woman distinct from one another." [13]

The firm stand on Christ's individuality as a man again raised the issue of the hypostatic union, for in Chalcedonian Christology the unique hypostasis or person of Christ is that of the Logos. Obviously, then, the notion of hypostasis cannot be identified with either the divine or the human characteristics; neither can it be identical with the idea of human consciousness. The hypostasis is the ultimate source of individual, personal existence, which, in Christ, is both divine and human.

For Theodore, an image can be the image only of an hypostasis, for the image of a nature is inconceivable.[14] On the icons of Christ, the only proper inscription is that of the *personal* God "He who is," the Greek equivalent of the sacred tetragrammaton ΥΗWΗ (Yahweh) of the Old Testament, never such impersonal terms as "divinity" or "kingship" which belong to the Trinity as such and thus cannot be represented.[15] This principle, rigidly followed in classical Byzantine iconography, shows that the icon of Christ is for Theodore not only an image of "the man Jesus," but also of the incarnate Logos. The meaning of the Christian Gospel lies precisely in the fact that the Logos assumed all the characteristics of a man, including describability, and His icon is a permanent witness of this fact.

The humanity of Christ, which makes the icons possible, is a "new humanity," having been fully restored to communion with God, deified in virtue of the communication of idioms, bearing fully again the image of God. This fact is to be reflected in iconography as a form of art: the artist thus receives a quasi-sacramental function. Theodore compares the Christian artist to God Himself, making man in His own image: "The fact that God made man in His image and likeness shows that iconography is a divine action." [16] In the beginning God created man in His image. By making an icon of Christ the iconographer also makes an "image of God," for this is what the deified humanity of Jesus truly is.

By position, temperament, and style, Nicephorus, Patriarch of Constantinople (806–815), was the opposite of Theodore. He belongs to the series of Byzantine patriarchs, between Tarasius and Photius, who were elevated to the supreme ecclesiastical position after a successful civil career. As patriarch he followed a policy of *oikonomia* and suspended the canonical penalties previously imposed upon the priest Joseph who had performed the "adulterous" marriage of Constantine VI. This action brought him into violent conflict with Theodore and the monastic zealots. Later deposed by Leo v (in 815) for his defense of icons, he died in 828 after having composed a *Refutation* of the iconoclastic council of 815, three *Antirrhetics,* one *Long Apology,* and an interesting treatise *Against Eusebius and Epiphanius,* the main patristic references of the iconoclasts.

Nicephorus' thought is altogether directed against the Origenist notion, found in Eusebius' letter to Constantia, that deification of humanity implies dematerialization and absorption into a purely intellectual mode of existence. The patriarch constantly insists on the New Testament evidence that Jesus experienced weariness, hunger, and thirst, like any other man.[17] In dealing with the issue of Jesus' ignorance, Nicephorus also tries to reconcile the relevant scriptural passages with the doctrine of the hypostatic union in a way which, for different reasons, was not common in Eastern theology. In Evagrian Origenism, ignorance was considered as coextensive with, if not identical to, sinfulness. The original state of the created intellects before the Fall was that of divine gnosis. Jesus was precisely the non-fallen intellect and, therefore, eminently and necessarily preserved the "knowledge of God" and, of course, any other form of inferior gnosis. The authors of the age of Justinian, followed by both Maximus and John of Damascus, denied any ignorance in Christ in virtue of the hypostatic union, but, probably also under the influence of a latent Evagrianism, they interpreted the Gospel passages speaking of ignorance on the part of Jesus as examples of his *oikonomia,* or pastoral desire, to be seen as a mere man, and not as expressions of real ignorance. Nicephorus stands in opposition to that tradition on this point, although he admits that the hypostatic union *could* suppress all human ignorance in Jesus, in virtue of the communication of idioms, the divine knowledge being communicated to the human nature. He maintains that divine economy in fact required that Christ assume all aspects of human existence, including ignorance: "He willingly acted, desired, was ignorant, and suffered as man."[18] In becoming incarnate the Logos assumed not an abstract, ideal humanity, but the concrete humanity which existed in history after the Fall, in order to save it. "He did not possess a flesh other than our own, that which fell as a consequence of sin; He did not transform it [in assuming it], . . . He was made of the same nature as we, but without sin, and through that nature He condemned sin and death."[19]

This fullness of humanity implied, of course, describability, for if Christ were undescribable, His Mother, with whom He shared the same human nature, would have to be considered as undescribable as well. "Too much honor given to the Mother," Nicephorus writes, "amounts to dishonoring her, for one would have to attribute to her incorruptibility, immortality, and impassibility, if what by nature belongs to the Logos must also by grace be attributed to her who gave Him birth."[20]

The same logic applies to the Eucharist which, as we have seen, the iconoclasts considered as the only admissible image or symbol of Christ. For Nicephorus and the other Orthodox defenders of images, this concept was unacceptable because they understood the Eucharist as the very reality of the Body and Blood of Christ, and precisely not as an "image," for an image is made to be *seen,* while the Eucharist remains fundamentally *food* to be eaten. By being assumed into Christ the Eucharistic elements do not lose their connection with this world, just as the Virgin Mary did not cease to be part of humanity by becoming the Mother of God. "We confess," writes Nicephorus, "that by the priest's invocation, by the coming of the Most Holy Spirit, the Body and Blood of Christ are mystically and invisibly made present . . ."; and they are saving food for us "not because the Body ceases to be a body, but because it remains so and is preserved as body." [21]

Nicephorus' insistence upon the authenticity of Christ's humanity at times leads him away from classical Cyrillian Christology. He evades Theopaschism by refusing to admit either that "the Logos suffered the passion, or that the flesh produced miracles. . . . One must attribute to each nature what is proper to it," [22] and minimizes the value of the communication of idioms which, according to him, manipulates "words." [23] Obviously Theodore the Studite was more immune to the risk of Nestorianizing than was Nicephorus. In any case, the necessity of reaffirming the humanity of Christ and, thus, of defending His describability, led Byzantine theologians to a revival of elements of the Antiochian tradition and, thus, to a proof of their faithfulness to Chalcedon.

5. LASTING SIGNIFICANCE OF THE ISSUE

The iconoclastic controversy had a lasting influence upon the intellectual life of Byzantium. Four aspects of this influence seem particularly relevant to theological development.

A. At the time of the Persian wars of Emperor Heraclius in the seventh century, Byzantium turned away culturally from its Roman past and toward the East. The great confrontation with Islam, which was reflected in the origins and character of iconoclasm, made this trend even more definite. Deprived of political protection by the Byzantine emperors, with whom they were in doctrinal conflict, the popes turned to the Franks and thus affiliated themselves with the emerging new Latin Middle Ages. As a result the social, cultural, and political background of this separation became more evident; the two halves of the Christian world began to speak different languages, and their frames of reference in theology began to diverge more sharply than before.

Byzantium's turn to the East, even if it expressed itself in a certain cultural osmosis with the Arab world, especially during the reign of Theophilus, did not mean a greater understanding between Byzantine Christianity and

Islam; the confrontation remained fundamentally hostile, and this hostility prevented real dialogue. John of Damascus, who himself lived in Arab-dominated Palestine, spoke of Mohammed as the "forerunner of the Anti-Christ." [24] Giving second-hand quotations from the Koran, he presented the new religion as nothing more than gross superstition and immorality. Later-Byzantine literature on Islam rarely transcended this level of pure polemics.

However, even if this orientation eastward was not in itself an enrichment, Byzantium remained for several centuries the real capital of the Christian world. Culturally surpassing the Carolingian West and militarily strong in resisting Islam, Byzantine Christianity kept its universalist missionary vision, which expressed itself in a successful evangelization of the Slavs and other Eastern nations. But its later theological development took place in an exclusively Greek setting. Still bearing the title of "Great Church of Constantinople–New Rome," it became known to both its Latin competitors and its Slavic disciples as the "Greek" Church.

B. Whatever role was played in the Orthodox victory over the iconoclasts by high ecclesiastical dignitaries and such theologians as Patriarch Nicephorus, the real credit belonged to the Byzantine monks who resisted the emperors in overwhelming numbers. The emperors, especially Leo III and Constantine V, expressed more clearly than any of their predecessors a claim to caesaropapism. Thus the iconoclastic controversy was largely a confrontation between the state and a non-conformist, staunchly independent monasticism, which assumed the prophetic role of standing for the independence of the Gospel from the "world." The fact that this role was assumed by the monks, and not by the highest canonical authority of the Church, underlines the fact that the issue was the defense, not of the Church as an institution, but of the Christian faith as the way to eternal salvation.

The monks, of course, took their role very seriously and preserved, even after their victory, a peculiar sense of responsibility for the faith, as we saw in the case of Theodore the Studite. Theologically they maintained a tradition of faithfulness to the past, as well as a sense of the existential relevance of theology as such. Their role in later-Byzantine theological development remained decisive for centuries.

c. The theological issue between the Orthodox and the iconoclasts was fundamentally concerned with the icon of Christ, for belief in the divinity of Christ implied a stand on the crucial point of God's essential indescribability and on the Incarnation, which made Him visible. Thus the icon of Christ is the icon *par excellence* and implies a confession of faith in the Incarnation.

The iconoclasts, however, objected on theological grounds, not only to this icon, but also to the use of any religious pictures, except the cross, because, as their Council of 754 proclaims, they opposed "all paganism."

Any veneration of images was equated with idolatry. If the goal pursued by Constantine v to "purify" Byzantine Christianity, not only of the image cult, but also of monasticism, had been achieved, the entire character of Eastern Christian piety and its ethos would have evolved differently. The victory of Orthodoxy meant, for example, that religious faith could be expressed, not only in propositions, in books, or in personal experience, but also through man's power over matter, through aesthetic experience, and through gestures and bodily attitudes before holy images. All this implied a philosophy of religion and an anthropology; worship, the liturgy, religious consciousness involved the whole man, without despising any functions of the soul or of the body, and without leaving any of them to the realm of the secular.

D. Of all the cultural families of Christianity—the Latin, the Syrian, the Egyptian, or the Armenian—the Byzantine was the only one in which art became inseparable from theology. The debates of the eighth and ninth centuries have shown that in the light of the Incarnation art could not retain a "neutral" function, that it could and even must express the faith. Thus through their style, through symbolic compositions, through the elaborate artistic programs covering the walls of Byzantine churches, through the permanent system which presided over the composition of the Byzantine iconostasis, icons became an expression and a source of divine knowledge. The good news about God's becoming man; about the presence among men of a glorified and deified humanity, first in Christ, but also through Him and the Holy Spirit in the Virgin Mary and in the saints—all this "adornment of the Church" was expressed in Byzantine Christian art. Eugene Trubetskoi, a Russian philosopher of the early-twentieth century, called this expression "contemplation in colors." [25]

NOTES

1. Porphyry, *Against the Christians,* fragment 77; ed. A. Harnack, *AbhBerlAk* (1916), 93.
2. Text of Eusebius' letter in Nicephorus, *Contra Eusebium,* ed. J. B. Pitra, *Spicilegium Solesmense* (Paris, 1852; repr. Graz, 1962), I, 383–386.
3. Mansi, XIII, 252AB, 256AB.
4. *Ibid.,* 261D–264C. See pseudo-Dionysius, *Celestial Hierarchy*; PG 3:124A.
5. Mansi, XI, 977–980.
6. Germanus I, *De haeresibus et synodis*; PG 98:80A.
7. John of Damascus, *Or.* I; PG 94:1236C.
8. *Ibid.*; PG 94:1245A.
9. Mansi, XIII, 377D.
10. *Ibid.,* XXXII, 103.
11. Theodore the Studite, *Antirrhetic* 1; PG 99:332D–333A.
12. *Ibid.,* III; PG 99:396C–397A.
13. *Ibid.,* 409C.

14. *Ibid.*, 405A.
15. Theodore the Studite, *Letter to Naucratius*, II, 67; PG 99:1296AB; see also *Antirrh.*, III; PG 99:420D.
16. *Antirrh.*, III; PG 99:420A.
17. Nicephorus, *Antirrh.*, I; PG 100:272B.
18. *Ibid.*, 328BD.
19. Nicephorus, *Contra Eusebium*, ed. Pitra, I, 401.
20. *Antirrh.*; PG 100:268B.
21. *Ibid.*, 440, 447.
22. *Ibid.*, 252B.
23. *Ibid.*, 317B.
24. John of Damascus, *De Haer.*; PG 94:764A.
25. E. Trubetskoi, *Umozrenie v Kraskakh* (Moscow, 1915–1916; repr. Paris: YMCA Press, 1965); trans. *Icons: Theology in Color* (New York: St. Vladimir's Seminary Press, 1973).

4

Monks and Humanists

IN 843 THE BYZANTINE CHURCH celebrated the "triumph of orthodoxy" over iconoclasm, a triumph which was interpreted as a victory over all the heresies which until that time had divided Christendom. The document composed for the occasion, the famous *Synodikon,* commemorates the champions of the true faith, condemns the heretics, and implicitly presupposes that Byzantine society had reached an internal stability which would never allow further division. In fact, new conflicts and crises did occur, and the *Synodikon* would have to be expanded. But the tendency to freeze history, to consider their empire and Church as expressing the eternal and unchangeable form of God's revelation, would be a permanent and mythological feature of Byzantine civilization, even though it was constantly challenged by historical realities. In the ninth century itself, Byzantine society was, in fact, a divided society—divided politically, intellectually, and theologically.

During the entire iconoclastic period, Byzantium had been culturally cut off from the West and fascinated with the military and intellectual challenge of Islam. When, in 787 and in 843, communion was finally reestablished with the Church of Rome, the hostile emergence of the Carolingian Empire prevented the restoration of the old *orbis Christianorum.* Moreover, the resumption of the veneration of icons was a victory of *Greek* traditions, as distinct from the Oriental, non-Greek cultural iconoclasm of the Isaurians. The result of these historical developments was the emergence of the Byzantine Church from the iconoclastic crisis as more than ever a "Greek" church. It might even have become a purely national church, such as the Armenian, if the empire had not expanded again in the ninth and tenth centuries under the great emperors of the Macedonian dynasty, and if the evangelization of the Slavs and the subsequent expansion of Byzantine Christianity into Eastern Europe, one of the major missionary events of Christian history, had not taken place. Unlike the West, however, where the papacy "passed to the barbarians" after their conversions, Constantinople, the "New Rome," remained the unquestionable and unique intellectual center of the Christian East until 1453. This "Rome" was culturally and intellectually *Greek,* so much so that Emperor Michael III, in a letter to Pope Nicholas I, could even designate Latin as a "barbarian" and "Scythian" tongue.

The Hellenic character of Byzantine civilization brought into theology the perennial problem of the relationship between the ancient Greek "mind" and the Christian Gospel. Although the issue was implicit in much of the theological literature in the sixth, seventh, and eighth centuries, it had not been raised explicitly since the closing of the pagan universities by Justinian. In the ninth century, following the intellectual renewal which had taken place under Theophilus (829–842), the last iconoclastic emperor, Byzantine scholars undertook more vigorously the study of ancient pagan authors. The University of Constantinople, endowed and protected by the Caesar Bardas and distinguished by the teaching of the great Photius, became the center of this first renaissance. Scholars such as Photius, Arethas, and Michael Psellos promoted encyclopedic curiosity and encouraged the copying of ancient manuscripts. Much of our knowledge of Greek antiquity is the direct result of their labors. On the whole, their interest in ancient philosophy remained rather academic, and coexisted easily with the equally academic and conservative theology which predominated in the official circles of the Church. When John Italos, in the eleventh century, attempted a new synthesis between Platonism and Christianity, he immediately incurred canonical sanction. Thus Byzantine humanism always lacked the coherence and dynamism of both Western Scholasticism and the Western Renaissance, and was unable to break the widespread conviction of many Byzantines that Athens and Jerusalem were incompatible. The watchdogs in this respect were the leading representatives of a monasticism which persisted in a staunch opposition to "secular wisdom."

This polarity between the humanists and the monks not only appeared on the intellectual level; it manifested itself in ecclesiastical politics. The monks consistently opposed the ecclesiastical "realists" who were ready to practice toleration toward former iconoclasts and imperial sinners, and toward unavoidable political compromises and, at a later period, state-sponsored doctrinal compromises with the Latin West. Conflicts of this sort occurred when Patriarchs Tarasius (784–806) and Methodius I (843–847) accepted into the episcopate former supporters of official iconoclasm, when the same Tarasius and Nicephorus I (806–815) condoned the remarriage of Emperor Constantine VI, who had divorced his first wife, and when in 857 Patriarch Ignatius was forced to resign and was replaced by Photius. These conflicts, though not formally theological, involved the issue of the Christian witness in the world, and, as such, greatly influenced Byzantine ecclesiology and social ethics.

THEODORE THE STUDITE

Theodore was, in the ninth century, both the model and the ideologist of the rigorist monastic party which played a decisive role in the entire life of Byzantine Christendom.

In the preceding chapter Theodore's contribution to the theology of images as an aspect of Chalcedonian Christological orthodoxy was discussed. His impact on the history of monasticism is equally important. Severely challenged by iconoclastic persecutions, Byzantine monasticism had acquired the prestige of martyrdom, and its authority in Orthodox circles was often greater than that of the compromise-minded hierarchy. Under Theodore's leadership it became an organized and articulate bulwark of canonical and moral rigorism.

For Theodore, monastic life was, in fact, synonymous with authentic Christianity:

> Certain people ask, whence arose the tradition of renouncing the world and of becoming monks? But their question is the same as asking, whence the tradition of becoming Christians? For the One who first laid down the apostolic tradition also ordained six mysteries: first, illumination; second, the assembly or communion; third, the perfection of the chrism; fourth, the perfections of priesthood; fifth, the monastic perfection; sixth, the service for those who fall asleep in holiness.[1]

This passage is important not only because monasticism is counted among the sacraments of the Church—in a list strikingly different from the post-Tridentine "seven sacraments"—but also, and chiefly, because the monastic state is considered one of the essential forms of Christian perfection and witness. Through detachment, through the vows of poverty, chastity, and obedience, through a life projected into the already-given reality of the kingdom of God, monasticism becomes an "angelic life." The monks, according to Theodore, formed an eschatological community which realizes more fully and more perfectly what the entire Church is supposed to be. The Studite monks brought this eschatological witness into the very midst of the imperial capital, the center of the "world," and considered it normal to be in almost constant conflict with the "world" and with whatever it represented. They constituted a well-organized group. Their abbot abhorred the spiritual individualism of the early Christian hermits, and built Studios into a regimented, liturgical, working community, in accordance with the best cenobitic traditions stemming from Basil and Pachomius.

For Theodore and his disciples, "otherworldliness" never meant that Christian action was not needed in the world. Quite to the contrary. The monks practiced and preached active involvement in the affairs of the city so that it might conform itself as far as possible to the rigorous criteria of the kingdom of God as they understood it. The iconoclastic emperors persecuted the monks for their defense of the icons, of course, but also for their attempts to submit the earthly Christian empire to the imperatives and requirements of a transcendent Gospel. Their Orthodox successors, obliged to recognize the moral victory of the monks and to solicit their support, also found it difficult to comply with all their demands. The conflict over the second marriage of Constantine VI (795) which Patriarchs Tarasius and Nicephorus tolerated, but which Theodore and the Studites considered "adulterous" ("moechian schism"), provoked decades of discussion over the nature of *oikonomia*—i.e., the possibility of circumventing the letter of the law for the ultimate good of the Church and of the individual's salvation. This principle, invoked by the council of 809, and discussed at greater length in the next chapter, was challenged by Theodore not so much in itself as in the concrete case of Constantine VI. "Either the emperor is God, for divinity alone is not subject to the law, or there is anarchy and revolution. For how can there be peace if there is no law valid for all, if the emperor can fulfill his desires—commit adultery, or accept heresies, for example—while his subjects are forbidden to communicate with the adulterer or the heretic?" [2]

Theodore was certainly not an innovator in his attitude toward the state. For his was the attitude of Athanasius, of John Chrysostom, of Maximus the Confessor, and of John of Damascus, and it would be that of a large segment of Byzantine churchmen in later centuries; it merely illustrates the fact that Byzantine society was far from having found the "harmony" between the two powers about which Justinian spoke in his *Novella* 6. The action and witness of the monks was always present in Byzantium to demonstrate that true harmony between the kingdom of God and the "world" was possible only in the *parousia*.

Theodore's ideology and commitments normally led him away from the Constantinian parallelism between the political structure of the empire and the structure of the Church, a parallelism endorsed in Nicaea and best exemplified in the gradual elevation of the bishop of Constantinople to "ecumenical patriarch." Theodore, of course, never formally denied the canonical texts which reflected it but, in practice, often referred to the principle of apostolicity as a criterion of authority in the Church, rather than to the political pre-eminence of certain cities. The support given to the Orthodox party during the iconoclastic period by the Church of Rome, the friendly correspondence which Theodore was able to establish with Popes Leo III (795–816) and Paschal I (817–824), contrasted with the internal conflicts which existed with his own patriarchs, both iconoclastic and Orthodox. These factors explain the very high regard he repeatedly expressed toward the "apostolic throne" of old Rome. For example, he addressed Pope Paschal as "the rock of faith upon which the Catholic

Church is built." "You are Peter," he writes, "adorning the throne of Peter." [3] The numerous passages of this kind carefully collected by modern apologists of the papacy[4] are, however, not entirely sufficient to prove that Theodore's view of Rome is identical to that of Vatican I. In his letters, side by side with references to Peter and to the pope as leaders of the Church, one can also find him speaking of the "five-headed body of the Church," [5] with reference to the Byzantine concept of a "pentarchy" of patriarchs. Also, addressing himself to the patriarch of Jerusalem, he calls him "first among the patriarchs" for the place where the Lord suffered presupposes "the dignity highest of all." [6]

Independence of the categories of "this world," and therefore of the state, was the only real concern of the great Studite. The apostolic claim of Rome, but also the no less real, but much less effective, claims of the other Eastern patriarchs, provided him with arguments in his fight against the Byzantine state and Church hierarchies. Still, there is no reason to doubt that his view of the unity of the Church, which he never systematically developed, was not radically different from that of his contemporaries, including Patriarch Photius, who, as we shall see, was always ready to acknowledge the prominent position of Peter among the apostles, but also considered that the authority of Peter's Roman successors was dependent upon, not the foundation of, their orthodoxy. In Rome, Theodore the Studite saw that foremost support of the true faith, and expressed his vision and his hope in the best tradition of the Byzantine superlative style.

The ancient monastic opposition to secular philosophy does not appear in Theodore's writings. Theodore himself seemed even to have liked exercises in dialectics, as his early correspondence with John the Grammarian, a humanist and later an iconoclastic patriarch, seems to show. But the anti-humanist tendency would clearly appear among his immediate disciples, the anti-Photians of the ninth century.

PHOTIUS (*ca.* 820–*ca.* 891)

The dominant figure in Byzantine religious, social, and political life in the ninth century, Photius is also the father of what is generally called Byzantine "humanism." In his famous *Library,* an original and tremendously important compilation of literary criticism, he covers Christian writers of the early centuries, as well as a number of secular authors; similarly, in his *Responses* to Amphilochius, a collection of theological and philosophical essays, he displays a wide secular knowledge and an extensive training in patristic theology.

In all his writings Photius remains essentially a university professor. In philosophy his main interest is logic and dialectics; hence, his very clear predisposition to Aristotle, rather than to Plato. In theology he remains faithful to the positions and problematics of the early councils and Fathers. His love for ancient philosophy does not lead him to any tolerance toward a man like Origen, whose condemnation by the Fifth Council he accepts without reservation,[7] or like Clement of Alexandria, in whose main writing, the *Hypotypōseis*, Photius found the "impious myths" of Platonism.[8]

His extensive erudition often provides us with detailed critical analysis of, and exact quotations from, authors about whom, without his notes, we should know nothing. The Christological controversies of the fifth and sixth centuries in particular attracted Photius' attention. Despite his predilection for Antiochian exegesis and for theologians of the Antiochian school,[9] he remains rigorously faithful to the Cyrillian exegesis of the Council of Chalcedon, which prevailed in Byzantium under Justinian, and devotes long and, for us, precious attention to some of its important spokesmen.[10]

On other theological issues, Photius remains in very formal agreement with traditional patristic and conciliar positions. But he does not seem to have accepted fully or to have understood the implications of the absolute apophaticism of a Gregory of Nyssa, and his doctrine of God in relation to creation seems to approach the Latin Scholastic concept of the *actus purus*.[11] But careful analysis of Photius' thought would be required to assert his exact position on this point. In any case, his authority was invoked by the Byzantine anti-Palamites of the fourteenth century against the real distinction between essence and "energy" in God maintained by Palamas and endorsed by the councils of the period.[12] In addition, his devotion to secular learning and his liberal use of *oikonomia* made him, during his lifetime and after, rather unpopular in monastic circles.

In one aspect, Photius obviously dominated his contemporaries and the Middle Ages as a whole: his sense of history, of historical development, and of tradition. This sense is apparent in every codex (chapter) of the *Library*. Thus, in analyzing the book of a priest Theodore, who defended the authenticity of the Dionysian writings, Photius carefully lists the arguments against authenticity and concludes with the simple statement that the author "tries to refute these objections and affirms that *in his opinion* the book of the great Dionysius is genuine."[13] Even if, on other occasions, Photius takes Dionysian authenticity for granted, the passage just cited clearly shows Photius' intellectual honesty in acknowledging the impossibility of explaining the way in which Dionysius can foretell "traditions which grew old only gradually in the Church and took a long time to develop."[14]

This acknowledgment of the development of tradition and also of a possible and legitimate variety in ecclesiastical practices and rules plays a significant role in Photius' attitude toward Pope Nicholas I and toward the Church of Rome. Accused by the pope of having been elevated from the lay state to the patriarchate in six days, a practice forbidden in Western tradition but never formally opposed in the East, Photius writes: "Everyone must preserve what is defined by common ecumenical decisions, but a particular opinion of a Church Father or a definition issued by a local council can be followed by some and ignored by others. . . ." He then refers to such issues as shaving, fasting on Saturdays, and a celibate priesthood, and continues: "When faith remains inviolate, the common and catholic decisions are also safe; a sensible man respects the practices and laws of others; he considers that it is neither wrong to observe them nor illegal to violate them." [15]

Photius' concern for the "common faith" and "ecumenical decisions" is illustrated in the *Filioque* issue. Since modern historical research has clearly shown that he was not systematically anti-Latin, his position in the dispute can be explained only by the fact that he took the theological issue itself seriously. Not only did he place the main emphasis on the *Filioque* in his encyclical of 866, but even after ecclesiastical peace had been restored with Pope John VIII in 879–880, and after his retirement from the patriarchate, Photius still devoted many of his last days to writing the *Mystagogy of the Holy Spirit,* the first detailed Greek refutation of the Latin interpolation of *Filioque* into the Creed.

As the *Mystagogy* clearly shows, Photius was equally concerned with this unilateral interpolation into a text which had won universal approval, and with the content of the interpolation itself. He made no distinction between the canonical and theological aspects of the issue and referred to the popes, especially to Leo III and to John VIII, who had opposed the interpolation, as opponents of the *doctrine* of the "double procession." The weakness of Photius' treatment of the issue lies in the fact that he had no access to the sources of Latin theology. He knew, however, that the Latin Fathers favored the *Filioque,* and refers specifically to Ambrose, Augustine, and Jerome (although the first and the last can hardly be regarded as proponents of the *Filioque*); but he obviously had not read their writings. His refutation of the Latin position is therefore based on oral information alone.

Whatever its shortcomings and its difficult and sharply dialectical style, the *Mystagogy* makes clear the basic Byzantine objection to the Latin doctrine of the Trinity: that it understands God as a single and philosophically simple essence, in which personal or hypostatic existence is reduced to the concept of mutual relations between the three Persons. If the idea of consubstantiality requires that the Father and the Son together be the one origin of the Spirit, essence in God necessarily precedes His personal existence as three hypostases. For Photius, however, "the Father is the origin [of the Son and of the Holy Spirit] not by nature, but in virtue of His hypostatic character." [16] To confuse the hypostatic characters of the Father and the Son by attributing to them the procession of the Spirit is to fall into Sabellianism, a modalist heresy of the third century, or rather into semi-Sabellianism. For Sabellius had confused the three Persons into one, while the Latins limit themselves to the Father and the Son, but then fall into the danger of excluding the Spirit from the Godhead altogether.[17]

Thus, Photius clearly demonstrates that behind the dispute on the *Filioque* lie two concepts of the Trinity: the Greek personalistic concept, which considers the personal revelation of the Father, the Son, and the Spirit as the starting point of Trinitarian theology; and the Latin, Augustinian approach to God as a simple essence, within which a Trinity of persons can be understood only in terms of internal relations.

In opposing the Latin view of the Trinity, Photius does not deny the *sending* of the Spirit through the Son to the world, in the "economy" of salvation, as the link between the deified humanity of Jesus and the entire body of the Church and of creation.[18] He would not be opposed, therefore, to speaking of a procession of the Spirit through, or from, the Son in this last sense. Neither does he oppose the West as such. He repeatedly acknowledges the authority of the Latin Fathers and of the Church of Rome where the interpolated creed was not yet used at the time. He claims —and there is no reason to doubt his sincerity—to be concerned only with the unity of the East and West in the one, catholic faith defined by the ancient councils. Unfortunately, after him history would drive the two halves of Christendom even further apart, and Photius' fundamental broadmindedness and sense of history would be sorely lacking on both sides.

MICHAEL PSELLOS (1018–1078)

After the age of Photius, Byzantine intellectuals found a freer and fuller access to the sources of ancient Greek philosophy. With Michael Psellos we discover a personality who is, to a large extent, the product of this early-medieval Byzantine renaissance. Psellos' contribution to theology is actually very limited and only indirect. Since in the accepted Byzantine world-view, religion and philosophy were in fact inseparable, he can and must be mentioned as a major phenomenon in the history of Byzantine Christianity.

"I want you to know," he writes, "that Hellenic wisdom, while it fails to render glory to the divine and is not unfailing in theology, *knows nature as the Creator made it*." [19] This acknowledgment of the ancients' competence in understanding nature implies a basis for natural theology, a knowledge of the Creator through the creatures. Elements of this approach existed, of course, among the Apologists of the second and third centuries and were developed by Origen and by the Cappadocian Fathers. But, first and foremost, responsible churchmen, they emphasized the religious gap between Christianity and ancient Hellenism. For them Hellenic wisdom was a tool for apologetics, not an end in itself. Occasionally, Psellos himself recognizes this incompatibility; for example, he refutes Plato's concept of a world of ideas subsistent in themselves, and not only in the divine intellect.[20] But these reservations come to his mind from explicit and formal definitions of the Church, rather than from any deep conviction. He certainly expresses the true state of his mind more accurately when he writes: "To be born to knowledge I am satisfied with the throes of Plato and Aristotle: they give me birth and form me." [21]

In fact, the rather formal theological conservatism which prevailed in official circles of the Church made possible, in men like Psellos, the resurgence of a Neoplatonism approximately identical to what it had been in the sixth century. In him and his contemporaries there was, in fact, very little true encounter between theology and philosophy. Psellos certainly remained a Christian, but if there is any emotional thrust to his thought, it consists in finding agreement, and not opposition, between Platonism and Christianity, and it is of little concern to him if the agreement is artificial. Psellos is quite happy, for example, to discover the Trinity, as well as the Biblical world of angels and saints, in Homer.[22]

This example of formal and artificial adaptation of Hellenism to the Gospel shows the limitations of what has been called Byzantine humanism. It obviously lacked the living stamina which made Western Scholasticism possible after the rediscovery of Aristotle or the Italian Renaissance after the decline of medieval civilization. Even if he knew Plato and Aristotle better than those in the West ever did, Psellos remained a medieval Byzantine—i.e., a man committed to tradition, and loyal, at least formally, to the rigid norms of official theology. He was not a great theologian, and his loyalty to official theology prevented him from becoming a really great philosopher. Fundamentally, his thought remains eclectic. The principles of Neoplatonism—fidelity to Aristotle in logic and natural philosophy, coupled with Platonic metaphysics—were precisely appropriate to his frame of mind. "As far as I am concerned," he confesses, "I collected the virtue and the potential of everyone; my reasoning is varied and is a melding of every single idea into one. And I myself am one out of many. If one reads my books, one discovers that they are many out of one." [23]

No brilliancy of expression, no exquisite sophistication of style was sufficient to transform this eclecticism into an original and creative system of philosophy. Real creativity and living thought continued in the circles which Psellos considered infested with unhealthy and irrational mysticism. It is doubtful, however, whether Psellos at any time even met or read the most authentic representatives of monastic spirituality, his contemporaries, such as Symeon the New Theologian. If he had, they would have been unlikely to understand each other at all.

THE TRIALS OF JOHN ITALOS (1076–1077, 1082)

A disciple of Psellos' and his successor as *hypatos tōn philosophōn,* i.e., as head of the university, John Italos ("the Italian," probably an Italo-Greek) was formally brought to trial on charges of heresy and condemned for his exaggerated use of ancient philosophy in general and, in particular, for holding Platonic views on the origin and nature of the world. The importance of his two successive trials is emphasized by the fact that, for the first time since 843, new extensive doctrinal paragraphs were added to the *Synodikon* to be read yearly on the Sunday of Orthodoxy. By condemning Italos, the Byzantine Church thus created a pattern which could be, and indeed was, used in later times.

The published writings of John Italos do not contain all the teachings of which he was accused, but it cannot be excluded *a priori* that he actually held them in his oral teaching. In any case, the decisions of the synod concerning him have an importance beyond his personality, as a position taken officially by the Church.

In the eleven anathemas referring to the case of Italos in the *Synodikon,* the first ten are purely doctrinal and were issued in 1076–1077; the final one is a formal personal condemnation published in 1082.[24] The doctrinal position taken by the synod concerns two major issues:

1) Ancient Greek philosophers were the first heresiarchs; in other words, all the major Christian heresies resulted from their influence and, therefore, the seven councils, by condemning the heretics, also implicitly condemned the philosophers (Anath. 5). Actually, after Tertullian, patristic literature frequently ascribed to philosophy the responsibility for all heresies. The position of the synod, therefore, was not entirely new, but its restatement in the eleventh century was of very great importance for medieval Byzantium. A distinction was admitted, however, between those who accept the "foolish opinions" of the philosophers and those who pursue "Hellenic studies" for instruction only (Anath. 7). The second attitude was not considered automatically wrong. The synodal decision corresponds somewhat to the positive attitude, accepted in conservative circles and present even in Psellos, toward the study of Aristotle's *Organon* as opposed to the study of Plato. Though Aristotle was generally considered to be a teacher of logic and physics, subjects useful "for instruction," Plato implied a metaphysical stand incompatible with Christianity.

2) The anathemas condemn a series of Platonizing positions attributed to Italos and almost identical with the Origenistic theses rejected by Justinian and the Council of 553: pre-existence and the transmigration of

souls, denial of bodily resurrection, eternity of matter, self-subsistent world of ideas, and so forth.

Even after the condemnation of Italos, learned Byzantines continued, of course, to read, to copy, and to study ancient Greek authors, but any attempt to follow the ancients' "foolish opinions" was now automatically a crime against the true faith. No doubt, the decisions of 1076–1077, while clearly encouraging the traditional monastic abhorrence of "Hellenism," constituted a serious new handicap for the development of humanism.

Greek in its language and culture, Byzantium thus took a much more negative stand toward Greek philosophy than the West ever did. On the eve of the period when the West would commit its mind to the philosophy of the ancients and enter the great epoch of Scholasticism, the Byzantine Church solemnly refused any new synthesis between the Greek mind and Christianity, remaining committed only to the synthesis reached in the patristic period. It assigned to the West the task of becoming more Greek than it was. Obviously, this was an option of the greatest importance for the future of theology and for relations between East and West.

NOTES

1. Theodore the Studite, *Ep.* II, 165 (to Gregory); PG 99:1524B.

2. Theodore the Studite, *Ep.* I, 36 (to Euprepianus); PG 99:1032cD.

3. Theodore the Studite, *Ep.* II, 12; PG 99:1152c.

4. See, for example, S. Salaville, "La primauté de Saint Pierre et du pape d'après Saint Théodore Studite (759–826)," *Échos d'Orient* 17 (1914), 23–42; and A. Marin, *Saint Théodore* (Paris: Lecoffre, 1906), p. 1, who calls Theodore "the last Catholic of Byzantium." Similarly, in his letter to Leo Sacellarius (PG 99:1417c) he wrote: "And who are their [the Apostles'] successors?—he who occupies the throne of Rome and is the first; the one who sits upon the throne of Constantinople and is the second; after them, those of Alexandria, Antioch, and Jerusalem. That is the Pentarchic authority in the Church. It is to them that all decision belongs in divine dogmas" (quoted in F. Dvornik, *Byzantium and the Roman Primacy* [New York: Fordham University Press, 1966], p. 101).

5. Theodore the Studite, *Ep.* II, 63 (to Naucratius); PG 99:1281B.

6. Theodore the Studite, *Ep.* II, 15; PG 99:1161AB.

7. Photius, *Library*, codex 8, 18, etc.

8. *Ibid.*, codex 109.

9. See the long article on Diodore of Tarsus, *Library*, codex 223, and his appreciation of Theodoret of Cyrus, *ibid.*, codex 46.

10. See codices on Eulogius of Alexandria, 182, 208, 225–227, which, in fact, are detailed monographs on this author. On Ephrem of Antioch, see *Library*, codex 228.

11. "The divine is in the universe both by essence and by energy." *Amphil.*, 75; PG 101:465BC.

12. See Akindynos, *Against Palamas*, in Codex Monacensis graecus 223, foll. 283^v, 293^v, 298^v, 305, 311^v, etc.

13. *Library*, codex 1.

14. *Ibid.*

15. *Ep.* 2 to Pope Nicholas; PG 102:604D–605D.

16. *Mystagogy of the Holy Spirit*, 15; PG 102:293A.

17. *Ibid.*, 9, 23; PG 102:289B, 313BC.

18. *Ibid.*, 94.

19. Michael Psellos, *Address to His Negligent Disciples,* ed. J. F. Boissonade (Nuremberg, 1838; repr. Amsterdam: Hakkert, 1964), p. 151.

20. Ed. C. Sathas, *Bibliotheca graeca medii aevi* (Venice, 1872), V, 442.

21. *Address to His Negligent Disciples,* p. 146.

22. See B. Tatakis, *La philosophie byzantine* (Paris: Alcan, 1949), p. 199.

23. Michael Psellos, *On the Character of Some Writings,* ed. J. F. Boissonade, p. 52.

24. See J. Gouillard, *Synodikon,* pp. 56–60, 188–202.

5

Monastic Theology

THE ROLE OF THE MONKS in the triumph of Orthodoxy over iconoclasm illustrates their traditional involvement in theological debates in Byzantium; Byzantine monasticism thus appears not only as a school of spiritual perfection, but also as a body which feels responsibility for the content of the faith and for the fate of the Church as a whole. At the same time, the particularity of the monastic polity and ideology, its foundation upon the notion that "the Kingdom of God is not of this world," and its opposition to all compromises with "this world's" requirements, gave rise in Byzantium to a theology which can properly be called "monastic." In contrast with the formal conservatism of official ecclesiastical circles and in opposition to the traditions of secular Hellenism, this theology happened also to be the most dynamic and creative current in Byzantine thought as a whole.

It is well known that, very early in its development, monasticism became a diversified movement. Between the extreme eremitism of Antony of Egypt and the absolute and organized cenobitism of Pachomius, there was a whole scale of intermediary forms of monastic life practiced everywhere in Eastern Christendom and gradually spreading to the West. Between the hermits—also frequently called "hesychasts"—and the cenobites there was often competition and, at times, conflict; but the entire Eastern monastic movement remained united in its basic "other-worldliness" and in the conviction that prayer, whatever its form, was the fundamental and permanent content of monastic life. Some monastic centers—such as the monastery of Studios—may have been relatively "activist," developing social work, learning, manuscript copying, and other practical concerns; but, even then, the liturgical cycle of the monastic office remained the absolute center of the community's life and, generally, comprised at least half of the monk's daily schedule.

As a whole, the monastic community taught the Byzantines how to pray. The cenobites developed a liturgical system (which was gradually adopted by the whole Church until today the Eastern Church knows no *ordo* but the monastic one), while the hesychasts created a tradition of personal prayer and continuous contemplation. In both cases, prayer was understood as a way to reach the goal of Christian life as such: participation in God, *theōsis* through communion with the deified humanity of Christ in the Holy Spirit. The cenobites generally emphasized the sacramental or liturgical nature of this communion, while the hesychasts taught that experience was to be reached through personal effort. In post-iconoclastic Byzantium, the two traditions generally interpenetrated to a greater extent, and we find, for example, that the prophet of personal mysticism, Symeon the New Theologian, spent most of his life in cenobitic communities located in the city of Constantinople. Since theologically and spiritually there was no opposition between the hermits and the cenobites, it is, therefore, possible to speak of a single monastic theology.

1. THE ORIGINS OF MONASTIC THOUGHT:
EVAGRIUS AND MACARIUS

The role of Evagrius Ponticus († 399) in the shaping of early monastic spirituality was recognized by historians early in this century. The authentic text of his *Gnostic Centuries,* with their quite heretical Christology, explains his condemnation by the Council of 553. Seen as an expression of his metaphysical system—a developed Origenism—Evagrius' spiritual doctrine itself becomes somehow suspect. But, in the Byzantine tradition taken as a whole, it will be used for centuries out of its original and heretical context; and its extraordinary psychological relevance will be exploited fully. We will mention here two major aspects of Evagrian thought because of their permanence in later tradition: the doctrine of the passions and the doctrine of prayer.

According to Evagrius, the true nature of the "mind" is to be fixed in God, and anything which detaches it from God is evil. Thus, since the Fall, the human mind is captured with self-love, which generates "thoughts"; "thoughts," a definitely pejorative term in Evagrius, imply interest in sensible things and distraction from God. Acting upon the passible part of the soul, they can lead it to *passions*. These passions form a very definite hierarchy, beginning with the casual attachment to the most inevitable of all human sensible needs, food, and ending with demonic possession, with love for oneself. The eight steps which constitute this hierarchy are: gluttony, fornication, avarice, grief, wrath, weariness, vainglory, and pride.[1] With very slight variations, this classification of the passions and the psychological structure of the human mind which it presupposes will be retained by John Cassian, John Climacus, Maximus the Confessor, and almost all the Eastern ascetical writers. The first goal of monastic "practice" is to subdue the passions and reach a state of "passionlessness"—a detachment from senses and "thoughts"—which makes a restoration of the true original relationship between the mind and God possible. Beginning with the elementary monastic virtues, fasting and celibacy, the life of the monk can gradually subdue the other passions and reach true detachment.

Union then becomes possible through prayer. It is Evagrius who first coins the term "prayer of the mind" which will become standard in Byzantine hesychasm. Prayer is "the proper activity of the mind," [2] "an impassible state," [3] the "highest possible intellection." [4] In this "state" of prayer, the mind is totally liberated from every "multiplicity"; it is "deaf and dumb" to every perception of the senses.[5] According to Evagrius, as we know now, prayer also means that the mind is in an "essential union" with the deity; thus Evagrian monks of the sixth century could boast that they were "equal to Christ." But Evagrius' teaching on prayer will be understood in a much more orthodox way by generations of Byzantine monks, and the credit for this reinterpretation of Evagrian spirituality belongs, in a large degree, to the writings attributed to Macarius of Egypt.

Macarius of Egypt was a contemporary and teacher of Evagrius' in the desert of Scete. Fifty *Homilies* and several other writings of an unknown author of the early-fifth century have been attributed to Macarius, who, it is now certain, was never a writer. The influence of this anonymous writer, conventionally called "Macarius," was enormous.

While Evagrius identifies man with the "intellect" and conceives Christian spirituality as a dematerialization, Macarius understands man as a psychosomatic whole, destined to "deification." To the Origenistic and Platonic anthropology of Evagrius, he opposes a Biblical idea of man, which makes it inconceivable for the "mind" or the "soul" to have its final destiny in separation from the body. From this anthropology follows a spirituality based upon the reality of Baptism and the Eucharist as ways of union with Christ and of "deification" of the entire human existence in all its aspects, including the corporeal. "The fire which lives inside, in the heart, appears then [on the last day] openly and realizes the resurrection of the bodies." [6]

In Macarius, the Evagrian "prayer of the mind" thus becomes the "prayer of the heart"; the center of man's psychosomatic life, the heart, is the "table where the grace of God engraves the laws of the Spirit";[7] but it also can be a "sepulcher," where "the prince of evil and his angels find refuge." [8] The human heart is thus the battlefield between God and Satan, life and death. And the monk devoting his entire existence to prayer chooses, in fact, to be at the forefront of this battle, in a direct and conscious way. For the presence of God is a real fact which the "inner man" perceives "as an experience and with assurance." [9] In Macarius, just as in some books of the Old Testament, and especially in the Psalms, the role played by the heart is undeniably connected with a physiology which sees in this particular organ the center of the psychosomatic life of man. This means, in practice, that whenever the "heart" is mentioned, the author simply means man's inner personality, the "I" at its very depth. In any case, the "heart" *never* designates the emotional side of man alone, as it sometimes will in the West.

The notion of the coexistence of God and Satan in the heart of man, and the call for a conscious experience of grace, have led some modern historians to identify the *Homilies* of Macarius with the writings of a Messalian leader. If this accusation were true, it would involve Macarius, as well as much of the later monastic spirituality of Byzantium, where Macarius enjoyed unquestionable authority and where his ideas, especially the notion of the conscious experience of God, remained dominant. But the exact definition of what Messalianism really means, and the absence in Macarius of some basic Messalian positions—such as anti-sacramentalism —makes the hypothesis highly improbable. Even if the unknown author of the Macarian *Homilies* belonged to a tradition which eventually bifurcated between sectarian and orthodox spiritualities, his anthropology and his concept of human destiny were certainly closer to the New Testament than was that of the Evagrian Origenists; and his influence, acting as a Biblical counterpart, contributed indirectly to salvaging for posterity the tradition of pure prayer which, in Evagrius, had a rather dubious context.

2. THE GREAT SPIRITUAL FATHERS

An Origenistic spiritualism and Messalian pseudo-prophetism—in which prayer and visions are supposed to replace the sacraments—were the two main temptations of Eastern Christian monasticism. The examples of Evagrius and Macarius show that in the fourth and fifth centuries it may not have been easy to draw a line in the monastic milieu between the orthodox and the sectarians. After several conciliar decrees against Messalianism (at Side in 390, at Constantinople in 426, and at Ephesus in 431), and the condemnation of Evagrius in 553, confusion became impossible; but clarification had begun to emerge in the monastic milieu itself at the very time when the councils were legislating on the issue. We will mention here briefly three authors of major importance who, after assimilating the major contributions of both the Evagrian and the Macarian traditions, gave to Eastern Christian spirituality its classical forms.

Diadochus, a bishop of Photice in Epirus, in the fifth century, and a participant at the Council of Chalcedon (451), is the author of *Gnostic Chapters* and of a few minor spiritual works. The title of his principal work betrays his relation to Evagrius; still, the major inspiration of Diadochus' doctrine of prayer approximates Macarius', though at a greater distance from Messalianism than that of the author of the *Spiritual Homilies*.

Baptism, for Diadochus, is the only foundation of spiritual life: "Grace is hidden in the depth of our mind from the very moment in which we were baptized, and gives purification both to the soul and to the body." [10] This concern for the wholeness of man is expressed by a mysticism of the "heart," as opposed to the Evagrian insistence on the "mind." Actually, Diadochus, just like Macarius, locates the mind, or soul, "in the heart":

> Grace hides its presence in the baptized, waiting for the initiative of the soul; but when the whole man turns toward the Lord, then grace reveals its presence to the heart through an ineffable experience. . . . And if man begins his progress by keeping the commandments and ceaselessly invoking the Lord Jesus, then the fire of holy grace penetrates even the external senses of the heart. . . .[11]

Diadochus, on several occasions in his *Chapters,* clarifies the ambiguity of the Macarian tradition on the issue of the coexistence of God and Satan in the heart; but he is fully in agreement with Macarius in affirming that Christians do, and even must, experience consciously and even "externally" (i.e., not only "intellectually" in the Evagrian sense) the presence of the Spirit in their hearts. His definition of the Christian faith as a personal experience will be appropriated by Symeon the New Theologian and other Byzantine spiritual writers. In the writings of Diadochus, the teaching on incessant prayer, adopted from Evagrius and Macarius, presupposes a constant invocation of the name of Jesus;[12] an essential orientation of spirituality toward the Person of the Incarnate Logos, with a resurgence of the role played in Biblical theology by the concept of the "name" of God, thus replaces in Diadochus the much more abstract and spiritualistic understanding of prayer in Evagrius.

Better known in the West since the Middle Ages and more exalted in the East (where a special celebration in its honor takes place on the Fifth Sunday of Lent), the personality of John Climacus—"the author of *The Ladder*"—abbot of the monastery on Mount Sinai, is another great witness of monastic spirituality based upon invocation of the "name of Jesus." Very little is known of his life, and even the date of his death is not solidly established (it is generally believed to have taken place some time around 649).

His famous book, *The Ladder of Paradise,* has more definite leanings toward Evagrianism than has the *Chapters* of Diadochus, as can be seen from its detailed classification of the passions and from the extreme forms of asceticism which John required from his monks and which certainly denote Origenist spiritualism. This extremism pleased the French Jansenists of the seventeenth century, who contributed to the popularity of *The Ladder* in the West. But John's positive teaching about prayer, like that of Macarius and Diadochus, is centered on the person and the name of Jesus: it thus denotes a purely Christian incarnational foundation, and involves the whole man, not just the "mind."

"Let the memory of Jesus be united to your breathing: then you will understand the usefulness of hesychia." [13] In John, the terms "hesychia" ("silence," "quietude") and "hesychasts" designate quite specifically the eremitic, contemplative life of the solitary monk practicing the "Jesus prayer." "The hesychast is the one who says 'My heart is firm' [Ps 57:8]; the hesychast is the one who says 'I sleep, but my heart is awake' [Sg 5:2]. Hesychia is an uninterrupted worship and service to God. The hesychast is the one who aspires to circumscribe the Incorporeal in a fleshly dwelling. . . ." [14]

The terminology which John uses will gain particular popularity among the later Byzantine hesychasts, in the thirteenth and fourteenth centuries, with their practice of connecting mental prayer with breathing; it is not *a priori* impossible that the practice was known in Sinai in the time of John. In any case, he understands "deification" as a communion of the whole man with the transfigured Christ. The "memory of Jesus" meant precisely this, and not a simple "meditation" on the historical Jesus or on any particular episode in His life. Warnings against any evoking, through imagination, of figures external to the "heart" is constant in Eastern Christian spiritual tradition. The monk is always called to realize in himself (his "heart") the objective reality of the transfigured Christ, which is neither an image nor a symbol, but the very reality of God's presence through the sacraments, independent of any form of imagination.

At this point one should understand the necessary and unavoidable link which exists in this tradition between spirituality and theology. If any single author succeeded in formulating this link, he is Maximus the Confessor.

We have already seen the heroic and lonely role of Maximus in the Christological controversy, and his ability to integrate into a consistent Christological and anthropological system the issues which were at stake between the orthodox and the Monothelites. His ability to view the problems of the spiritual life as they arose in his time in the light of the Evagrian and Macarian heritages on one side, and of orthodox Christology on the other, is similarly remarkable.

Origen and Evagrius certainly occupied the first place in Maximus' readings and intellectual formation. In his doctrine of the spiritual life he adopts the Evagrian hierarchy of passions, as well as the concept of "passionlessness," as the goal of ascetic *praxis*. In Evagrius the detachment from "passions" is a *negative* achievement, through which a total emptiness from any sensation of the soul or of the body is supposed to be achieved, in order for the mind to realize its divine nature and recover its essential union with God through knowledge; this concept obviously implies an Origenistic anthropology in which any connection of the "mind" with either a "soul" or a "body" is a consequence of the Fall. As a result, in Evagrius, true de-

tachment is also detachment from virtues; and active love itself is superseded by knowledge. In Maximus, however, love is understood, not only
as the highest virtue, but as the only true result of detachment. Because of
"passionlessness," love can be perfectly equal for all, since human prefer-
ences are the result of imperfection.[15] Ultimately, human love, which
necessarily includes an element of desire (erōs), must be transformed, by
a gift of God, and thus become agapē.[16]

This transformation of the Evagrian spirituality parallels in Maximus a
basic modification of Origenism in the doctrine of creation and implies a
positive view of man, whose ultimate destiny does not consist of an absorption into God's essence, but in a "natural activity" made possible
through a God-given active love. The total transcendence and inaccessibility
of the essence of God becomes, in Maximus—as, before him in Gregory
of Nyssa, and after him in later Byzantine theology—a matter of Christian
faith fundamental for spiritual life.[17] If love, and not "essential gnosis,"
is the highest goal of spiritual life, man, while united with God, remains
totally himself in his nature and activity; but he also enjoys communion
with the activity of God, which alone can guarantee his total liberation
from "passion" and transform his erōs into agapē. In Byzantine monastic
spirituality, to "follow the commandments," i.e., active love, will therefore
remain both a condition and a necessary aspect of the vision of God.

To achieve his balanced understanding of spiritual life, Maximus did not
rely only on the monastic spiritual tradition. He was first of all a consistent Chalcedonian, and thus he approached the problem with a fundamental conviction that each nature of Christ keeps, as nature, its characteristics and activity. "Deification" does not suppress humanity, but makes
it more authentically human.

3. OPPOSITION TO SECULAR PHILOSOPHY

The traditional unpopularity of Byzantium in the Western Middle Ages
and in modern times has been somewhat moderated by the recent recognition that it was Byzantine scholars who preserved the treasures of Hellenic
antiquity and transmitted them to the Italian Renaissance. If the transmission is, indeed, a fact (all the available manuscripts of the authors of
Greek classical antiquity are Byzantine, and often monastic, in origin), it
remains that, throughout Byzantine intellectual history, the positive interest in pagan philosophy, which kept reappearing in intellectual circles, was
always staunchly opposed, often by the official Church and always by the
monks. The official conciliar statements against the "Hellenic myths"—
the term implies essentially Platonic metaphysics—appeared in 553, under
Justinian, and later at the condemnation of Italos and at the Palamite councils of the fourteenth century. More subtly, but no less decisively, the

gradual abandonment of Origenistic concepts was also a victory of the Bible over the Academy.

In spite of a widespread view that Eastern Christian thought is Platonic, in contrast to Western Aristotelianism, an important corrective must be found in the fact that the above-mentioned condemnations of various forms of Platonism were repeated yearly, as part of the *Synodikon* of Orthodoxy, in all churches on the First Sunday of Lent. The universities taught Aristotle's logic as part of the "general curriculum" required from students under the age of eighteen; but the pious families prevented their children from continuing their education on a higher level, where students were required to read Plato. This generally explains the ever-recurring remark by hagiographers that saints, especially monks, stopped their education at eighteen to enter monasteries.

In monastic circles, denunciations of "secular philosophy" are constant; and the polarization which occurs in the ninth century between the party of the monastic "zealots" (often followers of Theodore the Studite) on the one hand, and that of the higher secular clergy on the other, is intellectual as well as political. The monks oppose compromises with the state, but they also reject the renaissance of secular humanism. Patriarch Ignatius, Photius' great competitor, supported by the monastic party, is known to have snubbed the promoters of secular philosophy;[18] Symeon the New Theologian writes virulent verses against them;[19] and Gregory Palamas († 1359) orients his entire polemic against Barlaam the Calabrian on the issue of the "Hellenic wisdom" which he considers to be the main source of Barlaam's errors. Perhaps it is precisely because Byzantium was "Greek-speaking" and "Greek-thinking" that the issue of Greek philosophy, in its relation to Christianity, remained alive among the Byzantines. In any case, monastic thought continued to remind them of their conversion to the faith preached by a Jewish Messiah and their becoming a "new Jerusalem."

4. CHRISTIAN FAITH AS EXPERIENCE: SYMEON THE NEW THEOLOGIAN

In Macarius and in Diadochus, we noted the identification of the Christian faith itself with *a conscious-experience* of God. Symeon the New Theologian (949–1022) will be the prophet of that idea in medieval Byzantium. Disciple of a Studite monk, the "New Theologian"—a title given to him by his later admirers in order to identify him with John the Evangelist and Gregory of Nazianzus, both often called "Theologians" in Byzantine literature—started his monastic life as a novice at the Studion. But the strict regimentation of the big monastery was obviously foreign to his temperament, and he withdrew to the small community of St. Mamas, also in

Constantinople, where he was soon elected abbot and ordained priest. His leadership at St. Mamas lasted more than twenty-five years, but ended in a conflict when a monastic party in his commmunity complained to the ecclesiastical authorities about the demands he imposed on his monks. Exiled, then rehabilitated, Symeon spent his last years composing spiritual writings quite unique in their mystical originality, their poetic quality, and their influence on later Byzantine thought. His works include *Catechetical Discourses* addressed to the monks of St. Mamas, *Theological and Ethical Treatises,* fifty-eight hymns, and several minor writings.

Symeon has often been classified as a major representative of the hesychast tradition in Byzantium, following in the line of Evagrius and Macarius, and anticipating Gregory Palamas. This classification should be accepted only with reservations, however, since Symeon neither makes any specific mention of "prayer of the mind" nor insists on any clearly formulated theological distinction between "essence" and "energy" in God. But it is clear that Symeon stands for the basic understanding of Christianity as personal communion with, and vision of, God, a position which he shares with hesychasm and with the patristic tradition as a whole. Like all prophets, he expresses the Christian experience without definite concern for precise terminology. It is, therefore, easy to find him at variance with any established tradition, or with any theological system. In the midst of the tradition-minded Byzantine society, Symeon stands as a unique case of personal mysticism, but also as an important witness of the inevitable tension in Christianity between all forms of "establishment" and the freedom of the Spirit.

Often autobiographical, Symeon's writings are centered on the reality of a conscious encounter with Christ; and here, obviously, he follows Macarius. "Yes, I beg you," he addresses his monks, "let us try, in this life, to see and contemplate Him. For if we are deemed worthy to see Him *sensibly,* we shall not see death; death will have no dominion over us [Rm 6:9]." [20] The notion of "sensible" vision makes Symeon, as well as Macarius, border on Messalianism; but it is generally recognized today[21] that Symeon's intent differs fundamentally from that of the sectarians who defined "experience" in opposition to the sacramental structure of the Church. What Symeon wants to make clear is that the Kingdom of God has indeed become an attainable reality, that it does not belong only to the "future life," and that, in this life, it is not restricted to the "spiritual" or "intellectual" part of man alone, but involves his entire existence. "Through the Holy Spirit," he writes, "the resurrection of all of us occurs. And I do not speak only of the final resurrection of the body. . . . [Christ] through His Holy Spirit grants, even now, the Kingdom of heaven." [22] And in order to affirm that this experience of the Kingdom is not, in any sense, a human "merit," a simple and due reward for ascetic practice, Symeon insists on its "sudden" and unexpected character. In passages where he recalls his own conversion, he likes to emphasize that he was not aware of *who* was pulling him out of the "mud" of the world to show him finally the beatitude of the Kingdom.[23]

Symeon's prophetic insistence that the Christian faith is an experience of the living Christ met with resistance; the legalistic and minimalistic view of Christianity, limiting the faith to the performance of "obligations," seemed much more realistic to monks and laymen alike. For Symeon, these minimalists were modern heretics:

> Here are those whom I call heretics [he proclaims in a homily addressed to his community]: those who say that there is no one in our time in our midst who would observe the commandments of the Gospel and become like the holy Fathers . . . [and] those who pretend that this is impossible. These people have not fallen into some particular heresy, but into all the heresies at once, since this one is worse than all in its impiety. . . . Whoever speaks in this way destroys all the divine scriptures. These anti-Christs affirm: "This is impossible, impossible!" [24]

Symeon was involved, at the end of his life, in violent conflict with Stephen, a former metropolitan of Nicomedia who had become a syncellus, or administrative official, of the patriarchate, on the issue of the canonization of his spiritual father, Symeon the Pious, which he had performed in his community without the proper hierarchical sanction. The New Theologian was given an opportunity to raise the question of authority in the Church, by opposing the charismatic personality of the saint to that of the institution. His statements on this problem can be very easily interpreted as anti-hierarchical in principle: according to Symeon, if one accepts the episcopate without having received the vision, one is nothing but an intruder.[25] On this point, Symeon reflects a frame of mind which had existed in both ancient and Byzantine Christianity, in pseudo-Dionysius, and in the Macarian tradition of monasticism; but the subjectivism, which may be involved in such an interpretation, is an ecclesiological problem in itself.

Here, as always, Symeon is not directly concerned with rationalization; his purpose is to formulate the tension between the Kingdom and "this world," to affirm that the tension between the "institution" and the "event" is built into the very existence of the Church in history. The New Theologian's realistic sacramentalism shows clearly that this tension, not the denial of the sacramental nature of the Church, is his true concern. The Byzantine Church canonized Symeon the New Theologian, and generations of Eastern Christians have seen in him the greatest mystic of the Middle Ages. By so doing, Byzantine Christianity has recognized that, in the Church, the Spirit alone is the ultimate criterion of truth and the only final authority.

5. THEOLOGY OF HESYCHASM: GREGORY PALAMAS

The debates which took place in fourteenth-century Byzantium involved a series of issues, including forms of monastic spirituality. The discussion, however, was fundamentally a theological one: the hesychast method of prayer was debated in the light of earlier tradition concerning knowledge of God, Christology, and anthropology. The endorsement given by the Byzantine Church to the hesychast theologians implied a stand on these basic issues of the Christian faith as well. The debate originated in a confrontation between an Athonite monk, Gregory Palamas (1296–1359), and a Calabrian Italo-Greek "philosopher," Barlaam. At the beginning, the issue was the doctrine of man's knowledge of God and the nature of theology. For Palamas, immediate knowledge of God, in Christ, is available to all the baptized and, therefore, is the real basis and criterion of true theology; Barlaam insisted, however, on the unknowability of God, except through indirect, created means—revealed Scripture, induction from creation, or exceptional mystical revelations. In fact, the issue was not radically different from the one which Symeon the New Theologian had debated with certain of his monks, who denied the possibility of a direct vision of God. At a second stage of the debate, Barlaam also attacked, as a form of Messalian materialism, the psychosomatic method of prayer practiced by Byzantine hesychasts.

Although this method is held by some as a return to the origins of monasticism, it appears only in explicit, written documents of the late-thirteenth and early-fourteenth centuries. It is described in particular by Nicephorus the Hesychast, an anonymous author whose *Method of Holy Prayer and Attention* is attributed, by some manuscripts, to Symeon the New Theologian, and to Gregory of Sinai (1255–1346), who became widely known in Slavic countries. Undoubtedly, the method was widely known, for Gregory Palamas quotes, among its adepts, such major figures of the Church as Patriarch Athanasius I (1289–1293, 1303–1310) and Theoleptus, Metropolitan of Philadelphia (1250–1321/26).[26] The method consisted in obtaining "attention" (*prosochē*)—the first condition of authentic prayer —by concentrating one's mind "in the heart," retaining each breath, and reciting mentally the short prayer: "Lord Jesus Christ, Son of God, have mercy upon me." Parallelisms in non-Christian Eastern spiritual practices are easy to find, and "materialistic" abuses may have occurred among Byzantine monks. But the major representatives of fourteenth-century hesychasm are unanimous in saying that the psychosomatic method is not an end in itself, but only a useful tool for placing a man literally "in attention," ready to receive the grace of God—provided, of course, he deserve it by "observing the commandments." Barlaam objected to this method with a Platonic view of man: any somatic participation in prayer can only be an obstacle to a true "intellectual" encounter. The Council of 1341 condemned Barlaam for his attacks on the monks. Still, several Byzantine theologians—Gregory Akindynos, Nicephorus Gregoras, and, later, the Thomist Prochoros Cydones—continued to protest against the theological positions of Palamas. Palamas, however, received final conciliar endorsement of his theology successively in 1347, 1351, and, posthumously, in 1368, when he was also canonized.

The theological positions of Gregory Palamas may be summarized in the three following points:

1) Knowledge of God is an experience given to all Christians through Baptism and through their continuous participation in the life of the Body of Christ in the Eucharist. It requires the involvement of the whole man in prayer and service, through love for God and neighbor; and then it becomes recognizable not only as an "intellectual" experience of the mind alone, but as a "spiritual sense," which conveys a perception neither purely "intellectual" nor purely material. In Christ, God assumed the whole of man, soul and body; and man as such was deified. In prayer—for example, in the "method"—in the sacraments, in the entire life of the Church as a community, man is called to *participation* in divine life: this participation is also the true knowledge of God.

2) God is totally inaccessible in His essence, both in this life and in the future; for only the three divine hypostases are "God by essence." Man, in "deification," can become God only "by grace," or "by energy." The inaccessibility of the essence of God was one of the basic affirmations of the Cappadocian Fathers against Eunomius and also, in a different context, against Origen. Affirming the absolute transcendence of God is only another way of saying that He is the Creator *ex nihilo*: anything which exists outside of God exists only through His "will" or "energy," and can participate in His life only as a result of His will or "grace."

3) The full force with which Palamas affirms God's inaccessibility and the equally strong affirmation of deification and of participation in God's life, as the original purpose and the goal of human existence, also give full reality to the Palamite distinction between "essence" and "energy" in God. Palamas does not try to justify the distinction philosophically: his God is a living God, both transcendent and willingly immanent, who does not enter into preconceived philosophical categories. However, Palamas considers his teaching to be a development of the Sixth Council decisions that Christ has two natures, or "essences," and two natural wills, or "energies." [27] For Christ's humanity itself, enhypostasized as it is in the Logos and thus having become truly God's humanity, did not become "God by essence"; it was penetrated with the divine energy—through the *circumincessio idiomatum*—and, in it, our own humanity finds access to God in His energies. The energies, therefore, are never considered as divine emanations, or as a diminished God. They are divine life, as given by God to

His creatures; and they are God, for in His Son He truly gave Himself for our salvation.

The victory of Palamism in the fourteenth century was therefore the victory of a specifically Christian, God-centered humanism for which the Greek patristic tradition always stood, in opposition to all concepts of man which considered him as an autonomous or "secular" being. Its essential intuition that "deification" does not suppress humanity, but makes man truly human, is, of course, greatly relevant for our own contemporary concerns: man can be fully "human" only if he restores his lost communion with God.

NOTES

1. Evagrius Ponticus, *Praktikos*; PG 40:1272–1276.
2. Pseudo-Nilus (Evagrius), *De Oratione,* 84; PG 79:1185B.
3. *Ibid.,* 52.
4. *Ibid.,* 34A.
5. *Ibid.,* 11.
6. Macarius of Egypt, *Hom.,* 11, 1; ed. Dörries, pp. 96–97.
7. *Ibid.,* 15, 20; p. 139.
8. *Ibid.,* 11, 11; p. 103.
9. *Ibid.,* 1, 12; p. 12.
10. Diadochus, *Cap.* 77, 78; ed. E. des Places, SC, 5 bis (Paris: Cerf, 1955), pp. 135–136.
11. *Ibid.,* 85; pp. 144–145.
12. See *ibid.,* 31, 32, 61, 88.
13. John Climacus, *The Ladder of Paradise,* Degree 28; PG 88:1112c.
14. *Ibid.,* Degree 27; PG 88:1097AB.
15. On Evagrius and Maximus, see Lars Thunberg, *Microcosm and Mediator: The Theological Anthropology of Maximus the Confessor* (Lund: Gleerup, 1965), pp. 317–325.
16. See P. Sherwood, in Maximus the Confessor, *The Ascetic Life,* ACW 21 (Westminster: Newman, 1955), p. 83.
17. See Lossky, *Vision of God,* pp. 9–10.
18. Anastasius Bibliothecarius, *Preface to the Eighth Council,* Mansi XVI, 6.
19. I. Hausherr, ed., in *OrientChr* 12 (1928), 45.
20. Symeon the New Theologian, *Cat.* II; ed. B. Krivochéine, *Syméon le Nouveau Théologien, Catéchèses,* SC 96 (Paris: Cerf, 1963), pp. 421–424.
21. See J. Darrouzès, SC 122, Introduction, p. 26.
22. Symeon the New Theologian, *Cat.* VI, ed. Krivochéine, pp. 358–368.
23. Symeon the New Theologian, *Euch.* 2; ed. Krivochéine, pp. 47–73.
24. *Cat.* 29; ed. Krivochéine, pp. 166–190.
25. *Cap. Eth.,* 6; ed. J. Darrouzès, pp. 406–454.
26. Gregory Palamas, *Triads,* I, 2; ed. J. Meyendorff, *Défense des saints hésychastes,* Specilegium Sacrum Lovaniense 30 (Louvain, 1959), p. 99.
27. Synodal Tome of 1351; PG 151:722B.

6

Ecclesiology: Canonical Sources

In Greek patristic literature, accepted throughout the entire Byzantine period as the ultimate expression of Church tradition, there was, generally speaking, no systematic treatment of "ecclesiology." This does not mean, however, that such factors of Christian life as Church order, the sacraments, and tradition were not central for the Byzantines. A major source of our knowledge of Byzantine ecclesiological ideas is constituted by ancient canonical texts: conciliar decrees, commentaries, and later synodal legislation. Even imperial laws concerning the Church, inasmuch as they were accepted as guiding principles of ecclesiastical polity, often witness to ecclesiastical consciousness essentially identical to that of the conciliar canons.

Viewed from a juridical point of view, the entire body of Byzantine canonical sources hardly constitutes a coherent whole. The attempts at codification, which we shall mention later, are far from exhaustive and do not eliminate important contradictions. They were never intended to provide the Byzantine Church with a complete *corpus juris*. Many Western polemicists have pointed to this state of affairs as an essential weakness of Eastern Christianity, which has failed to provide itself with an independent and consistent canon law, and, thus, has surrendered to the power of the state. These judgments, however, have generally taken for granted that the Church is a divine "institution" whose internal existence could be adequately defined in juridical terms, a presupposition which Byzantine Christians did not consider. For them the Church was, first of all, a sacramental communion with God in Christ and the Spirit, whose membership —the entire Body of Christ—is not limited to the earthly *oikoumene* ("inhabited earth") where law governs society, but includes the host of angels and saints, as well as the divine head. The management of the earthly Church was certainly recognized as a necessary task, and there the use of juridical terms and concepts was unavoidable; but these concepts never exhausted the ultimate reality of the Church of God, and could be determined occasionally by the councils, or even left to the benevolent and, in principle, Christian care of the emperors.

This attitude did not mean, however, that the Byzantines were either indifferent toward the canons or juridically incompetent. Quite the contrary. They were generally aware that at least certain canons reflected the eternal and divine nature of the Church, and that it was a Christian and absolute duty to obey them. Yet, Roman traditions were always strong enough in Byzantium to maintain almost permanently a series of highly competent ecclesiastical lawyers who advised the emperors on decrees concerning the Church, and also introduced principles of Roman Law into ecclesiastical legislation and jurisprudence. But again, they always understood their role as subordinate to the more fundamental and divine nature of the Church, expressed in a sacramental and doctrinal communion, uniting heaven and earth. And they recognized that there was no canonical legislation in heaven (for if "justification comes by law, then Christ died in vain" [Ga 2:21]), and that their task was a limited one.

1. THE COUNCILS AND THE FATHERS

The standard Byzantine canonical collection—which will also form the basis of canon law in Slavic countries and in the modern Orthodox Church —the so-called *Nomocanon in XIV Titles* (its origin and development will be mentioned later)—contains the following canonical texts of purely ecclesiastical origin:

i. The Apostolic Canons, an early collection of eighty-five disciplinary rules, which served, in the first half of the fourth century, as a standard canonical text in Syria. Its content, in many ways, reflects the practices of the pre-Nicaean period, but is certainly not of genuinely apostolic origin. A shorter collection (fifty canons) was translated into Latin by Dionysius Exiguus (late-fifth century), and was widely accepted in the West. The introduction of the full series of eighty-five canons into the canon law of the Church of Constantinople was the work of Patriarch John iii Scholasticus (565–577) and was endorsed by the Quinisext Council (692). The difference between the shorter and the longer collections will play a role in Greco-Latin polemics.

ii. The Canons of the Ecumenical Councils:
1. Nicaea (325)—20 canons.
2. Constantinople i (381)—7 canons.
3. Ephesus (431)—8 canons.
4. Chalcedon (451)—30 canons.
5. The Quinisext (or "Fifth–Sixth") Council; also known as the Council *in Trullo* and often referred to in Byzantine texts as the

"Sixth Council" (692), because its entire canonical *corpus* was given *post factum* an "ecumenical" status in being procedurally attributed to the ecumenical councils of 553 and 680—102 canons.
6. Nicaea II (787)—22 canons.

III. The Canons of local Councils:
1. Ancyra (314)—25 canons.
2. Neocaesarea (314–325)—15 canons.
3. Antioch (341)—25 canons.
4. Sardica (343)—20 canons.
5. Gangra (first half of fourth century)—21 canons.
6. Laodicea (fourth century?)—60 canons.
7. Constantinople (394)—1 canon.
8. Carthage (419)—133 (sometimes 147) canons; also known as *Codex canonum ecclesiae Africanae,* this collection of canons resulted from the continuous legislation by African councils, which was compiled in 419.
9. Constantinople (859–861); also known as "First–Second," because the two councils of 859 and 861 were, for reasons of convenience, considered as a single assembly—17 canons.
10. Constantinople (879–880), sometimes referred to as "Eighth Ecumenical"—3 canons.

IV. The Canons of the Holy Fathers: The patristic texts gathered in this category were, for the most part, occasional letters or authoritative answers written to individuals. In collections they are often divided, or classified, in "canons." The following authors appear in the *Nomocanon*:
1. Dionysius of Alexandria († 265).
2. Gregory of Neocaesarea († 270).
3. Peter of Alexandria († 311)
4. Athanasius of Alexandria († 373).
5. Basil of Caesarea († 379) [a very authoritative collection of 92 "canons"].
6. Gregory of Nyssa († 395).
7. Gregory of Nazianzus († 389).
8. Amphilochius of Iconium († 395).
9. Timothy of Alexandria († 355).
10. Theophilus of Alexandria († 412).
11. Cyril of Alexandria († 444).
12. Gennadius I of Constantinople († 471).

Later Byzantine collections also include texts by the patriarchs of Constantinople, Tarasius († 809), John the Faster († 595), Nicephorus († 818), and Nicholas III (1084-1111), which also entered the Slavonic *Kormchaya Kniga*. Obviously, this entire series of authoritative canonical texts is conceived, first of all, as a frame of references and standards, different in kind and in importance. The most important collection of canons is probably that of the Council *in Trullo* (692), conceived by its convener, Emperor Justinian II, as a first attempt to codify earlier conciliar legislation. Actually, most of these texts—including the Apostolic Canons and the Canons of the Fathers—receive their authority from the Trullan Council. It must be noted, however, that although the Quinisext is invested with "ecumenical" authority in the Byzantine Church tradition, it has never been received as such in the West. Actually, since it explicitly condemns several Latin liturgical and canonical practices, it already clearly implies an understanding of Church tradition and authority differing from that of the Latin Church.

2. IMPERIAL LEGISLATION

The principle stated earlier about the transitory and relative significance of law in Church polity can serve now as a key for the understanding of the easy and practically unchallenged acceptance in the East of imperial legislation in the field of Church administration, once the emperor himself became a member of the Church and had agreed to protect the basic sacramental and doctrinal principles upon which the Church is built. No text ever gave the emperor the power to define or formulate these principles; but it was universally accepted that he had a responsibility for relating them to the empirical realities of history, and thus to manage, where necessary, the practical affairs of the visible Church. This is the meaning of the famous words attributed to Constantine—"I have been established by God as the supervisor of the external affairs of the Church" [1]—and consistently applied in the legislation of Justinian. The *Codex* and the *Novellae* contain a set of laws concerning the Church which cover a much wider range of ecclesiastical functions and activities than does the entire conciliar legislation before and after Justinian. A fine example of Justinian's style is his edict of 528 concerning the mode of selecting candidates for the episcopacy:

> Taking ever every forethought for the most holy churches and for both honor and glory of the Holy Immaculate and Consubstantial Trinity, through which we have believed that both we ourselves and the common polity will be saved, and also following the holy apostles' teaching . . . , by the present law we ordain that, as often as in any city whatever it should happen that the episcopal see is vacant, a vote by the persons inhabiting the said city should be taken concerning three persons who have borne a character for correct faith and holiness of life and the other virtues, so that from these the most suitable should be selected for the episcopates. . . . [2]

The famous *Novella* 6 contains, on the other hand, a full set of bylaws for the Church's existence in the framework of the Roman imperial system.

It was self-evident that, in principle, there could be no contradiction between ecclesiastical canons and imperial laws. Justinian himself ordered that canons had "force of law"[3] (*legum vicem,* Nov. 131, 1), but later Byzantine commentators admitted the possibility of a contradiction between canons and imperial laws; in that case the canons were to be preferred.[4] Actually, it is always important to remember that, in spite of all the power which was accorded them in ecclesiastical affairs, the emperors were above neither the dogmas nor the canons of the Church. The explicit denial of doctrinal authority to the emperors by anti-iconoclastic writers like John of Damascus and Theodore the Studite, and the opposition of Patriarch Nicholas I Mystikos (901–907, 912–925) to the uncanonical fourth marriage of Emperor Leo VI (886–912), are among the many examples available. The above reservations in no way exclude the fact that it is impossible to understand Byzantine ecclesiastical polity and consciousness without taking imperial legislation into consideration. After the *Code* of Justinian, the greatest body of important texts is found among the *Leges Novellae,* which were promulgated by Justinian and by his successors, especially Leo VI (886–912), as complements to the *Code.*

Other important collections of laws relevant for the Church are the *Ecloga* of the Isaurians, issued between 739 and 741, which includes modifications of Justinian's legislation, especially in marriage and divorce laws. Basil I (867–886) published major legislative texts, partly codifying, partly modifying, earlier legislation: the *Procheiron,* which appeared between 870 and 878, was a handbook for lawyers which, like the *Ecloga,* contains laws on marriage and on ecclesiastical affairs—a Title VII on forbidden marriages, a Title XI on divorce, a Title XXVIII on qualifications and procedure for clergy appointments. The so-called *Basilics,* which appeared partly under Basil I and partly under his successor Leo VI, reproduced some of Justinian's laws, but omitted others, thus making a selection important for medieval Byzantine and Slavic ecclesiastical practices. The exact character of another text, which also appeared under the Macedonians and was probably drafted by Patriarch Photius, is not so clear: the *Epanagogē* ("Recapitulation of the Law") is well known for its description of the emperor and the patriarch of Constantinople as "the most exalted and the most necessary members of society"; it also contains legislation on matters of clerical discipline (Titles VIII and IX), on the legal status of Church property (Title X), and on marital law (Titles XVII and XXI). It is not quite clear whether the *Epanagogē* was ever formally promulgated and acquired force of law, but it is often quoted and reproduced in later legal collections. Its scheme of a God-established dyarchy of the emperor and of the patriarch—in line with Justinian's theory of "symphony" between Church and state, but exalting in particular the unique position of the "ecumenical patriarch" of Constantinople as a high official of the empire—is close to the ideology which prevailed in Byzantium in the ninth century after the victory over imperial iconoclasm. Later, this scheme became a standard program in Slavic countries, where national "patriarchs" shared the dyarchy with various local rulers.

3. CODIFICATIONS OF ECCLESIASTICAL LAW

Besides the famous *Codex,* the era of Justinian naturally saw the appearance of codified ecclesiastical legislation, although various forms of chronological and systematic collections had existed earlier. Both during the reign of Justinian and in the years which followed his death, John III Scholasticus, Patriarch of Constantinople (565–577), a lawyer by formation, contributed most to this codification. He is credited with having composed a *Collection of Fifty Titles* which divided the conciliar canons according to subjects, as well as a parallel collection of imperial laws, divided into eighty-seven chapters (*Collectio LXXXVII capitulorum*). The end of the sixth century was marked by the appearance of another, anonymous collection similar to that of John Scholasticus', but subdivided into fourteen Titles, with a parallel collection of imperial laws under the same headings. The anonymous author was familiar with the work of a Western contemporary and colleague, the monk Dionysius Exiguus († 555), the author of the first Latin collection of conciliar canons, and adopted from him the "African canonical code," which, as "the canons of the Council of Carthage," enjoyed great authority in Byzantium. The entire work of John Scholasticus, as well as that of the anonymous author, was re-edited and completed in the following centuries in the form of *Nomocanons.* The principle of this new form of canonical handbook obviously reflects the need of a Byzantine lawyer, canonist, or ecclesiastical official to have under systematically arranged headings the entire active legislation on problems arising in the life of the Church.

The *Nomocanon in Fifty Titles,* the final form of which took shape in 883 probably under the supervision of Photius, covered a much greater number of texts, and, in general, gave greater satisfaction to generations of canonists. Moreover, it often served as a basis for later canonical commentaries. Both *Nomocanons* were translated into Slavic. The *Nomocanon in Fourteen Titles* served as the basis for the standard Slavic canonical collection in its various versions, the so-called *Kormchaya Kniga.* Together with the *Nomocanons,* several canonical reference books circulated in the Byzantine world. A *Canonical Synopsis* by Stephen of Ephesus, dating probably from the sixth century, later revised and completed, included a commentary by Aristenos. In the fourteenth century, two prominent lawyers of Thessalonica published systematic collections in which canons were clearly separated from imperial laws: Constantine Harmenopoulos, well known by historians of Roman Law for his *Hexabiblon,* also compiled an *Epitome* of canons, which served as the appendix to his compendium of civil law; and Matthew Blastares, a priest and monk, produced a canonical "collection," accompanied by several more-recent documents and critical articles on canonical issues.

4. AUTHORITATIVE COMMENTARIES AND CRITICISM

Under the reign of John II Comnenos (1118-1143), John Zonaras, an encyclopedic Byzantine scholar and historian, composed a commentary on the anonymous canonical collection in fourteen titles. A systematic mind, Zonaras clarifies the canonical texts in order of importance. In doing so, he adopts a logically coherent, but historically artificial, scheme which considers the so-called Apostolic Canons to be of greater authority than conciliar texts, and the decisions of ecumenical councils of greater weight than those of local councils; he attributes the least value to the canons of individual "fathers." The difficulty in applying this logical principle consistently (for ecumenical councils often issued decrees of passing and casual significance, while important doctrinal and ecclesiological points are made in texts which Zonaras would consider "secondary") was undoubtedly felt by Zonaras' contemporary, Alexios Aristenos, the author of a more literal and brief commentary based upon a shortened collection, or *epitome,* of canons. His aim is mainly to explain the meaning of the texts in their historical setting, rather than to judge their relation to each other and their respective importance.

The third great commentator of the twelfth century, Theodore Balsamon, in his major work based on Photius' *Nomocanon* in its entirety, pursued a specific task, entrusted to him by Emperor Manuel I Comnenos (1143-1180) and ecumenical Patriarch Michael of Anchialos (1170-1178): a coordination between ecclesiastical and imperial legislation. The task implied, in fact, a codification of the imperial laws, some of which contained contradictions in their stipulations concerning the Church. Balsamon's concrete task involved those instances when a law of Justinian included in the *Nomocanon* was either omitted or contradicted in the *Basilics.* As a principle, he gives preference to the *Basilics* over Justinian and, consequently, in some cases, over Photius' *Nomocanon.* Balsamon's greater emphasis on imperial legislation in its more recent form does not prevent him from affirming explicitly the precedence of ecclesiastical canons over laws,[5] though in practice he does, at times, overrule clear conciliar definitions by referring to imperial laws.[6] This emphasis on the role of the emperor prompts Balsamon also to stress the authority of the ecumenical patriarch in general Church affairs; he always visualizes the Church as centralized in the framework of an ideally universal Christian empire.

An abundant canonical literature, whose authors it would be impossible to enumerate here, discussed issues arising from the canons, from imperial legislation, and from the commentaries: this literature, mostly polemical in nature, constitutes one of the major sources for our understanding of Byzantine medieval ecclesiology, which otherwise was not expounded in any systematic way.

One of the major issues arising in this literature is the canonical relationship between the patriarch and the provincial primates, or metropolitans. Actually, the controversies on this issue touched implicitly upon the role of the emperor in Church affairs; for it was an agreed fact that the ecumenical patriarch was not only an ecclesiastical, but a *state,* official. His secular function was expressed in the right to crown the emperor (a privilege which dated from the tenth century), and through the custom of his assuming the regency in case of need. The patriarch's appointment as a state official formally depended upon an "investiture" by the emperor, which followed an election of three candidates by the synod.[7] Meanwhile, the texts foresaw no official intervention of the emperor in the election of local metropolitans, and several canons even severely condemned it. Thus, dependence or independence of the metropolitans upon the patriarch as civil servants involved their relation to the emperor as well.

In the tenth century, a discussion arose between Euthymios, Metropolitan of Sardis, who defended the right of the patriarch to choose metropolitans from among the three candidates presented by the synod, and an anonymous author who interpreted the canons as attributing to the patriarch the right of the ordination of the metropolitans, but not that of election. Nicetas, Metropolitan of Amaseia, then wrote a treatise in favor of patriarchal rights.[8]

It seems that the debate ended in favor of imperial and patriarchal centralization, an idea which had also been expressed in Balsamon's commentaries (particularly on Canon 28 of Chalcedon). But, in the thirteenth and fourteenth centuries, as the imperial power weakened, the patriarchate acquired greater prestige independent of the empire. A series of patriarchs of the Paleologan period simultaneously asserted a greater independence from the state and a wider authority over the metropolitans. Patriarch Athanasius I (1289–1293, 1303–1310) even dismissed the synod altogether. His unedited correspondence and encyclicals offer a considerable canonical and ecclesiological interest.[9] The example of Athanasius will be followed by the patriarchs of the fourteenth century, especially Callistos and Philotheos, with their concept of "universal leadership" (*ķēdemonia pantōn*), which they attribute to the patriarch of Constantinople, and which is reflected in the patriarchal *Acts* of their time.

5. SYNODAL AND PATRIARCHAL DECREES

During the entire Byzantine period, the patriarch of Constantinople was the *de facto* head of the Eastern Church as a whole. His authority was first described as a "privilege of honor after the Bishop of Rome" (Second Ecumenical Council, Canon 3); the Fourth Council in its famous Canon 28 spoke of privileges "equal" to those of Rome and gave to the bishop of the capital a wide patriarchal jurisdiction, as well as a right to receive appeals against the judgments of regional primates. These privileges and rights were based only on the prestige of the "imperial city" and never led to any notion of patriarchal infallibility. It was inevitable, however, that major doctrinal issues were solved in Constantinople by the patriarch and the bishops who, around him, constituted a permanent synod. More representative assemblies, sometimes presided over by the emperor and including the other Eastern patriarchs or their delegates, met on exceptional occasions to solve the more important issues. Major decisions of this permanent magisterium are included in the *Synodikon* of Orthodoxy, a lengthy liturgical text which, since 843, has been read in all churches on the First Sunday of Lent and commemorates the end of iconoclasm. The *Synodikon* in its various versions and the documents issued by the patriarchal synod are primary sources for our knowledge of Byzantine ecclesiological self-understanding.

Beginning with a solemn thanksgiving for the triumph of Orthodoxy over "all heresies," the text of the *Synodikon* contains a particular commemoration of the defenders of the true faith during the iconoclastic period; it adds praises for the orthodox patriarchs of the subsequent period and, finally, anathemas against various heretics. Since the end of the ninth century, the document has received some additions as a result of several later doctrinal disputes, which were solved by synodal decrees in Constantinople.

The listing of the patriarchs for the period between 715 and 1416 is, in itself, an important witness to the ways in which various internal and external problems were solved. The successive mention of Ignatius, Photius, Stephen, Anthony, Nicholas, and Euthymius as "orthodox patriarchs of eternal memory" [10] shows that the famous schisms which occurred in the ninth and tenth centuries between Ignatius and Photius, and between Nicholas and Euthymius, and the mutual excommunications which ensued, were simply considered as not having taken place. But the omission among the names of the patriarchs of the late-thirteenth century of the names of Nicephorus II (1260–1261), Germanus III (1265–1267), John XI Beccos (1275–1282), Gregory II of Cyprus (1283–1289), and John XII Cosmas (1294–1303) reflects the rejection of the Union of Lyons (1274) and the terms of the reconciliation of the "Arsenites" with the official Church in 1310. The Arsenites had refused to recognize the deposition of Patriarch Arsenius Autoreianus in 1260, and obtained in 1310 his full rehabilitation, as well as a partial *damnatio memoriae* for several of his successors.[11]

The *Synodikon* also portrays the Byzantine magisterium in action against the Platonism of John Italos (1076–1077, 1082), as well as the Christo-

logical deviations of John's contemporary, Nilus the Calabrian, those of
Eustratius of Nicaea (1117), Soterichos Panteugenos (1155–1156), Constantine of Corfu, and John Eirenikos (1169–1170), and, finally, the solution given to the great doctrinal disputes on "deification" and the "energies" in the fourteenth century. The *Acts* of the patriarchal synod, unfortunately, are not preserved for the entire period, but only for the last two centuries of the Byzantine Empire. They represent an inexhaustible source of information on Church–state relations, canonical procedures, and the practice of *oikonomia,* one of the important illustrations of the manner in which the Byzantines understood the relationship of law and grace in the Christian Church.

6. OIKONOMIA

In both historical and theological literature, the principle of *oikonomia* is often referred to to illustrate the particularly Byzantine ability to interpret the law arbitrarily to suit political or personal purposes. Such a use betrays an obvious misunderstanding of the term, and is an injustice both to the principle itself and to its proper application. The term *oikonomia* does not belong originally to legal vocabulary; meaning "household management," it designates in the New Testament the divine *plan of salvation*: "He has made known to us in all wisdom and insight the mystery of his will, according to his purpose which he set forth in Christ as a *plan* [*oikonomia*] for the fullness of time, to recapitulate all things in him, things in heaven and things on earth" (Ep 1:9–10; v. also 3:2–3). But this divine plan for the management of history and of the world has been entrusted to men. For Paul, preaching of the word is an *oikonomia,* entrusted by God (1 Co 9:17), and, therefore, we should be regarded as "servants of Christ and stewards [*oikonomoi*] of the mysteries of God" (1 Co 4:1). More specifically, the "management" or "stewardship" belongs to those who fulfill the ministry of leading the Church: "The Church, of which I became a minister according to the divine office [*oikonomia*] which was given to me for you" (Col 1:24–25). In the Pastorals, the *oikonomia* belongs particularly to the *episkopos*: "For a bishop, as God's steward [*oikonomos*], must be blameless" (Tt 1:7).

Among the Greek Fathers, *oikonomia* has the standard meaning of "incarnation history," especially during the Christological controversies of the fifth century. In a subsidiary way it is also used in canonical texts, and then, obviously, places the pastoral "management" entrusted to the Church in the context of God's plan for the salvation of mankind. Thus, in his famous *Letter to Amphilochius,* which became an authoritative part of the Byzantine canonical collections, Basil of Caesarea, after reaffirming the Cyprianic principle about the invalidity of baptism by heretics, continues: "If, however, this becomes an obstacle to [God's] general *oikonomia,* one should again refer to custom and follow the Fathers who have man-aged [the Church]." The "custom" to which Basil refers was current "in Asia," where "the management of the multitude" had accredited the prac-tice of accepting baptism by heretics. In any case, Basil justifies "economy" by the fear that too much austerity will be an obstacle to the salvation of some.[12] In the Latin versions of the New Testament, and in later ecclesi-astical vocabulary, the term *oikonomia* is very consistently translated by *dispensatio*. In Western canon law, however, the term *dispensatio* acquired a very definite meaning of "exception to the law granted by the proper authority." The text of Basil quoted above, and innumerable references to *oikonomia* in Byzantine canonical literature, clearly interpret it in a much wider sense. What is at stake is not only an exception to the law, but an obligation to decide individual issues in the general context of God's plan for the salvation of the world. Canonical strictures may sometimes be in-adequate to the full reality and universality of the Gospel, and, by them-selves, do not provide the assurance that, in applying them, one is obedient to the will of God. For the Byzantines—to use an expression of Patriarch Nicholas Mystikos (901–907, 912–925)—*oikonomia* is "an imitation of God's love for man" [13] and not simply an "exception to the rule."

Occasionally, *oikonomia*—whether the word itself is used or not—be-comes part of the rule itself. Canon 8 of Nicaea, for example, specifies that Novatian bishops be received as bishops whenever the local episcopal see is vacant, but that they be accepted as priests, or *chorepiskopoi,* when a Catholic bishop already occupies the local see. In this case, the unity and welfare of the Church are concepts which supersede any possible notion of the "validity" of ordination outside the canonical boundaries of the Church, and *oikonomia*—i.e., God's plan for the Church—represents a living flexibility extending beyond a legalistic interpretation of sacramental validity.

Oikonomia, on the other hand, plays an important role in Byzantine marriage law. This law, as we shall see later, aims fundamentally at ex-pressing and protecting the notion that the unique Christian marriage, a sacramental reality, is projected—"in reference to Christ and the Church" (Ep 5:32)—into the eternal Kingdom of God. Marriage, therefore, is not simply a contract, which is indissoluble only while both parties remain in this world, but an eternal relationship not broken by death. In accordance with St. Paul (1 Co 7:8–9), second marriage is tolerated, but not con-sidered "legitimate" in itself, whether it is concluded after the death of one partner or after a divorce. In both cases, it is tolerated twice only "by economy," as a lesser evil, while a fourth marriage is excluded.

Of its nature, *oikonomia* cannot be defined as a legal norm, and prac-tical misuses and abuses of it have frequently occurred. Throughout its entire history, the Byzantine Church has known a polarization between a party of "rigorists," recruited mainly in monastic circles, and the generally more lenient group of Church officials supporting a wider use of *oikonomia*, especially in relation to the state. In fact, *oikonomia*, since it permits various possible ways of implementing the Christian Gospel practically, implies conciliation, discussion, and, often, unavoidably, tension. By admitting representatives of the two groups in the catalogue of its saints—Theodore the Studite, as well as the patriarchs Tarasius, Nicephorus, and Methodius; Ignatius, as well as Photius—the Church has given credit to them all, as long as it recognized that the preservation of the orthodox faith was their common concern. In fact, no one in Byzantium ever denied the principle of *oikonomia*; rather everyone agreed with Eulogius, Patriarch of Alexandria (581–607), when he wrote: "One rightly can practice *oikonomia* whenever pious doctrine remains unharmed." [14] In other words, *oikonomia* concerns the practical implications of Christian belief, but it never compromises with the truth itself.

NOTES

1. *De Vita Constantini*, 4, 24; PG 20:1172AB.
2. *Codex Justinianus* I, 3, 41; English text in P. R. Coleman-Norton, *Roman State and Christian Church*, III (London: SPCK, 1966), no. 579, p. 1017.
3. *Novella* 131, 1.
4. Balsamon, *Commentary on Nomocanon*, I, 2; PG 104:981c.
5. *Ibid.*
6. See his commentary on Laodicea 58 and Quinisext 59 forbidding celebration of sacraments in private homes, but overruled by *Novella* 4 of Leo VI; *ed. cit.*, II, 440; See *Les novelles de Léon VI*, edd. P. Noailles and A. Dain (Paris: Belles Lettres, 1944), pp. 20–21.
7. Constantine Porphyrogenetos, *De ceremoniis*, II, 14; PG 112:1044A; Symeon of Thessalonica, *De sacris ordinibus*; PG 155:440D.
8. All texts and French translation in J. Darrouzès, *Documents inédits d'écclesiologie byzantine* (Paris: Institut français d'études byzantines, 1966).
9. R. Guilland, "Correspondance inédite d'Athanase, patriarche de Constantinople," *Mélanges Diehl* 1 (Paris, 1930), pp. 131–140; M. Banescu, "Le patriarche Athanase I et Andronic II," *Académie roumaine, Bulletin de la section historique* 23 (1942), 1–28.
10. *Synodikon*, ed. J. Gouillard, II, 103.
11. On the Arsenites, see I. Troitsky, *Arseny i Arsenity* (St. Petersburg, 1874; repr. London: Variorum, 1973 [with introduction and bibliographical updating by J. Meyendorff]).
12. Basil of Caesarea, *Ep. ad Amphilochium*; PG 32:669B.
13. Nicholas Mystikos, *Ep.* 32 (to the pope), ed. A. Mai, *Spicilegium Romanum* 10 (1844), 300; PG 111:213A.
14. Eulogius, quoted by Photius in *Library*, 227; ed. R. Henry (Paris: Belles Lettres, 1965), 4:112.

The Schism Between East and West

THE CHRISTOLOGICAL CONTROVERSIES of the fifth century, as we have seen, provoked a final break between Byzantine Christendom and the other ancient spiritual families of the East: Syriac, Egyptian, and Armenian. The Greeks and the Latins remained alone, in their common faithfulness to Chalcedon, as the two main cultural expressions of Christianity inside the Roman world. The schism which finally separated them cannot be identified with any particular event or even be dated precisely. Political opposition between Byzantium and the Frankish Empire, gradual estrangement in thought and practice, divergent developments in both theology and ecclesiology, played their respective parts in this process. But in spite of the historical factors which pushed the two halves of Christendom further and further apart, there were political forces working in favor of union: the Byzantine emperors, for example, systematically tried from the thirteenth to the fifteenth centuries to re-establish ecclesiastical communion with Rome and thus gain Western support against the Turks.

In fact, neither the schism, nor the failure of the attempts at reunion can be explained exclusively by socio-political or cultural factors. The difficulties created by history could have been resolved if there had been a common ecclesiological criterion to settle the theological, canonical, or liturgical issues keeping the East and the West apart. But the medieval development of the Roman primacy as the ultimate reference in doctrinal matters stood in obvious contrast with the concept of the Church prevailing in the East. Thus, there could not be agreement on the issues themselves, or on the manner of solving them, as long as there was divergence on the notion of authority in the Church.

1. THE *Filioque*

The Byzantines considered the *Filioque* issue as the central point of disagreement. In their eyes, the Latin Church, by accepting an interpolated creed, was both opposing a text adopted by the ecumenical councils as the expression of the universal Christian faith, and giving dogmatic authority to an incorrect concept of the Trinity. Among the Byzantines, even the moderates, like Peter, Patriarch of Antioch, who objected to the systematic anti-Latinism of his colleague in Constantinople, Michael Cerularius, considered the interpolation as an "evil, and even the worst of evils." [1]

Generally, the Byzantines lacked a full knowledge of the complicated historical circumstances which led to the acceptance of the *Filioque* in the West: the interpolation of the creed in Spain in the sixth century as a means of strengthening the anti-Arian position of the Spanish Church; the spreading of the interpolated creed in the Frankish Empire; Charlemagne's use of it in his anti-Greek polemic; the *post factum* reference by Frankish theologians to Augustine's *De Trinitate* to justify the interpolation (which Augustine never envisaged), and, finally, the acceptance of the *Filioque* in Rome, probably in 1014. Photius offered the first open Greek refutation in 866, when he saw in the interpolated creed not only an alteration by some Frankish "barbarians" in the distant West, but also a weapon of anti-Byzantine propaganda among the nearby Bulgarians, who had recently been converted to Christianity by the Greeks and for whom the Byzantine patriarch considered himself directly responsible.

In his encyclical to the Eastern patriarchs (866), Photius considers the *Filioque* as the "crown of evils" introduced by the Frankish missionaries in Bulgaria.[2] We have already seen that his major theological objection to the interpolation was that it presupposed a confusion of the hypostatic characters of the Persons of the Trinity and was, therefore, a new form of modalism, or "semi-Sabellianism." After the Council of 879–880, which solemnly confirmed the original text of the creed and formally anathematized anyone who would either "compose another confession of faith" or corrupt the creed with "illegitimate words, or additions, or subtractions," [3] Photius considered himself fully satisfied. To celebrate what he considered a final victory of Orthodoxy, he composed a detailed refutation of the doctrine of the "double procession"—his famous *Mystagogy*—in which he also praised Pope John VIII for having made the triumph possible.[4]

After the final adoption of the *Filioque* in Rome and throughout the West, the issue was bound to be raised at every encounter, polemical or friendly, between Greeks and Latins. Byzantine literature on the subject is extremely voluminous and has been reviewed in reference works by Martin Jugie, Hans-Georg Beck, and others. The arguments raised by Photius— "the *Filioque* is an illegitimate interpolation," "it destroys the *monarchy* of the Father" and "relativizes the reality of personal, or *hypostatic* existence, in the Trinity"—remained at the center of the discussion. But often, the controversy was reduced to an interminable enumeration by both sides of patristic texts collected in favor of the respective positions of the Greeks and of the Latins.

The battles around ancient authorities often concentrated on texts by those Fathers—especially Athanasius, Cyril of Alexandria, and Epiphanius of Cyprus—whose main concern was anti-Arian or anti-Nestorian polemics, i.e., the establishment of Christ's identity as the eternal and pre-existing divine Logos. In reference to the Holy Spirit, they unavoidably used expressions similar to those also adopted in sixth-century Spain where the interpolation first appeared. Biblical texts, such as John 20:22 ("He breathed on them and said: Receive the Holy Spirit"), were seen as proofs of the divinity of Christ: if the "Spirit of God" is also the "Spirit of Christ" (cf. Rm 8:9), Christ is certainly "consubstantial" with God. Thus it is also possible to say that the Spirit is the "proper" Spirit of the Son,[5] and even that the Spirit "proceeds substantially from both" the Father and the Son.[6] Commenting upon these texts and acknowledging their correspondence with Latin patristic thought, Maximus the Confessor rightly interprets them as meaning not that "the Son is the origin of the Spirit," because "the Father alone is the origin of the Son and of the Holy Spirit," but that "the Spirit proceeds through the Son, expressing thus the unity of nature."[7] In other words, from the activity of the Spirit in the world after the Incarnation, one can infer the consubstantiality of the three Persons of the Trinity, but one cannot infer any causality in the eternal personal relationships of the Spirit with the Son.

However, those whom the Byzantines called *Latinophrones*—the "Latin-minded"—and especially John Beccos (1275-1282), enthroned as patriarch by Emperor Michael VIII Paleologus with the explicit task of promoting in Byzantium the Union of Lyons (1274), made a significant effort to use Greek patristic texts on the Spirit's procession "through the Son" in favor of the Latin *Filioque*. According to the *Latinophrones,* both "through the Son" and "from the Son" were legitimate expressions of the same Trinitarian faith.

The usual counter-argument of the Orthodox side was that in Biblical or patristic theology procession "from" or "through" the Son designates the *charismata* of the Spirit, and not His hypostatic existence.[8] For indeed *pneuma* can designate the giver and the gift; and, in the latter case, a procession of the "Spirit" from or through the Son—i.e., through the Incarnate, historical Christ—happens *in time,* and thus does not coincide with the eternal procession of the Spirit from the hypostasis of the Father, the only "source of divinity."

This counter-argument was recognized as insufficient, however, by the major Orthodox Byzantine theologians of the thirteenth and the fourteenth centuries. Gregory of Cyprus, a successor of Beccos' on the patriarchal throne (1283-1289) and chairman of the council (1285) which officially rejected the Union of Lyons, had this assembly approve a text which, while condemning the *Filioque,* recognized an "eternal manifestation" of the Spirit through the Son.[9] What served as a background to the council's position is the notion that the *charismata* of the Spirit are not temporal, created realities, but the eternal, uncreated grace or "energy" of God. To this uncreated divine life, man has access in the body of the Incarnate Logos. Therefore, the grace of the Spirit does indeed come to us "through" or "from" the Son; but what is being given to us is neither the very hypostasis of the Spirit nor a created, temporal grace, but the external "manifestation" of God, distinct from both His persons and His essence. The argument was also taken over and developed by Gregory Palamas, the great Byzantine theologian of the fourteenth century, who, like Gregory of Cyprus, formally recognizes that as *energy*, "the Spirit is the Spirit of Christ, and comes from Him, being breathed and sent and manifested by Him, but in His very being and His existence, He is the Spirit *of* Christ, but is not *from* Christ, but from the Father." [10]

As time went on, it became increasingly clear that the *Filioque* dispute was not a discussion on words—for there was a sense in which both sides would agree to say that the Spirit proceeds "from the Son"—but on the issue of whether the hypostatic existence of the Persons of the Trinity could be reduced to their internal relations, as the post-Augustinian West would admit, or whether the primary Christian experience was that of a Trinity of Persons, whose personal existence was irreducible to their common essence. The question was whether tri-personality or consubstantiality was the first and basic content of Christian religious experience. But to place the debate on that level and to enter into a true dialogue on the very substance of the matter, each side needed to understand the other's position. This unfortunately never occurred. Even at the Council of Florence, where interminable confrontations on the *Filioque* issue took place, the discussion still dealt mainly with attempts at accommodating Greek and Latin formulations. The council finally adopted a basically Augustinian definition of the Trinity, while affirming that the Greek *formulations* were not in contradiction with it. This, however, was not a solution of the fundamental issue.

2. OTHER CONTROVERSIES

Photius, in his encyclical of 867, also had criticized several liturgical and canonical practices introduced by Frankish missionaries in Bulgaria (opposition to a married priesthood, confirmation performed only by bishops, fasting on Saturdays), but his criticism was directed at the fact that the missionaries were requiring from the newly-baptized Bulgarians complete abandonment of Greek usages. He did not yet consider diversity in practice and discipline as an obstacle to Church unity. The Latin interpolation of the creed and the doctrine which it reflected were the only doctrinal issues which, according to Photius, were leading to schism.

This attitude will generally predominate among the best theologians of Byzantium. Peter of Antioch (*ca.* 1050) and Theophylact of Bulgaria (*ca.*

1100) explicitly state that the *Filioque* is the only issue dividing East and West. And even at a later period, when the separate development of the two theologies was bound to create new problems, one finds many prominent Byzantines failing to raise any issue in their anti-Latin treatises other than that of the procession of the Holy Spirit.

On the less enlightened level of popular piety, however, polemics took a sharper tone and were often oriented toward peripheral issues. When well-intentioned, but ill-informed, Frankish reformers in Bulgaria under Photius, or in Italy under Michael Cerularius, attacked the practices of the Greek Church, the Church often answered with a counterattack on Latin discipline and rites. Thus, the schism of the eleventh century was almost exclusively a dispute about ritual practices. In addition to the issues quoted by Photius, Michael Cerularius mentions among "Latin heresies" the use of unleavened bread in the Eucharist, the leniency of the Latin fast, baptism by one and not three immersions, and other similar issues.[11]

Cerularius' list of heresies was frequently repeated, and often expanded, by later polemicists. Of the problems mentioned in the list, however, the only one to be viewed consistently by the Greeks as a theological issue—and even sometimes placed on a level of importance comparable to that of the *Filioque*—is that of the azymes, the use of unleavened bread in the Latin Eucharistic celebration. Thus, in the late Middle Ages, Greek and Slavic peoples often characterized the Latins as azymites.

The arguments brought against the Latin practice by Cerularius' friends and contemporaries—Leo of Ohrid and Nicetas Stethatos—and repeated by their successors can be reduced to three: (1) the use of unleavened bread is Judaic; (2) it contradicts the historic evidence as recorded in the Synoptics (Jesus took "bread"); and (3) its symbolic value is that of "death," not of "life," for yeast in the dough is like the soul in the body. The weakness of these arguments requires no demonstration. The second point in particular implies the solution of several exegetical and historical problems: Was the Last Supper a paschal meal? In that case unleavened bread would have been used. Or did Jesus deliberately violate the law in order to institute a "new" covenant? Can the word *artos,* which normally designates ordinary bread, also mean "unleavened bread"?

The third argument was also raised by Greek polemicists in the Christological context of anti-Armenian polemics. Nicetas Stethatos himself was involved in arguments against the Armenians, who, after the conquests of the Macedonian emperors of the tenth century, were in close contact with Byzantium. The Armenians were using unleavened bread in the Eucharist, and the Greeks drew a parallel between this practice and the Monophysite —or, more precisely, Apollinarian—Christology of the Armenians: bread, symbolizing Christ's humanity, in order to reflect Chalcedonian orthodoxy, must be "animated" and dynamic, in full possession of the living energies of humanity. By imitating the Monophysite Armenians in their use of the "dead" azymes, the Latins themselves were falling into Apollinarianism, and denying that Christ, as man, had a soul. Thus, during the Middle Ages and afterward, in Greek and Slavic countries, Latins were considered as having fallen into the "Apollinarian heresy": the charge appears, for example, in the writings of the monk Philotheus, the famous Russian sixteenth-century ideologist of "Moscow, the third Rome."

After the late-thirteenth century, the growing Scholastic precisions, which appeared in contemporary Latin theology, concerning the fate of the souls after death and purgatory fire, were reflected in the various encounters between Latin and Greek theologians. The unionist Profession of Faith, which had to be signed by Emperor Michael VIII Paleologus (1259–1282), included a long clause affirming that the souls, before enjoying the fruits of repentance in heaven, "were purified after death through the fire of Purgatory" and that prayer for the departed was able to alleviate their "pains." [12] Although the Byzantine tradition had always acknowledged that prayers for the dead were both licit and necessary, that the solidarity of all the members of the Body of Christ was not broken by death, and that, through the intercession of the Church, the departed could get closer to God, it ignored the notion of redemption through "satisfaction," of which the legalistic concept of "purgatory pains" was an expression. On this point most Byzantine theologians were more puzzled than impressed by the Latins, and they never succeeded in placing the issue in the wider context of the doctrine of salvation, the only level on which a successful refutation and alternative could be found. Even in Florence, where, for the first time, a prolonged dialogue on the issue took place, the discussion was limited to particulars and was never concerned with the notion of redemption as such.[13] It ended with the weary acceptance, by the Greek majority, of a detailed and purely Latin definition of the issue.

In the decades preceding the Council of Florence, the growing knowledge among Byzantines of the Latin liturgical practices led to the emergence of another issue between the churches, that of the relationship in the Eucharist canon between the words of institution and the invocation of the Spirit, or epiclesis. Reproaching the Latins for the absence of an epiclesis in the Roman canon of the Mass, Byzantine polemicists pointed out the fact that all sacramental acts are effected through the Holy Spirit. Nicholas Cabasilas († before 1391), the famous spiritual writer, in his *Explanation of the Divine Liturgy*,[14] invokes in favor of this point the authority of the Latin rite itself, whose Christian authenticity he thus explicitly recognizes. He recalls that an invocation of the Spirit is part of the Latin rite of ordination and that the Roman Mass includes in the oration *supplices te rogamus* a prayer *for the gifts,* which follows the words of institution, a fact which, according to Cabasilas, means that the words of institution are not consecratory in themselves. Whatever the strength of this last argument, it is clear that the Greek insistence on an explicit invocation of the

Spirit is very much in line with the traditional patristic theology of the sacraments, especially when it considers the epiclesis not as a "formula" of consecration, opposed to the Latin one, but as the normal and necessary fulfillment of the Eucharistic prayer, of which the words of institution also constitute a fundamental part.

3. AUTHORITY IN THE CHURCH

Most of the controversy which set Greek against Latin in the Middle Ages could have been solved easily if both churches had recognized a common authority able to solve the unavoidable differences created by divergent cultures and historical situations. Unfortunately, behind the various doctrinal, disciplinary, and liturgical disputes stood an ecclesiological dichotomy. Any historian today would recognize that the medieval papacy was the result of a long doctrinal and institutional development in which the Eastern Church had either no opportunity or no desire to participate. Orthodox and Roman Catholics still argue whether this development was legitimate from the point of view of Christian revelation.

The reformed papacy of the eleventh century used a long-standing Western tradition of exegesis when it applied systematically and legalistically the passages on the role of Peter (especially Mt 16:18, Lk 22:32, and Jn 21:15-17) to the bishop of Rome. This tradition was not shared by the East, yet it was not totally ignored by the Byzantines, some of whom used it occasionally, especially in documents addressed to Rome and intended to win the popes' sympathy. But it was never given an ultimate theological significance. The personal role of Peter as the "rock" upon which the Church was built was readily recognized by Byzantine ecclesiastical writers. Only late polemicists, systematically anti-Latin, tended to diminish it; but this was not the case among the most enlightened of the Byzantine theologians. Thus, according to Photius, Peter is "the chief of the apostolic choir, and has been established as the rock of the Church and is proclaimed by the Truth to be keybearer of the Kingdom of Heaven." [15] Numerous passages, similar to that of Photius, can be found in Byzantine ecclesiastical literature and hymnography. Their true significance, however, cannot be understood apart from more general presuppositions on the nature of the Christian faith and the manner of its preservation and continuity in the Church.

Origen, the common source of patristic exegetical tradition, commenting on Matthew 16:18, interprets the famous *logion* as Jesus' answer to Peter's confession: Simon became the "rock" on which the Church is founded because he expressed the true belief in the divinity of Christ. Origen continues: "If we also say 'Thou art the Christ, the Son of the living God,' then we also become Peter . . . for whoever assimilates to Christ, becomes rock. Does Christ give the keys of the kingdom to Peter alone, whereas

other blessed people cannot receive them?" [16] According to Origen, therefore, Peter is no more than the first "believer," and the keys he received
opened the gates of heaven to him alone: if others want to follow, they can
"imitate" Peter and receive the same keys. Thus the words of Christ have
a soteriological, but not an institutional, significance. They only affirm
that the Christian faith is the faith expressed by Peter on the road to
Caesarea Philippi. In the whole body of patristic exegesis, this is the prevailing understanding of the "Petrine" *logia,* and it remains valid in
Byzantine literature. In the twelfth-century Italo-Greek homilies attributed
to Theophanes Kerameus, one can still read: "The Lord gives the keys to
Peter and to all those who resemble him, so that the gates of the Kingdom
of heaven remain closed for the heretics, yet are easily accessible to the
faithful." [17] Thus, when he spoke to Peter, Jesus was underlining the
meaning of the faith as the foundation of the Church, rather than organizing the Church as guardian of the faith. The whole ecclesiological
debate between East and West is thus reducible to the issue of whether
the faith depends on Peter, or Peter on the faith. The issue becomes clear
when one compares the two concepts of the *succession* of Peter.

If many Byzantine ecclesiastical writers follow Origen in recognizing
this succession in *each believer,* others have a less individualistic view of
Christianity; they understand that the faith can be fully realized only in
the sacramental community, where the bishop fulfills, in a very particular
way, Christ's ministry of teaching and, thus, preserves the faith. In this
sense, there is a definite relationship between Peter, called by Christ to
"strengthen his brethren" (Lk 22:32), and the bishop, as guardian of the
faith in his local church. The early Christian concept, best expressed in
the third century by Cyprian of Carthage,[18] according to which the "see
of Peter" belongs, in each local church, to the bishop, remains the long-
standing and obvious pattern for the Byzantines. Gregory of Nyssa, for
example, can write that Jesus "through Peter gave to the bishops the keys
of heavenly honors." [19] Pseudo-Dionysius, when he mentions the "hierarchs"—i.e., the bishops of the earthly Church—refers immediately to the
image of Peter.[20] Examples taken from the later period, and quite independent of anti-Latin polemics, can easily be multiplied. Peter's succession
is seen wherever the right faith is preserved, and, as such, it cannot be
localized geographically or monopolized by a single church or individual.
It is only natural, therefore, that the Byzantine will fail to understand the
developed medieval concept of Roman primacy. Thus, in the thirteenth
century, shortly after the capture of Constantinople by the Crusaders (1204),
we can read Nicholas Mesarites, addressing the Latins:

> You try to present Peter as the teacher of Rome alone. While the divine
> Fathers spoke of the promise made to him by the Savior as having a *catho-*
> *lic* meaning and as referring to all those who believed and believe, you

force yourself into a narrow and false interpretation, ascribing it to Rome alone. If this were true, it would be impossible for every church of the faithful, and not only that of Rome, to possess the Savior properly, and for each church to be founded on the rock, i.e., on the doctrine of Peter, in conformity with the promise.[21]

Obviously, this text of Mesarites' implies a concept of the Church which recognizes the fullness of catholicity in each *local* church, in the sense in which the Apostolic Fathers could speak, for example, of the "catholic church sojourning in Corinth." Catholicity, and therefore also truth and apostolicity, thus become God-given attributes belonging to each sacramental, Eucharist-centered community possessing a true episcopate, a true Eucharist, and, therefore, an authentic presence of Christ. The idea that one particular church would have, in a full theological sense, more capacity than another to preserve the faith of Peter was foreign to the Byzantines. Consensus of bishops, and not the authority of one particular bishop, was for them the highest possible sign of truth. Hence their constant insistence on the authority of the councils and their inability to understand the Roman concept of the papacy. It is not, however, that the very idea of primacy was foreign to the Byzantines; but they generally understood it as a matter for conciliar legislation, not as a God-given function of a particular church.

4. TWO IDEAS OF PRIMACY

One important difference between eastern and western attitudes deserves particular emphasis. . . . The idea of apostolicity played a very limited role in the development of the Church in the eastern provinces, but . . . Rome owed its prestige in Italy and in other western provinces . . . to the veneration in which young Christian communities of the West held St. Peter . . . whose successors the Roman bishops claimed to be.[22]

Historians have often cited the fact that Rome was the only local church of the West which could claim "apostolic" foundation and attract pilgrimages *ad limina apostolorum*. In the East, innumerable cities, or lesser localities, could authentically attribute their foundation to Peter, Paul, John, Andrew, or other Apostles. These various "apostolicities" did not entail any jurisdictional claims: the bishop of Jerusalem was still, in the fourth century, only a suffragan of the metropolitan of Caesarea, the civil capital of Palestine.

When the Council of Nicaea, in its famous Canon 6, vaguely mentioned the "ancient customs" which recognized an exceptional prestige to the churches of Alexandria, Antioch, and Rome, the selection of these particular churches was determined not by their apostolic foundation, but by the fact that they were located in the most important cities of the empire.

For if apostolicity were the criterion, as later Western interpretations insist, the position of Alexandria, purported to have been founded by a minor apostolic figure, Mark, could not be greater than Antioch's, where Peter's presence is attested by the New Testament.

The East remained pragmatic in its definition of universal or local primacies among the churches, and this attitude made conflict inevitable as soon as Rome recognized an absolute and dogmatic significance to the "apostolic" criterion of primacy. Actually, in the Byzantine Empire, "pragmatism" meant adjustment to the structure of the state, and this adjustment explains the text of Canon 28 of the Council of Chalcedon:

> The Fathers rightly granted privileges to the throne of old Rome, because it was the imperial city. And one hundred and fifty most religious bishops [of Constantinople, 381], actuated by the same considerations, gave equal privileges to the most holy throne of new Rome, justly judging that the city, which is honored with the presence of the emperor and the senate and enjoys equal privileges with the old imperial Rome, should, in ecclesiastical matters also, be magnified as she is and rank next after her.

This text was in no way meant to suppress the prestige of Rome (it was directed against the pretentions of Dioscorus of Alexandria, whom the Council of Chalcedon deposed); but it certainly excluded the "Petrine" interpretation of Roman primacy, and

> was in conformity with the logical development of ecclesiastical organisms in the Byzantine period which, since the era of Constantine, had admitted the principle that ecclesiastical administration coincided with the secular structure of the Empire.[23]

As we have seen above, the succession of Peter was considered to be involved in the episcopal office present in every church, and was envisaged as a responsibility in which any "successor of Peter," including the bishop of Rome, could fail. A theologian of the fifteenth century, Symeon of Thessalonica, could thus write:

> One should not contradict the Latins when they say that the bishop of Rome is the first. This primacy is not harmful to the Church. Let them only prove his faithfulness to the faith of Peter and to that of the successors of Peter. If it is so, let him enjoy all the privileges of Peter. . . .[24]

5. THE MEANING OF THE SCHISM

Cultural and historical differences may easily lead to theological divergences; but such divergences need not become contradictions and incompatibilities.

There were differences and even violent conflicts between the East and West as early as the fourth century, but in spite of ever-recurring tension, there existed, until the eleventh century, a mutually recognized procedure for solving difficulties: the council. Joint councils, meeting generally in the East, convened by the emperor, and at which Roman legates were given a place of honor, served as the ultimate tribunals to solve the standing issues. Thus the crisis which set Photius against Pope Nicholas I was finally ended at the last council (879–880) to follow that procedure and one which still ranks, according to the Orthodox Church, on almost the same level as the earlier ecumenical councils.

The German-oriented reformed papacy of the eleventh century was definitely no longer attuned to this type of conciliarity. The Crusades did much to antagonize the two culturally distinct civilizations of the East and of the West. And when the papacy, shaken by the Great Western Schism, and Byzantium, threatened by the Turks, finally agreed to hold a union council at Florence, it was too late to create the atmosphere of mutual respect and trust which alone would have permitted an authentic theological dialogue.

NOTES

1. Peter of Antioch, *Letter to Michael*; ed. Cornelius Will, *Acta et scripta quae de controversiis ecclesiae graecae et latinae extant* (Leipzig, 1856), p. 196.

2. Photius, *Encyclical*, 8; PG 102:725c.

3. Mansi, XVII, 520E.

4. Photius, *Mystagogy*, 89; PG 102:380–381.

5. Athanasius, *To Serapion*, III, 1; PG 26:625B.

6. Cyril, *Thesaurus*; PG 68:148A.

7. Maximus the Confessor, *Letter to Marinus*; PG 91:136AD.

8. The argument is found in Photius, *Mystagogy*, 59; PG 102:337.

9. Gregory of Cyprus, *Tome of 1285*; PG 142:240c.

10. Gregory Palamas, *Apodictic Treatise*, I, 9; ed. B. Bobrinskoy, in P. Chrestou, *Palama Syngrammata* (Thessaloniki, 1962), I, 37.

11. Michael Cerularius, *Letter to Peter of Antioch*; ed. Will, *Acta et Scripta*, pp. 179–183.

12. Mansi, XXIV, 70A.

13. See the major documents on this discussion published by L. Petit in *PatrOr*, 15 (Paris, 1903), pp. 1–168.

14. Nicholas Cabasilas, *Explanation of the Divine Liturgy*, chs. 29–30; ed. Perichon, SC 4 bis (Paris: Cerf, 1967), pp. 179–199; trans. J. M. Hussey and P. A. McNulty (London: SPCK, 1960), pp. 71–79.

15. Photius, *Hom.*, 1; trans. in C. Mango, *The Homilies of Photius* (Cambridge: Harvard University Press, 1958), p. 50.

16. Origen, *Hom. in Matt.*, XII, 10; ed. Klostermann GCS 40 (Leipzig, 1935), pp. 85–89.

17. Theophanes Kerameus, *Hom.*, 55; PG 142:965A. For a more general view of patristic exegesis on Matthew 16:18, see particularly J. Ludwig, *Die Primatworte Mt. 16, 18, 19 in der altkirchlichen Exegese* (Münster, 1952); and J. Meyendorff, "St. Peter in

Byzantine Theology," *The Primacy of Peter in the Orthodox Church,* ed. J. Meyendorff (London: Faith Press, 1963), pp. 7–29.

18. On Cyprian, see, for example, A. d'Alès, *La théologie de St. Cyprien* (Paris: Beauchesne, 1922); P.-Th. Camelot, "St. Cyprien et la primauté," *Istina* 4 (1957), 421–434; cf. also M. Bévenot's introduction and notes for Cyprian *De catholicae ecclesiae unitate* in ACW 25. (Westminster: Newman, 1957.)

19. Gregory of Nyssa, *De castigatione*; PG 46:312c.

20. Pseudo-Dionysius, *Eccl. hier.,* VII, 7; PG 3:561–564.

21. Nicholas Mesarites, in A. Heisenberg, ed., *Neue Quellen zur Geschichte des lateinischen Kaisertums und der Kirchenunion,* II. *Die Unionverhandlungen von 30. Aug. 1206,* in *AbhMünchAk,* phil. Klasse (1923) II, 34–35.

22. Francis Dvornik, *The Idea of Apostolicity in Byzantium* (Cambridge: Harvard University Press, 1958), p. 39.

23. J. Meyendorff, *Orthodoxy and Catholicity* (New York: Sheed & Ward, 1956), p. 74.

24. Symeon of Thessalonica, *Dialogus contra haereses,* 23; PG 155:120ab.

8

Encounter with the West

WITH THE EXCEPTION of Barlaam the Calabrian, no major participant of the great theological controversies, which ended in 1351, had anything but a casual knowledge of Western theology. Discussions between Greeks and Latins revolved around formulae which were used by both sides, each in a totally different context. And Barlaam himself, in spite of his double theological formation, was hardly a prominent representative of Western theological thought; he was, rather, a manipulator of ideas, and probably influenced by Nominalism.

Meanwhile, the formal conciliar decisions of 1341 and 1351, endorsing a theology of real "participation" of man in God and, therefore, of a real distinction between "essence" and "energy" in God, were clearly incompatible with the prevailing Latin theology of the time. A significant dialogue on the content of these decisions, as well as on their true relation to patristic tradition on the one hand and Latin Scholasticism on the other, would have required much time, wide historical knowledge, and true openness of mind. These conditions were obviously lacking on both sides but—and this will be the main point of this chapter—they were in the process of being realized in Byzantium during the last century of the empire.

1. THE CIRCLE OF CANTACUZENOS

Father-in-law of the legitimate emperor John v Paleologos, and himself emperor between 1347 and 1354, John Cantacuzenos exercised a decisive influence in assuring the triumph of Palamism in Byzantium, and, after his abdication, remained for almost forty years a powerful political and intellectual force in Byzantine society. Having accepted monastic tonsure in 1354, he nonetheless kept at his personal disposal enough funds and influence to act as a generous Maecenas for Byzantine intellectuals. Traveling between Constantinople and Mistra in the Peloponnesus, he sponsored, in both his main residences, the copying of manuscripts and the development of scholarly projects.

A theologian himself, he is the author of learned apologies of Palamism and of a lengthy refutation of Islam. During his entire life, however, he never lost sight of Western Christianity and, several times, participated in debates with papal envoys. Ecclesiastical union with Rome was consistently on the diplomatic agenda of the time as a condition for a Western crusade against the menacing Turks. Many Byzantines, including Emperor John v Paleologus, who succeeded Cantacuzenos, were ready to accept hastily all papal conditions in order to achieve immediate military relief. Supported by a majority in Church circles—especially by the disciples of Palamas who were occupying major positions in the hierarchy—Cantacuzenos defended the idea that union could be achieved only through a solution, at a joint council, of the theological issues dividing East and West. He was probably, and justifiably, skeptical that Western help could be decisive in any case, and, together with a majority of the Byzantine population, envisaged Turkish conquest as a possibility preferable to a betrayal of Orthodoxy.

He was never opposed to contacts with the West, however, repeatedly proposed a serious theological dialogue, and actively supported careful preparation on the Byzantine side for this eventual encounter. Knowledge of Latin theological thought was a necessary precondition, of course, and it is in the circle of Cantacuzenos that Latin theological sources were systematically translated into Greek. The emperor himself used some of them in his polemics against Islam, but his secretary and friend Demetrios Cydones devoted his entire life, with Cantacuzenos' approval and support, to the translation and study of Thomism. Meanwhile, another friend, Nicholas Cabasilas, was reviving sacramental mysticism in the best tradition of the Greek Fathers. Speaking to the legate Paul in 1367, Cantacuzenos develops his conviction that union will never be achieved by imperial decree: "This is impossible in our Church," he said, "since faith can never be forced." [1] His view of the situation was all the more realistic since the greater part of the Orthodox world was then out of the reach of the Byzantine emperor. The greater mass of the Greeks were already under Turkish occupation, the Balkan Slavs were politically and ecclesiastically independent, and the Russians were unlikely to accept lightly any union schemes drafted without their participation. Byzantium could not hope to legislate in Church matters as it had in the time of Photius, but could hope only to provide intellectual leadership in the forthcoming dialogue. Cantacuzenos did what he could to give Byzantium the necessary intellectual tools to produce, as a condition for Church union, what he and his contemporaries considered a real possibility: a theological victory of the East over the West at a union council.

Out of the groundwork laid by the circle of Cantacuzenos grew two or three generations of intellectuals who often adopted radically divergent attitudes toward the main theological options of the day. Investigation of their writings and thought has only recently begun but, at the present stage of our knowledge, it is already clear that, in spite of several individual casualties and major mistakes, an "in depth" encounter with Western theology was in the making.

2. HUMANISTS AND THOMISTS

The encyclopedic interests of Cantacuzenos led him to grant support to all forms of knowledge, including the study of secular philosophy—a tradition at all times alive in a small group of Byzantine aristocrats and intellectuals. Synodal decrees of the eleventh and twelfth centuries had warned the humanists against the dangers of considering Greek philosophy as a criterion of theological thought, but Barlaam of Calabria—originally a protégé of Cantacuzenos'—went beyond the permissible by reducing theology to the level of intellectual wisdom and discursive knowledge. The Council of 1341 signaled his defeat and condemnation. The capture of imperial power by Cantacuzenos in 1347 coincided with the total victory of Palamas and the Hesychasts, and was seen as a disaster by the humanists, among whom the Antipalamite party recruited most of its members. Clearly, the Byzantine Church was rejecting Platonizing humanism and refusing to accept the very patterns of humanistic civilization which the West was in the process of adopting.[2] It is precisely at this time that several prominent humanists, whose intellectual forefathers—Photius, Michael Psellos, Theodore Metochites—had despised the Latins as "barbarians," discovered in the Latin West, and particularly in Italy, the last refuge of true Hellenism.

Demetrios Cydones (*ca.* 1324–*ca.* 1398), a close political associate of Cantacuzenos', certainly belongs to this category. Staunchly Orthodox in his youth, he sometimes worried that the protocol requirements for an imperial ambassador to the pope, which would force him to address the Roman pontiff as "beatitude," "holiness," "common pastor," "Father," and "Vicar of Christ," might be harmful to his faith.[3] But then, suddenly, he discovered Thomism. When his diplomatic functions led him to learn Latin from a Dominican of Pera, he used the *Summa contra Gentiles* as an exercise book, and the effect on this friend of Barlaam, disappointed by the recent victory (in 1347) of the Hesychasts, was astounding. The Latins, whom the Byzantines considered incapable of rising above the military or merchant professions,[4] knew Greek philosophy! "Because the Byzantines did not care for their own [Greek] wisdom, they considered Latin reasonings to be Latin inventions." In fact, if only one took the time to unveil the meaning of Latin books, hidden by a foreign tongue, one would find that "they show great thirst for walking in those labyrinths of Aristotle and Plato, for which our people never showed interest."[5]

With the approval and support of Cantacuzenos, Demetrios continued his work of translation. The entire *Summa contra Gentiles,* most of *Summa theologica,* as well as important texts of Augustine and Anselm, were made accessible, in Greek versions, to Demetrios' contemporaries and to the following generations of Byzantine theologians. Cantacuzenos himself used Demetrios' translation of the *Refutation of the Koran* by the Dominican Ricoldo da Montecroce as a source book for his writings against Islam.

Translation work, contacts with Latins, travels to Italy, confirmed Demetrios Cydones in his conviction that Thomism was actually more "Greek" than Palamism. And in that he was certainly right. His enthusiasm for the intellectual possibilities of both Scholasticism and the Italian Renaissance finally led him to become the main adviser of Emperor John v in his union policies. Around 1363 he, unofficially, joined the Roman Catholic Church. He published several treatises in defense of the *Filioque,* written from the Thomist point of view which he had adopted; but after the synodal condemnation of his brother Prochoros (also a translator of Thomas and convinced Antipalamite) in 1368 by the reigning patriarch, Philotheos, he could have no further hope about the future of secular Hellenism in Byzantium. He continued, however, with conviction and obvious sincerity to play a political role as a promoter of union until his death. But in order to understand the true significance of his conversion, we should remember that it is ancient Greece—and not Rome or Constantinople—which for him is the ultimate criterion of wisdom. In 1365–1369, for example, in a letter to the philosopher George, his preference for St. Thomas is determined by Thomas' superiority over Plato;[6] and his charming little treatise *De contemnenda morte*[7] discusses immortality in purely Platonic terms, without a single reference to the Christian faith. Of course, Demetrios simultaneously wrote technical theological treatises and sermons without direct philosophical overtones. This double intellectual life was characteristic of Byzantine humanists before and after Cydones. The religious evolution of many *Latinophrones* of the fourteenth and fifteenth centuries followed the same pattern.

Whatever the case of the brothers Cydones, the effect exercised by their translations was much wider than their personal options and convictions, and led some Greeks to adopt straightforwardly the Roman Catholic faith and even to join the Dominican order. Such is the case of Manuel Calecas († 1410) and of Maximus Chrysoberges (*ca.* 1430), in whose conversions Greek humanism seems to have played a lesser role than in Demetrios'. Others, like the scholar Manuel Chrysoloras († 1415) found in St. Thomas not so much theological "truth" as a proof of Latin intellectual respectability. Manuel accepted an offer to teach Greek in Florence and later played a leading role at the Council of Constance, where he was even a candidate for the papacy. In the next generation, the famous Cardinal Bessarion followed a very similar intellectual and personal career, without personally becoming a Thomist. For all these intellectuals imbued with "Greek wisdom," Palamism symbolized a rejection of secular humanism. It was Prochoros

Cydones who, for the first time, wrote refutations of Palamism using Thomist arguments: Thomism and *Latinophrony* thus became the obvious solution for the small group of intellectuals who opposed Palamite thought.

But Palamite theologians also profited from the translations. Some of them even tried to overcome the dilemma between Palamism and Thomism. Nilus Cabasilas, who succeeded Gregory Palamas as Archbishop of Thessalonica († 1363), but who earlier had been the teacher of Demetrios Cydones, is described by Demetrios as "passionately enthusiastic about the books of Thomas." [8] He was the first among the Greeks with a full knowledge of Latin theology to write in favor of Palamism and against the *Filioque.* To a lesser extent, the same is true of Joseph Bryennios († 1439), a learned "teacher," knowledgeable in Latin, ambassador to the Council of Constance, who nevertheless remained fiercely opposed to any doctrinal compromise with the Latins. Another Thomist–Palamite, George-Gennadios Scholarios, was active in Florence before becoming the first patriarch under Turkish occupation.

3. PALAMITE THEOLOGIANS: NICHOLAS CABASILAS

The persistence of opposition against Palamism by isolated but influential intellectuals and the implications of the controversy for East–West relations explain the very great number of Byzantine Palamite writings during the period. Together with those of Nilus Cabasilas and Joseph Bryennios, the names of John Cantacuzenos and of Patriarch Philotheos Kokkinos (1353–1354, 1364–1376) are particularly important.

Also found among the members of the close circle of Cantacuzenos is the remarkable lay theologian Nicholas Cabasilas (*ca.* 1320–*ca.* 1390). A nephew of Nilus Cabasilas, Nicholas was an intimate friend and correspondent of Demetrios Cydones. His background was very similar to Demetrios', and he pursued a like political career in the shadow of Cantacuzenos. But after Cantacuzenos' abdication (1354), Cydones committed himself totally to the cause of union with the Latins, and Cabasilas became an original exponent of traditional and patristic sacramental theology.

The main theological writings of Nicholas Cabasilas are *The Life in Christ,* a vast spiritual and theological commentary on the sacraments, an *Explanation of the Divine Liturgy,* and three Mariological sermons. Occasionally, important theological thought is also to be found in his *Encomia* ("laudations") of various saints. Although some authors have seen little rapport between his theology and Palamas',[9] between them there is, in fact, total unity of inspiration and purpose: to affirm that communion with God in Christ through the Spirit is the only true meaning of human life. Cabasilas actually did write a brief but violent pamphlet against the Antipalamite Nicephoros Gregoras and clearly took sides in the controversy. His major theological writings are also conceived as an implicit manifesto against the ideology of the humanists, many of them his personal friends. His thought represents anything but a mystical escape from the issues of the day. He did not explicitly quote Palamas, but many passages of *The Life in Christ* are paraphrases of Palamas' *Triads*. Similarly, he practically never quotes the Fathers of the Church, but parallels with the sacramental passages of John Chrysostom or Cyril of Alexandria can be found on almost every page of *The Life in Christ*. The greatness of Cabasilas is that he succeeded in defending a theology of communion with God in a challenging age without being either scholastic, or polemical. What Palamas rendered in terms of concepts, Cabasilas expressed as an existential reality not only for Hesychast monks but also for every Christian. To understand the theological achievement of fourteenth-century Byzantium, it is essential to read Palamas and Cabasilas together.

In his *Interpretation of the Divine Liturgy*, Cabasilas still sometimes seems derivative of pseudo-Dionysius and his symbolism. But when he is compared with Dionysius himself and with other medieval liturgical writers, it becomes clear that Cabasilas represents a step toward a sacramental realism more congenial with the early Christian understanding of the sacraments. This realism permeates *The Life in Christ,* where the author is more concerned with sacramental theology and spirituality than with explaining individual details of the rites. In the first chapter, Cabasilas takes pains to show that the divine life, which will be "perfected" in the *eschaton,* is, nonetheless, a living experience, accessible in the present age.[10] Baptism is a new birth to this life. As in the earlier Greek Fathers, the positive notion of "new birth," rather than the negative concept of a "remission of sin," dominates Cabasilas' theology of baptism. In the new life, which he enters by baptism, man receives an "experience": "He becomes eye to see the light." [11]

If baptism gives new being, chrismation—the gift of the Spirit—bestows "energy" and "movement," i.e., the *free* personal enjoyment of baptismal grace.[12] In the Eucharist, Christ gives man not "something of Himself, but Himself"; "this is the most-praised wedding, to which the Bridegroom leads the Church as a Virgin Bride . . . , when we become flesh of His flesh and bone of His bone." [13] The paradox of the Church's existence is that "as children, we remain free, but we also depend on Him as His members." [14] Sanctification comes only from Christ,[15] but sanctity consists in conforming our *wills* to His divine will. Cabasilas makes this last point clear when he discusses the concept of "sainthood" in the Church: miracles are unmerited gifts of God and do not constitute sanctity—a free human achievement.[16]

Side by side with the Pauline image of Christ as Head of the Church, Cabasilas will speak of Jesus as the "heart" of the Body: "As the risen Christ does not know death, so the members of Christ will never taste

death. How can death touch members in communion with a living heart?"
This passage and its parallels lead us to an understanding of the very personal manner in which Cabasilas describes the Christian mystery,[17] and
show his indebtedness to the anthropology of Macarius, which was predominant in Hesychast circles, and which locates the center of the psychosomatic human complex precisely in the heart.

An ecclesiology understood through the Eucharist—which, for Cabasilas,
is the "completion" of all sacraments, not simply one of them;[18] a spirituality founded on a living experience of Christ; and a theocentric anthropology:
these legacies of Cabasilas are clearly in contrast with the ideology of the
humanists. This contrast does not mean, however, that Cabasilas expressed,
at any time, even in his polemics, any systematic prejudice against the
Latin West. We have already seen that even when he accuses the Latins
of having dropped the epiclesis from the Eucharistic canon, he involves
the authority of the Latin rite itself, whose legitimacy he thus recognizes.
Obviously, his attitude toward the Western Church is similar to that of
his friend Cantacuzenos, who took some pains to explain Palamite theology
to the legate Paul and sought a free dialogue at a joint council; or even
to that of Patriarch Philotheos who endorsed the project and invited the
other patriarchs to take part, expressing the wish, however, that "at the
council, our doctrine may be shown better than that of the Latins, so that
they may join us in a common confession." [19] In the following century,
when the conciliar project was finally accepted by the pope, the Palamite
Mark of Ephesus will take the boat for Ferrara with the same aspirations
and hopes.

4. FLORENCE

In spite of the numerous non-theological factors which contributed to the
circumstances in which the Council of Ferrara–Florence was held, the event
itself is of great theological significance. Its convocation represented a major
concession on Rome's part—a concession which the popes of the thirteenth
and fourteenth centuries had systematically refused to make, in spite of
numerous Byzantine requests. The holding of a union council where all
differences would be freely discussed—including those to which Rome had
already agreed—would in fact put Western doctrinal developments somehow on trial. This papal concession was possible only because of the "con-
ciliarist" challenge by the Councils of Constance and Basel. In order to
show that there could not be a council without a pope, Eugene iv con-
ceded that the pope also needed a council.

But if a small group of "Latin-minded" humanists among the Byzantines
were ready for union through the simple acceptance of papal teachings, the
vast majority—including the conservative Palamites—considered the coun-

cil as the normal way to union on the basis of Orthodoxy. Yet the impressive and formally very representative Byzantine delegation which came to Ferrara was hampered by serious handicaps. First, it was internally divided on the issue of knowledge: although they had formally ascribed to Palamism at their episcopal consecrations, several important members actually were Barlaamites, and therefore skeptical on the issue of whether true knowledge of divine truths is actually attainable. Secondly, in spite of prolonged contacts with the West in the previous decades, the Byzantines (perhaps under the influence of their theory of "pentarchy" which recognized the pope as patriarch of the whole West) seemed not to have understood the deep implications of the ecclesiological problems which were dividing the West, and they failed to capitalize on the division. They chose to negotiate with the pope, under the impression that he was able to speak for all Latins and to raise immediate military help against the Turks. And, finally, the representative character of the Byzantine delegation was only formal—the delegation, in fact, had been selected from among the tiny élite of Constantinople, which by then was a moribund city of fewer than 50,000 inhabitants,[20] and of a few scattered possessions in the Aegean. The millions of Eastern Christians—bishops, clergy, laity—in the Middle East, Asia Minor, and the Balkans were already under Turkish occupation, adapting themselves to the new situation and generally skeptical of eventual Latin Crusades. Muscovite Russia, meanwhile, was suspicious of the West anyhow.

Still, these handicaps did not prevent the Council of Ferrara–Florence from providing an occasion for useful, dramatic, and fundamentally free theological dialogue.

The decree *Laetentur caeli,* finally signed on July 6, 1439, was the result, and it was quite different from the theological "victory" expected by the circle of Cantacuzenos. The decree eliminates one point of contention between Greeks and Latins: the problem of the Eucharistic bread, by declaring that both leavened and unleavened bread may be used in the sacrament; and includes three doctrinal definitions: on the procession of the Holy Spirit, on purgatory, and on the Roman primacy.

Concerning the *Filioque,* the decree affirms the presupposition that no substantial difference exists between the Greek and Latin Fathers in their theology of the Trinity and defines the procession in traditional Latin, Augustinian terms (*ex utroque aeternaliter tanquam ab uno principio et unica spiratione procedit*). Furthermore, it explicitly reaffirms that the word *Filioque* was legitimately (*licite ac rationabiliter*) added to the creed. It was understood, however, that the Greeks would not be required to modify the text of the creed in their own use of it.

The definition on purgatory—as long and as detailed as the text dealing with the procession—was equally out of line with the generally accepted

Eastern thinking on the soul's fate after death. It formulated the Latin medieval doctrine on purification after death, which was required whenever no sufficient "fruits of repentance" were manifested before death. The definition included the formal statement that unbaptized souls "descend immediately to hell" (*mox in infernum descendere*).

The definition on the primacy affirmed that the Roman pontiff, "true vicar of Christ," is "the head of the whole Church, the Father and Teacher of all Christians," and that to him, in the blessed Peter, "was given full power to feed, to rule, and to govern the universal Church." The definition was manifestly directed at the Western conciliarists, even more than at the Greeks, and, in this particular respect, it achieved the desired result—actually the only major result of the Council of Florence.[21] The Byzantines relieved their consciences by securing an insertion, which in their minds was a limitation of papal power: it was to be exercised "in accordance with the acts of the ecumenical councils and the holy canons."

Orthodox apologetics has frequently maintained that the Greeks were under physical and mental strain when they signed this text, but this position is difficult to support since Mark of Ephesus refused to sign and left for home unharmed. One must therefore presume that the others, at the moment of signing, thought themselves right either theologically or, at least, politically. Most of them soon changed their minds, and those who remained faithful to their signature integrated themselves fully into the world of the Italian Renaissance and papal politics and had no further theological influence upon their compatriots.

Four personalities of the Greek delegation played a leading intellectual role in Ferrara, in Florence, and in the years immediately following the council: Mark, Metropolitan of Ephesus; Bessarion, Metropolitan of Nicaea; and two lay Archontes, George Scholarios and Gemisthos Pletho. Bessarion led the majority of Greeks who finally signed the decree of union; the others represent three rather different forms of opposition to union.

Mark Eugenikos (1392–1444) was made Metropolitan of Ephesus in the year before the council (1437). In theology, he had studied with Joseph Bryennios, and in philosophy, with Gemistos Pletho; under Pletho, he had received a much more elaborate philosophical training than was customary in monastic circles. Mark's view of the Latin West coincided with that of the circle of Cantacuzenos in the preceding century; and he had been willing to recognize the council as ecumenical until he lost hope that what he considered to be the truth would prevail at the assembly. At the beginning of the sessions in Ferrara, prompted by Cardinal Cesarini, Mark delivered to Pope Eugenius a preliminary address in which he called upon the "most holy Father" to receive "his children coming from the East" and "seeking his embrace." But he also stressed the minimum condition for true unity: the removal of the interpolation introduced unilaterally by the Latins into the common creed.[22] As discussions progressed in quite an opposite direction, his attitude, understandably, grew bitter. In the discussions, he and Bessarion were usually the main Greek spokesmen. His weakest point was a certain inability to go beyond the formal points under discussion—purgatory, *Filioque,* epiclesis—and to reach real issues, such as the juridical Anselmian concept of "justification," or the difference between the Cappadocian and Augustinian Trinitarian theologies. A lack of historical perspective on both sides and the conviction that all the Fathers must always agree with one another created an impasse: there were no alternatives but to accept or reject the Latin view. When Mark refused to sign, the pope is said to have declared: "We have accomplished nothing." [23] Obviously, Eugenius IV was aware by then of the real situation in the East and knew that Mark represented much better the prevailing mentality of the East than did the other members of the Greek delegation. Until his death, Mark remained the head of the anti-unionists in Constantinople. He is a saint of the Orthodox Church.

A lifelong admirer of Thomism and a Thomist theologian in his own right, George Scholarios is an intellectual enigma awaiting modern scholarly investigation. "O excellent Thomas," he writes in a preamble to some of his treatises, "why did heaven give you birth in the West? [If you had been born in the East,] you would not have defended the deviations of the Western Church on the procession of the Holy Spirit and on the distinction between the essence of God and His energy, and you would be our impeccable master in doctrine, just as you still are in the field of ethics." [24] With this attitude, similar to that of Nilus Cabasilas'—acceptance of Thomism, except on the points of the procession and of Palamism —he went to Florence and acted there in full support of union until shortly before the council's conclusion. He then left for Constantinople but avoided an explicit stand until, in 1444, Mark of Ephesus, on his deathbed, entrusted him with the leadership of the Orthodox party. He accepted, assumed the monastic garb under the name of Gennadios, and was affirmed patriarch by Mohammed II in 1453, after the fall of Constantinople. It is quite possible that men like Scholarios—if Byzantine theology had not died a violent death in 1453—would have been able to prepare the dialogue in depth which failed in Florence but which alone could have led to true union.

George Gemistos (*ca.* 1360–1452), a layman like Scholarios and better known by his surname "Pletho"—consonant with "Plato"—was among the orators chosen by the Greeks as their spokesmen at the Council of Ferrara–Florence. He did not make great use of the privilege in the public sessions but was quite active in the behind-the-scenes discussions of the Greeks. What was probably unknown to many and discovered only later, especially by Scholarios, is that Pletho had dropped his essential commitment to the Christian religion and had replaced it, for himself and for a group of disciples, with a Platonizing paganism. According to the best available study on Pletho, his involvment in Christian theologial discussions was therefore "perfectly hypocritical." [25] In Florence, he supported Mark Eugenikos, but left with Scholarios before the proclamation of union; still he seems to have accepted the union later. In any case, none of these gestures could have an ultimate significance for him. A convinced determinist in his philosophy of history,[26] he could not believe that either Western help or faithfulness to Orthodoxy could do anything to change the predetermined fate of the Hellenes. In Pletho, therefore, "secular humanism" reached its greatest extent, and seems to have amounted almost to an escape from the realities of history.

Pletho's defeatism was certainly not acceptable, as such, to all Byzantine humanists: the case of one of his pupils and close friends, Bessarion of Nicaea (1402-1472), is the best example. Already a monk in 1429, Bessarion was chosen metropolitan in 1436 when the council was in the making; his ecclesiastical career, however, did not prevent him from maintaining close humanist sympathies and concerns. His obviously sincere religious evolution in Florence (which followed a path directly opposite to that of Scholarios: originally a staunch proponent of Orthodoxy, Bessarion eventually became a leader of the unionist party) can best be explained by his fundamental attitude toward theological knowledge, which was similar to that of Barlaam of Calabria. Since no fundamental and experiential knowledge could be obtained on the main issue dividing Greeks and Latins, the *Filioque,* there was no reason why the Latin West could not play the role of savior, or at least become the refuge for the eternal values of Hellenism. It is significant that the entire literary legacy of Bessarion, with the exception of the few theological orations immediately required by the debates in Ferrara and Florence, deals with Greek philosophy. His monumental *Refutations of the Blasphemies Directed Against Plato* represents a manifesto of the principles which constitute the philosophy of his master, Pletho. The letter of totally pagan inspiration which he addressed to the son of Pletho after Pletho's death seems even to indicate that he was a secret member of Pletho's pagan sect.[27] The presence, in Bessarion's library, of Pletho's autograph with the sacred *ordo* of the sect seems to confirm the fact, which can certainly not be disproved by Bessarion's long, honorable diplomatic service in the curia of the humanist popes of the second half of the fifteenth century. Greek in spirit he indeed remained, much more successfully than his compatriots in the East; but how much of a Christian theologian?

The personality and intellectual evolution of Bessarion is the best possible illustration of the fact that if "the definition of Florence about the primacy of the papacy had dealt a death-blow to Conciliarism" [28] and thus changed the course of Western Church history by making the Reformation inevitable, it actually bypassed the issues dividing East and West and, stiffening the positions of both sides, made the schism a much deeper reality than it had been.

NOTES

1. See J. Meyendorff, "Projets de Concile oecuménique en 1367: un dialogue inédit entre Jean Cantacuzène et le légat Paul," *Dumbarton Oaks Papers* 14 (1960), 174.

2. See J. Meyendorff, *Introduction à l'étude de Grégoire Palamas* (Paris: du Seuil, 1959), p. 194.

3. Demetrios Cydones, Letter 1 in *Demetrius Cydonès, Correspondance*, ed. G. Camelli (Paris: Belles Lettres, 1930), p. 2.

4. Demetrios Cydones, *Apology I*, in G. Mercati, "Notizie di Procoro e Demetrio Cidone . . . ," *Studi e Testi* 56 (1931), 365.

5. *Ibid.*, 366.

6. Demetrios Cydones, *Letter 33*; ed. R. J. Loenertz, SeT 186 (1956), 66.

7. Demetrios Cydones, *De contemnenda morte*; PG 154:1169–1212.

8. Demetrios Cydones, *Apology III*; in Mercati, "Notizie," 391.

9. See, for example, H.-G. Beck, KTLBR, p. 781.

10. Nicholas Cabasilas, *Life in Christ*; PG 150:496D.

11. *Ibid.*; PG 150:560c–561A.

12. *Ibid.*; PG 150:569A–580c.

13. *Ibid.*; PG 150:593D.

14. *Ibid.*; PG 150:600A.

15. For this see Cabasilas' commentary on the exclamation "The holy things to the holy" in the liturgy; see also *Life in Christ*, PG 150:613A.

16. Cabasilas, "On St. Theodora," PG 150:753–772.

17. A good discussion of this can be found in M. Lot-Borodine, *Nicholas Cabasilas* (Paris: l'Orante, 1958), pp. 114–116.

18. Cabasilas, *Life in Christ*; PG 150:585B.

19. Patriarch Philotheos, *Letter to the Patriarch of Bulgaria*; PG 152:1412B.

20. See A. M. Schneider, "Die Bevölkerung Konstantinopels im XV. Jahrhundert," Göttingen Akademie der Wissenschaften, *Nachrichten phil.-hist. Klasse* (Göttingen, 1949), 235–237.

21. J. Gill, *The Council of Florence* (Cambridge: Harvard University Press, 1959), p. 411.

22. *Ferrariae gesta*, ed. I. Gill (Rome: Pontificium Institutum Orientalium Studiorum, 1952), Vol. 5, fasc. 1, pp. 28–34.

23. Syropulos, *Mémoire*, X, 15; *Les "Mémoires" du Grand Ecclesiarque de l'Eglise de Constantinople Sylvestre Syropoulos* (Paris: Centre National de la Recherche Scientifique, 1971), p. 496.

24. G. Scholarios, *Oeuvres complètes*, edd. L. Petit and M. Jugie (Paris: Bonne Presse, 1928–1936), VI, 1.

25. F. Masai, *Pléthon et le Platonisme de Mistra* (Paris: Belles Lettres, 1956), p. 321.

26. *Ibid.*, p. 98.

27. *Kardinal Bessarion*, ed. L. Mohler (Paderborn: Schöningh, 1942), III, 468–469; see the comments and French translation in Masai, *Pléthon*, pp. 306–307.

28. Gill, *Council of Florence*, p. vii.

Lex Orandi

BYZANTINE CHRISTIANITY is known for the wealth of its liturgy, a wealth which reflects indeed a theological—or, rather, an ecclesiological—position. Through the liturgy a Byzantine recognized and experienced his membership in the Body of Christ. While a Western Christian generally checked his faith against external authority (the magisterium or the Bible), the Byzantine Christian considered the liturgy both a source and an expression of his theology; hence, the very great conservatism which often prevailed both in Byzantium itself and in post-Byzantine times in matters of liturgical tradition and practice. The liturgy maintained the Church's identity and continuity in the midst of a changing world.

This conservatism does not mean, however, that the liturgical structures of the Byzantine Church did not undergo substantial evolution. Since neither theology nor liturgical piety could remain completely aloof from the issues arising from history, by studying them together we can follow the evolution of the religious mind of Byzantium. In spite of its conservatism as a living Christian tradition, Byzantine liturgy responded creatively to the changes of history. The interplay of continuity and change, unity and diversity, faithfulness to a central prototype and local initiative, is unavoidable in the *lex orandi* of the Church. The study of this interplay in Byzantium is a prerequisite for an understanding of its *lex credendi*.

1. THE "GREAT CHURCH" OF CONSTANTINOPLE

The famous temple built by Justinian and dedicated to Christ, "the Wisdom of God," or "Hagia Sophia," remained for centuries the greatest religious edifice in Christendom. Serving as a cathedral for the "archbishop of New Rome," the "ecumenical" patriarch, it provoked amazement in the whole world and had a great aesthetic and, therefore, missionary impact. When the ambassadors of the Russian prince Vladimir of Kiev visited it in 988, they confessed that they wondered whether "they were still on earth, or in heaven," and the Russian Chronicle interprets the adoption of Byzantine Christianity by the Russians as an effect of their report.[1] But the influence of the "Great Church" was felt not only by the "barbarians"; other Christian communities, possessing a tradition of their own, accepted it as well. During the Byzantine occupation of Italy (sixth–seventh centuries), the Roman Church adopted a great number of Byzantine hymns.[2] The Syrian Jacobites, in spite of their separation from Orthodoxy on the Christological issue, translated and adopted much of Byzantine hymnography, mostly during the Byzantine reconquest of the Middle East under the Macedonian dynasty (867–1056).[3] A similar influence on Armenia is well known.

This prestige accorded Constantinople is particularly remarkable since there is no evidence of any ecclesiastical or imperial policy of imposing its usages by law or by administrative measures. In the Orthodox world itself, which was directly in the orbit of Constantinople and which became even more liturgically centralized than the Roman world, liturgical diversity persisted until the fifteenth century (cf. Symeon of Thessalonica). But this liturgical centralization resulted, not from the deliberate policy of a central power, but from the extraordinary cultural prestige of Constantinople, the imperial capital. The adoption of a liturgical practice or tradition by the "Great Church" meant a final sanction and, ultimately, a quasi-guarantee of universal acceptance.

With the exception of the few, rather superficial, elements which were borrowed from imperial court ceremonial, the liturgy of the "Great Church" was a synthesis of disparate elements, rather than an original creation.[4] This synthetic and "catholic" character reflects faithfully the role of Byzantium in politics and in theology. As an empire, Byzantium had to integrate the various cultural traditions which composed it, and as the center of the imperial Church, it continually attempted to maintain a balance between the various local theological trends which divided Christendom after the fourth century.

The form of the Byzantine liturgy—and hence its theology—was determined by the following main elements:

A. The early Christian, pre-Constantinian nucleus, to which the Byzantine Church (as well as all the other major traditions of the Christian East) remained very closely faithful in the celebration of the two mysteries which "recapitulate" all the others: baptism and the Eucharist.[5] In spite of the totally different conditions of Christian life and of the adoption of infant baptism as a universal pattern, the rite of baptism retained the wording and the essential forms shaped in the second and third centuries. Performed by full immersion, it remained an elaborate and solemn representation of the paschal mystery, and of the "passage" from the old life to the new, of the renunciation of Satan, and the union with Christ. The rite remained virtually free of later forms of symbolism and unaffected by extra-sacramental theological developments. Confirmation, performed by a priest with "holy chrism" blessed by a bishop, was never separated from baptism; the neophyte, even if only a child, was then admitted immediately to the Eucharist.

The pre-Constantinian nucleus is less in evidence in the developed Byzantine Eucharist, whose peripheral parts have been embellished with symbolism and interpreted as a sacramental re-enactment of the life of Christ. Its central part—i.e., the Eucharistic canon itself—retains very faithfully, however, the original form and the Jewish root of the Eucharist. This is true of both Eucharistic liturgies which replaced, in the Byzantine world, the more ancient Palestinian liturgy of "St. James"—the liturgies of Basil and of John Chrysostom. Both date essentially from the fourth or fifth century, with the direct authorship by Basil of Caesarea († 379) almost certain in the case of the canon bearing his name. But Basil used a more ancient tradition which he attributed to the apostles themselves.[6] His Eucharistic prayer "is assuredly one of the most beautiful and most harmonious formulas of this type bequeathed to us by Christian antiquity. . . , very close to the most ancient wording of the Christian prayer, with expressions that are still very near to the Jewish prayer itself." [7]

According to the medieval Byzantine *ordo* reflected by the twelfth-century canonist Balsamon,[8] the liturgy of John Chrysostom is the usual Eucharistic form celebrated throughout the year, except during Lent; Basil's is used only on ten solemn occasions. The ancient liturgy of "St. James," however, was not entirely forgotten in Jerusalem and a few other local communities. Of ecclesiological importance is the fact that the Eucharist remained a solemn, festal celebration in Byzantium, and presupposed, in principle, the gathering around the Lord's table by the entire local Christian community. The contrast with Western medieval developments is, in this respect, quite striking. Not only does the Byzantine Church ignore "low Masses," or Masses of intention; it does not consider the daily celebration of the Eucharist as a norm, except in monasteries. Moreover, a priest is not allowed to celebrate more than once on the same day; nor can a single altar serve each day for more than one Eucharist. These rules place the ecclesiological reality of the one Church, realized in the one Eucharist, above all pastoral conveniences or practical considerations. As in the early Church, the Eucharist is never the action of a particular group of faithful, nor does it serve any partial or accidental purpose; it is always offered "on behalf of all and for all" by the entire Church.

B. The liturgical evolution of the so-called "cathedral" rite, a designation applied by A. Baumstark to the practice of the major city-churches, as distinct from the monastic communities.[9] A manuscript preserves a description of this rite as it was practiced at Hagia Sophia from 802 to 806,[10] and Symeon of Thessalonica († 1429) describes a "chanted vigil" belonging to the same tradition, although he recognizes that, in his times, it was no longer practiced in its pure form even at Hagia Sophia.[11]

Devoting comparatively little time to scriptural reading, or psalmody, this rite had favored the mushrooming of hymnography and the development of the liturgy as a "mystery," or "drama." It was indeed difficult to preserve the communal concept of Christian worship, or the notion that the Eucharist is a communion *meal,* when the liturgy began to be celebrated in huge basilicas holding several thousand worshippers. But since the early Christian community was now transformed into a crowd of nominal Christians (a transformation described as a real tragedy by Chrysostom in his famous sermons at Constantinople), it was necessary for the Church to emphasize the *sacred* character of the Christian sacraments, to protect them from secular profanation, and to surround them with veils and barriers, thus practically excluding the mass of the laity from active participation in their celebration, except through the singing of hymns.

This evolution, which could have been a purely practical and pastoral, and thus justifiable, development, acquired a not altogether healthy theological expression, of which the *Ecclesiastical Hierarchy* of pseudo-Dionysius is the most explicit witness. We described earlier the way in which the "earthly" liturgy was explained by Dionysius as a symbolic—and only symbolic—representation of an unchangeable hierarchy of beings who stand between the individual Christian and his God. After Dionysius, the liturgy began to play the role of a Gnostic initiation, and the notion of common life in Christ was often lost. But sacramental realism and a more traditional view of the liturgy were preserved in the rite itself, and theologians like Nicholas Cabasilas, in their writings about the liturgy, were able to overcome the ambiguous tradition of individualism and Gnostic symbolism which Dionysius had introduced in the sixth century.

c. Monasticism: From the beginning of the Constantinian era, a monastic type of worship existed concurrently with the emerging "cathedral" type and soon entered into competition with it. It was characterized by a number of autonomous units of common worship (vespers, compline, midnight prayer, matins, and the four canonical hours, completed in Jerusalem with "mid-hours"), by its almost exclusive use of psalmody, and by its original opposition to hymnography.[12] A monastic office could be practically continuous through day and night as it was, for example, in the monastery of the "Non-sleepers" in Constantinople. The monastic communities also developed the penitential aspects of the later Byzantine synthesis: Lenten cycle, prostrations, fasting.

The earliest available descriptions of the *Typikon* of the monastery of Studion in Constantinople and of the Palestinian *Typikon* of St. Sabbas preserve the liturgical orders of these two major monastic centers around the tenth century. At that time both had already lost the original sobriety of monastic worship: not only had they dropped opposition to hymnography; both had become major centers of hymn-writing (Theodore at the Studion, John of Damascus at St. Sabbas). On the other hand, the symbolic Gnosticism of pseudo-Dionysius had by then widely influenced monastic circles: if the goal of the earthly Church was to imitate the "celestial hierarchies," the monks considered themselves as fulfilling *a fortiori* the purpose of the "angelic life." Actually, a common acceptance of the Dionysian understanding of the liturgy must have brought the "monastic" and the "cathedral" type closer together.

But their initial integration did not occur in Constantinople. There the *Typikon* of the "Great Church" and that of the Studion were still clearly distinct in the tenth century (when the Studite rule, as modified by Patriarch Alexis, was brought to Kiev and adopted by Theodosius of the Caves). Integration occurred in Jerusalem, where monastic practices were accepted within the original "cathedral" rite around the eleventh century. The Latin occupation of Constantinople (1204–1261) and the subsequent decadence of the Studion may have contributed to the adoption of the integrated *Typikon* of Jerusalem by the "Great Church" of Constantinople and its generalization in the Byzantine world.[13] The great Hesychast patriarchs of the fourteenth century, especially Philotheos Kokkinos, were the main agents of this liturgical unification.

The adoption of a single system of liturgy for both secular and monastic churches facilitated liturgical unification throughout the Church. Byzantine dominance in the Christian East led, in fact, to an even greater liturgical centralization than Rome could ever achieve in the West. The difference, however, was that no particular ecclesiological significance was attached to this centralization, which was due only to the inimitable cultural prestige of the "Great Church." Actually, the Byzantine rite was not Constantinopolitan by origin, but Syrian in its first version and Palestinian in the second. Yet the opportunity presented to newly converted peoples to translate the liturgy into their respective tongues counterbalanced the disadvantages of centralization and constituted a powerful tool for missionary activity. In any case, the liturgy remained, in the Orthodox Church, a major expression of unity.

Equally important was the adoption, by the Byzantine Church, of a monastic *Typikon* to regulate the liturgical life of the entire Christian community. Actually, on this point, the other Eastern Christian spiritual families—the Copts, the Jacobites, the Armenians—were in the same predicament. By accepting monastic spirituality as a general pattern for its worship, the Christian East as a whole expressed the eschatological meaning of the Christian message. The very magnitude of the liturgical requirements described in the *Typikon*, the impossibility for an average community to fulfill them integrally, and the severity of penitential discipline implied in the liturgical books always served as a safeguard against any attempt to identify the Church too closely with the present *aion,* and as a signpost of the Kingdom to come. If properly understood, the Eastern liturgy places the Church in a state of permanent eschatological tension.

2. THE LITURGICAL CYCLES

In its fully developed form, reached in the fourteenth century, the Byzantine rite is still essentially dominated by the *paschal* theme of the early Christian message: in Christ, man *passes* from slavery to freedom, from darkness to light, from death to life. Byzantine liturgy may frequently use conceptual definitions, formal doctrinal confessions, or romantic poetry —as we shall see in our discussion of hymnography—but it is impossible to understand its structure and the internal logic of its cycles without grasping the dynamic suggestion of a *passage* from the "old" to the "new," which is the central theme of almost every liturgical unit. Variations on this theme appear everywhere. The misery of man's existence in the "old Adam" is given more or less emphasis, just as the bliss of new life is considered either as an already present reality or as a goal still to be achieved.

Each cycle normally corresponds to a particular liturgical book. The daily cycle, found in the *Expanded Psalter,* or its abbreviated form, the *Horologion,* uses the paschal theme in connection with the daily alternation of light and darkness. Following, in its permanent, unchangeable structure, the ancient monastic patterns, which used to shun hymnography, Byzantine vespers and matins select almost exclusively scriptural texts to connect the coming of night with man's fall and separation from God and sunrise with the advent of Christ, the "true light." Vespers begin with an evocation of creation (Ps 104) and a suggestion of man's helplessness after the Fall (Pss 140, 141, 129, 116), and end with the prayer of Simeon (Lk 2:29-32), the hope of salvation, the idea that night and death can also become blessed repose for those who hope in the coming of the Messiah. Alternating the themes of repentance and hope, matins represent an ascension toward the meeting of light: the ten Biblical canticles —including the eminently paschal Canticles of Moses (Ex 15:1-18; Dt 32:1-43) and of the Three Youths in Babylon (Dn 3:26-56, 67-88)—are part of a psalmodic ensemble, called a canon, which culminates in the *Magnificat* (Lk 1:46-55) and the *Benedictus* (Lk 1:68-79) combined. At sunrise the triumphant Psalms 148, 149, 150 (the Latin lauds), the exclamation "Glory to Thee, who has shown us the light," and the doxology reflect the Christian joy and assurance of God-given salvation.

Vespers obviously aim at suggesting the "old" situation of man, and thus the developed Byzantine rite includes Old Testament readings only at vespers. Matins, by contrast, are highlighted on certain appointed days by readings from the Gospels. The weekly cycle also uses the theme of the "old" and the "new," centering it on Sunday, the "eighth day," [14] the "day of the Lord" and of His second coming (Rv 1:10), the day of His resurrection and of His presence in the Eucharist. Still, the "old" Jewish Sabbath is not simply discarded: it is the day of awaiting, of commemoration of the dead, who expect resurrection, and also the day when Christ, in the tomb, descended into Hell to assure the dead of the forthcoming liberation. Thus Saturday is considered, together with Sunday, as a Eucharistic day, even during Lent.

The feast of Easter serves as the movable center of the yearly cycle. It has a period of preparation (Lent) and a fifty-day celebration (Pentecost), and its date determines the following liturgical year. For each of these periods there is a corresponding liturgical book containing the pertinent hymnography: the *Triodion* for Lent, the *Pentecostarion* for the period between Easter and Pentecost, and the *Oktoekhos* (Book of eight tones) containing the cycle of eight weeks, which repeats itself between the Second Sunday after Pentecost and the following Lent.

Finally, the twelve volumes of the *Menaion* (Book of months) contain proper offices for each day of the calendar year. The very great amount of hymnographic material which was gradually accepted into the *Menaion* through the centuries is very uneven in quality, but the offices of the major feasts and of principal saints are generally celebrated with hymns composed by the best liturgical poets of Byzantium. Like the Western Sanctoral, the *Menaion* represents a later, post-Constantinian development of the liturgy, based on historical interest for past events, on local piety connected with the veneration of particular saints and their relics, and on pilgrimages to holy places in Palestine. In each case, however, the *Menaion* establishes a connection with the central, paschal content of the Christian faith. Thus, for example, the feasts of the Nativity (December 25) and of the Epiphany of Christ (January 6) are preceded by periods of preparation which are patterned, hymnographically and musically, on the offices of Holy Week. Through this evocation, the cross and the Resurrection are shown as the ultimate goal of the Incarnation.

The three major cycles of the yearly feasts commemorate the lives of Christ, the Virgin Mary, and John the Baptist. The Christological cycle includes the feasts of the Annunciation, Nativity, Epiphany, Circumcision, "Meeting" with Simeon (February 2), and the Transfiguration. The feast of the Exaltation of the Cross (September 14) is also part of this cycle. The cycle of the Virgin includes the commemoration of her conception, nativity, presentation, and dormition. The cycle of John the Baptist is an early Palestinian creation with a Biblical foundation and serves as the model for the Mariological cycle. It includes the feasts of conception, nativity, and decollation. This entire system, represented iconographically on the so-called "Deisis"—a composition often shown centrally in the iconostasis and including the central figure of Christ flanked by Mary and John—suggests a parallelism between the Mother and the Precursor, the two representatives of the human race who stood closest to Jesus. No particular liturgical attention is paid to St. Joseph, except for a relatively modest commemoration on December 26, when he is included with other "ancestors" of Christ.

The *Menaion* contains explicit commemoration, however, of numerous Old Testament figures—prophets, kings, and others—the theological implication being that, after Christ's descent into Hell, they, as well as those who pleased God in the new dispensation, are alive in Him.

3. HYMNOLOGY

The introduction of massive hymnology in the "cathedral" rite is generally connected with the name of Romanos the Melode. There is very little historical evidence showing the reasons why the *kontakia* by Romanos and his imitators were very soon replaced, in Byzantine liturgical cycles, by different types of hymnography, but it may be assumed that the *kontakion* had to face monastic opposition. Although it dealt primarily with Biblical themes and often paraphrased Biblical texts, the *kontakion* nevertheless constituted a substitute for the Biblical psalms or canticles themselves, and encouraged the use of music which the monks considered too secular. The long poetical pieces of Romanos of course had no organic place in the increasingly rigid and strictly Biblical framework of vespers, matins, and other liturgical units as they were being elaborated in the monastic *Typika*. Yet the fact that Romanos' poetry, though explicitly Chalcedonian and Cyrillian, generally stood aloof from the great Christological disputes of the sixth and seventh centuries may also have contributed to the emergence of a hymnography more distinctly theological and doctrinal than the *kontakia.*

The original ascetic opposition of many monastic centers against hymnographical creativity did not persist. By the fifth century, Auxentios († in Bithynia ca. 470) was composing *troparia,* short poetical pieces of two or three sentences, sung according to the pattern of Biblical psalmody and probably in conjunction with Biblical psalms or canticles.[15] This style of hymnography served as the alternative for the long and independent *kontakia* of Romanos. Short *troparia,* or *stikhera,* were composed to be sung *after* each verse of the regular Biblical texts accepted as parts of vespers and matins, rather than as independent liturgical services. Complete series of *troparia* were written to accompany the ten Biblical canticles of matins. These series received the convenient appellation of canon, or "rule." They often include, after the sixth ode, a vestigial remnant of a *kontakion* of Romanos, while parts of the same *kontakion* are paraphrased in other *stikhera* or *troparia* (Nativity services, for example). Thus a few short pieces of Romanos' poetry were kept in the liturgical books after the final adoption, in the ninth or tenth century, of the new patterns of hymnography. Palestinian monks of the Lavra of St. Sabbas (Andrew, who later became bishop in Crete, John of Damascus, Cosmas of Maiuma) seem to have played, in the early-eighth century, a decisive role in the reform, which was in fact a compromise between the original Biblical strictness of the monastic rule and the free lyricism of Romanos.

In the final form it assumed in the ninth century—the later enrichments were only peripheral—the Byzantine hymnographical system is a poetic encyclopedia of patristic spirituality and theology. Its importance for our understanding of Byzantine religious thought cannot be exaggerated. Medieval Byzantium never attributed to schools, to intellectual speculation, or even to the magisterium the importance which they acquired in the West, but the centuries-old hymnographical tradition will be referred to —for example by Gregory Palamas against Barlaam—as a certain criterion of orthodoxy and as an expression of Church tradition *par excellence*. It will remain so in the Slavic and other areas, where Byzantine Christianity will be spread.

The difficulty in using hymnographical materials as a source for theology lies in the tremendous volume and diversity of the hymns. Of course, the many hagiographical legends and poetic exaggerations found in them can be used only in the context in which they were originally written. The Byzantines, however, obviously understood the difference between doctrinal statements and poetry, for some hymns are explicitly called *dogmatika troparia*; those of Saturday vespers, for example, which were always dedicated to the meaning of the Incarnation in terms of the Chalcedonian definition:

> Who will not bless you, O all-holy Virgin? Who will not sing praises to the One whom you bore? The only-begotten Son, who shone forth before all ages from the Father, the same came forth from you, O pure one. Ineffably He became incarnate, being by nature God, and became man by nature for our sakes; not being divided in two persons, but known in two natures without confusion. Him do you beseech, O pure and blessed one, that He will have mercy on our souls [Tone 6].

This text, obviously, is meant to be a confession of faith as well as a prayer or a piece of religious poetry. Other boundlessly emotional hymns addressed to Mary, the *Theotokos*, use Biblical images and symbols to describe her role in salvation history:

> Hail, O earth unsown! Hail, O bush which burned, yet was not consumed! Hail, O abyss unfathomable! Hail, O bridge leading to heaven, and lofty ladder, which Jacob saw! Hail, O divine container of manna! Hail, O abrogation of the curse! Hail, O recall of Adam! The Lord is with you [Annunciation vespers].

The Marian emotionalism displayed by Byzantine hymnographers—the same ones who were able to use the strictest possible theological language in other texts—is often an expression of liturgical wisdom and common sense. The liturgy of the Church, a sacred play involving the *whole of man,* must assume and transform all forms of human feeling and must not be restricted to satisfying only his intellectual capacity. The alternation and correlation between the various aspects of religious experience is probably the secret of the lasting impact exercised by Byzantine Church hymnography upon generations of human souls.

This humaneness of Byzantine hymnography is also shown in the *Triodion,* a book for use during the Lenten period, composed in large part by Theodore the Studite and his immediate disciples. A monument of monastic spirituality, the *Triodion* assumes a patristic system of anthropology according to which man is truly man only when he is in real communion with God: then also is he truly free. In his present fallen state, however, man is a prisoner of Satan and, as we saw in connection with the spiritual doctrine of Evagrius, his liberation and salvation presuppose the suppression of his "passions"—i.e., of that which makes him love creatures rather than God. The way to "passionlessness" (*apatheia*) is through repentance:

> O how many are the good things I miss! How beautiful the Kingdom I lost through my passions! I spent the wealth I once possessed by transgressing the commandment. Alas, O impassionate soul! You were condemned to fire eternal. But, before end comes, call on Christ, our God. Accept me as the prodigal son, O God, and have mercy on me [Sunday of the prodigal son, vespers].

Abstinence and asceticism are the tools proposed to fight passions, but, even if the ascetic note is somewhat exaggerated, the true dimension of the Christian life and hope is never lost: "The Kingdom of God is neither food nor drink, but joy in the Holy Spirit," proclaims a *stikheron* of the first week of Lent; "Give money to the poor, have compassion on the suffering: this is the true fast which pleases God." Monastic-oriented asceticism does not make the authors lose sight of marriage, family life, and social responsibility:

> Marriage is honorable, the couch is blameless; for Christ, in advance, blessed the one and the other by partaking food in the flesh and by changing water into wine in Cana . . . , so that you may change, O soul [Canon of Andrew of Crete, ode 9].

But all the appeals to "repentance" and to "change" would be meaningless if a foretaste of the blessed and joyful Kingdom to come were not also given. The triumphant hymns of the paschal night, composed by John of Damascus, paraphrasing a paschal sermon of Gregory of Nazianzus, are an immortal monument of Christian joy:

This is the day of resurrection!
Let us shine joyfully, O peoples!
The Pascha of the Lord, the Pascha!
From death to life, and from earth to heaven,
Christ has led us, and we sing hymns of victory.

O Christ, the great and holy Pascha,
O wisdom, Word, and Power of God!
Permit us to partake more fully of Thee
In the unending day of Thy Kingdom.

NOTES

1. "The Russian Primary Chronicle," trans. S. H. Cross, *Harvard Studies in Philology and Literature* 12 (1930), 199.

2. A. Baumstark, *Liturgie comparée* (Chévtogne, 1953), pp. 109–113.

3. *Ibid.*, pp. 104–106.

4. See A. Schmemann, "The Byzantine Synthesis," *Introduction to Liturgical Theology* (London: Faith Press, 1966), pp. 116–166.

5. Gregory Palamas, *Hom.* 60; ed. S. Oikonomos (Athens, 1861), p. 250.

6. Basil of Caesarea, *On the Holy Spirit,* 27; ed. B. Pruche, SC 17 (Paris: Cerf, 1945), p. 233.

7. Louis Bouyer, *Eucharist* (Notre Dame: University of Notre Dame Press, 1968), pp. 302–303.

8. PG 119:1033.

9. Baumstark, *Liturgie comparée,* p. 124.

10. MS Patmos 266, published by A. Dmitrievsky, *Opisanie Liturgicheskikh Rukopisei* (Kiev, 1901) I, 1–152.

11. Symeon of Thessalonica; PG 155:556D.

12. Baumstark, *Liturgie comparée,* p. 114.

13. See M. Skaballanovich, *Tolkovyi Tipikon* (Kiev, 1910), pp. 410–416.

14. Basil of Caesarea, *On the Holy Spirit,* 27; Pruche ed., p. 237.

15. See the *Life* of Auxentios, *ActSS.,* Feb. 11, 770ff.

II

Doctrinal
Themes

The historical outline found in the first nine chapters of this book was an attempt to cover the theological controversies, the distinctive tendencies, and the basic sources of theological thought in Byzantium. We now turn to a more systematic picture of Byzantine theology. No Byzantine theologian ever attempted to write a *Summa*. This does not mean, however, that behind the issues debated by theologians there was not a basic unity of inspiration, and the sense of a single, consistent tradition of faith. Of course, the East was less prone than the West to conceptualize or to dogmatize this unity of tradition. It preferred to maintain its faithfulness to the "mind of Christ" through the liturgy of the Church, through the tradition of holiness, through a living *gnosis* of the Truth. In any systematic presentation of Byzantine theology, there is, therefore, a danger of forcing it into the mold of rational categories foreign to its very nature. This is precisely what occurred in many textbooks of dogmatic theology which appeared in the Orthodox East after the eighteenth century, which claimed to remain faithful to the theology of the Byzantine Fathers. They have been ably characterized by Georges Florovsky as expressions of a "Western captivity" of the Orthodox mind. For, it is not enough to quote an abundance of proof-texts from patristic or Byzantine authors: true consistency requires a unity of method and congeniality of approach.

I have attempted to achieve this by adopting in the following chapters a plan of exposition which conforms to the content of the Christian experience itself: man, created and fallen, meets Christ, accepts the action of the Spirit, and is thus introduced into communion with the Triune God. The reader will judge for himself whether or not this plan is more adequate than the other to the subject matter itself.

Inevitably, a systematic exposition of doctrinal themes in Byzantine theology requires frequent reference to writings which sometimes fall outside the chronological limits defined in the Introduction. It is impossible, for example, to speak of either anthropology or Trinitarian theology in Byzantium without referring to Origen and to the doctrines of the great Fathers of the fourth century, whom the Byzantines recognized as their teachers *par excellence*.

It was also inevitable, on the other hand, that my treatment of the Byzantine authors be influenced by the fact that, as an Orthodox theologian, I personally see the great tradition of the undivided Church as continuing in Byzantium and, through it, carrying its message to modern times as well.

10

Creation

PATRISTIC THOUGHT ON CREATION developed within the framework of age-long polemics against Origenism. The issue in the debate was the Greek concept of an eternal cosmos and the Biblical linear view of history, which began with the creative *fiat*. The starting point of Origen's view on the origin of the world was that the act of creation was an expression of God's *nature* and that, since this nature is changeless, there could never be a "time" when God would not be creating. Consequently, the world has always existed, because God's goodness has always needed an object.[1] In Origenism, eternity of creation was, in fact, ontologically indistinguishable from the eternity of the Logos. Both proceeded eternally from God. This identification led Arius, after he had rejected the eternity of creation, to the concept that the Logos had also been generated in time. The anti-Arian theology of Athanasius of Alexandria defined the categories which became standard in later Byzantine authors: the distinction between generation and creation.

1. CREATOR AND CREATURES

For Athanasius,[2] creation is an act of the *will* of God, and will is ontologically distinct from *nature*. By nature, the Father generates the Son—and this generation is indeed beyond time—but creation occurs through the will of God, which means that God remains absolutely free to create or not to create, and remains transcendent to the world after creating it. The absence of a distinction between the nature of God and the will of God was common to Origen and to Arius. To establish this distinction constitutes the main argument of Athanasius.

It is totally impossible to consider the Father without the Son, because "the Son is not a creature which came into being by an act of will; by nature He is the proper Son of the essence [of the Father]."[3] The Son, therefore, is God by nature, while "the nature of creatures which came into being from nothing is fluid, impotent, mortal, and composite."[4] Refuting the Arian idea that the Logos was created in view of the world, Athanasius affirms that "it is not He who was created for us, but we were created for Him." [5] In God the order of nature precedes the order of volitive action,[6] and is both superior to and independent of it. Because *God is what He is,* He is not determined or in any way limited in what He *does,* not even by His own essence and being.

Divine "nature" and created "nature" are, therefore, separate and totally dissimilar modes of existence. The first is totally free from the second. Yet creatures depend upon God; they exist "by His grace, His will, and His word . . . so that they can even cease to exist, if the Creator so wishes." [7] In Athanasius, therefore, we have advanced quite far from Origen's cosmos, which was considered a necessary expression of God's goodness identified with divine nature itself. At this point one discovers that the notion of creation, as expressed by Athanasius, leads to a distinction in God between His transcendent essence and His properties, such as "power" or "goodness," which express His existence and action *ad extra,* not His essence.

The difference *in nature* between God and His creatures, as well as the distinction between the "natural" generation of the Son by the Father, and creation "by act of will," is emphasized by both Cyril of Alexandria[8] and John of Damascus.[9] The difference also represents the ontological *raison d'être* of the Chalcedonian definition on the "two natures" of Christ. The two natures can be understood as being in "communion" with each other, as "hypostatically" united, but they can never be "confused" i.e., considered as "one nature."

Athanasius' insistence on the transitory character of creation should not mislead us. What he wants to show is a *contrast* between the absolute, self-sufficient nature of God, and the dependence upon Him of all created nature. He certainly does not want to reduce created existence to a mere "phenomenon." God's creative act produced a new "created" order, another "essence" distinct from His own; an "essence" worthy of God, deserving of His love and concern, and fundamentally "very good." God does not create, as in Origen, simply a collection of equal intellects, which find a meaning of existence only in contemplating the essence of God and which are diversified only as a consequence of their Fall. Because creation is an essence, and not simply a phantom or a mirage, there is a sense in which its meaning is found in itself, for even God "loves" the world, i.e., considers it as a reality vis-à-vis Himself. Even when it is assumed by the Logos in a hypostatic union, created nature, according to the Chalcedonian definition, "preserves its properties." The implication of this created autonomy was developed in particular by Maximus the Confessor and by the Orthodox theologians of the iconoclastic period. Let us only emphasize here that the very ideas of providence, love, and communion, which reflect the creator's action toward the world, presuppose difference and distinction between Him and His creation.

2. THE DIVINE PLAN

Creation in time—i.e., the possibility of a true *beginning* of created existence—presents the major cleavage between Greek thought and Biblical Revelation. But the idea of an eternal *plan,* which God put into effect when He created the world in time, is not inconsistent with the concepts found in the Jewish "wisdom" literature, and even more concretely in the Johannine theology of the Logos, and responds to at least some preoccupations of Greek philosophical thought.

Throughout its history, Byzantine theology, both "Greek" and Biblical as it was, struggled with the possibility of integrating, into a consistent Christian view of creation, a theory of divine "ideas" about the world. The Platonic *kosmos noētos* had to be rejected, inasmuch as it represented an eternal reality outside of God, both impersonal and "substantial," which would limit the absolute freedom of the creative act, exclude creation *ex nihilo,* and tend to diminish the substantial reality of visible creation by considering it only as a shadow of eternal realities. This rejection was accomplished implicitly by the condemnation of Origen in 553 and explicitly in the synodal decisions against John Italos in 1081. Meanwhile, patristic and Byzantine thought developed in reaction to Origenism. Gregory of Nazianzus, for example, speaks of "images of the world" as thoughts of God.[10] These "thoughts" do not limit the freedom of a personal God, since they remain distinct from His nature. Only when He creates in time do they become "reality."[11] The thoughts are the expressions also of divine will,[12] not of divine nature; they are "perfect, eternal thoughts of an eternal God."[13] Since there cannot be anything created "in God," the thoughts, or ideas about the world, are uncreated expressions of divine life, which represent the unlimited potentiality of divine freedom. God creates the world, not "out of them," but out of nothing. The beginning of the world is the beginning of a totally new reality, put forward by the *act* of creation which comes from God and conforms to His eternal plan.

The existence in God of eternal, uncreated "potentiality," which is not God's essence, nor the world's, nor an essence in itself, but which implies a certain *contingency* toward creation, presupposes an antinomical concept of God which will find different forms of expression in Byzantine theology. To describe it, Georges Florovsky writes that "we have to distinguish, as it were, *two modes of eternity*: the *essential eternity* in which only the Trinity lives, and the *contingent eternity* of the free acts of Divine grace."[14] Actually, on this point, Byzantine theology reached a direct sense of the difference between the impersonal philosophical notion of God as an absolute, and the Biblical understanding of a God personal, transcendent, and free.

To express the relationship between creator and creatures, the great Maximus the Confessor uses the old theology of the Logos as center and living unity of the *logos* of creation. The terminology already existed in Philo and Origen. But, whereas for Origen the *logoi* as *logoi* exist only in an essential unity with the one Logos, for Maximus their real and "logical" existence is also expressed in their *diversity*. The great difference between Origen and Maximus is that Maximus rejects Origen's view of visible creation as diversified only through the Fall. The "goodness" of creation, according to Maximus, resides in creation itself, and not only in its unity with divine essence. But creation cannot be truly "good" unless its differentiated *logoi,* which pre-existed as "thoughts" and "wills" of God, are fixed in Him and preserve communion with the one "super-essential" divine Logos.[15] Creatures, therefore, do not exist only "as *logoi*," or only by the fact that God eternally "knows them"; they exist "by themselves" from the very moment when God put His foreknowledge into action. In His thought, eternally, creatures exist only potentially, while their actual existence occurs in time. This temporal, actual existence of created beings is not autonomous, but centered in the one Logos, and is in communion with Him. There is a sense, therefore, in which "the one Logos is many *logoi,* and the many are one"; "the One is many according to creative and unifying procession of the One into the many, but the many are One according to the providence which leads the many to turn up toward the One, as their all-powerful principle."[16] Paradoxically, therefore, the creatures are one in the one Logos, who, however, is "super-essential" and above participation.[17] "Thus, the *logoi* are to Maximus not identical either with the essence of God or with the existence of the things in the created world. In fact, an apophatic tendency is combined in Maximus with an anti-pantheistic tendency. . . . This is effected, above all, thanks to the understanding of the *logoi* as decisions of God's will."[18]

By remaining faithful to the Athanasian distinction between *nature* and *will,* Maximus succeeds in building an authentically Christian ontology of creation, which will remain, throughout the history of Byzantine thought, a standard and virtually unchallenged authority.[19] This ontology presupposes a distinction in God between "nature" (or "essence") and "energy," a distinction which will later be called "Palamism." It presumes a personal and dynamic understanding of God, as well as a dynamic, or "energetic," conception of created nature.

3. THE DYNAMISM OF CREATION

For Origen, the original, intellectual creation is static. It finds its true *logical* existence in the contemplation of God's essence, and its first *move-*

ment is a form of rebellion against God. Change and diversity in creation are consequences of the Fall and, therefore, are fundamentally evil. For Maximus, and the entire Byzantine theological tradition, the *movement* (*kinesis*) of creatures is the necessary and natural consequence of their creation by God.[20] God, therefore, in creating the world, placed outside of Himself a system of dynamic beings, which are different from Him in that they change and move toward Him.[21] The *logos* of every creature consists, therefore, in being essentially *active*;[22] there is no "nature" without "energy" or movement.

This dynamic conception of created nature constitutes Maximus' main argument against the "Monoenergists" of the seventh century, whose Christology considered Christ's humanity as having lost its genuinely *human* "energy" or will because of its union with divinity. But, for Maximus, created nature would lose its very existence if it were deprived of its *proper* energy, its proper purpose, and its proper dynamic identity. This proper movement of nature, however, can be fully itself only if it follows its proper goal (*skopos*), which consists in striving for God, entering into communion with Him, and thus fulfilling the *logos,* or divine purpose, though which and for which it is created. The true purpose of creation is, therefore, not contemplation of divine essence (which is inaccessible), but communion in divine energy, transfiguration, and transparency to divine action in the world. We shall discuss later the anthropological and Christological dimensions of this concept of creation. But it also has obvious cosmological implications.

In general, the Byzantines accepted cosmological concepts inherited from the Bible or from antiquity. So hesitant were they to push scientific knowledge further that it has even been written that "the meager accomplishment of the Byzantines in the natural sciences remains one of the mysteries of the Greek Middle Ages." [23] In any case, it does not seem that Byzantine theology is to blame for that failure, for theology affirmed the dynamism of nature and, therefore, contained the fundamental incentive for studying and, eventually, controlling its development.

During the entire Byzantine Middle Ages, Basil's homilies *On the Hexaemeron,* were the standard and most authoritative text on the origin, structure, and development of the world. Supporting Athanasius' opposition to the Hellenic and Origenistic concept of creation as an eternal cyclical repetition of worlds, and affirming creation in time, Basil maintains the reality of a created movement and dynamism in creatures. The creatures do not simply receive their form and diversity from God; they possess an energy, certainly also God-given, but authentically their own. "Let the earth bring forth" (Gn 1:24): "this short commandment," says Basil, "immediately became a great reality and a creative *logos,* putting forth, in a way which transcends our understanding, the innumerable varieties of plants. . . . Thus, the order of nature, having received its beginning from the first commandment, enters the period of following time, until it achieves the overall formation of the universe." [24] Using scientific knowledge as it existed in his time, as well as the Stoic terminology of the "seminal reasons," Basil remains theologically independent from his non-Biblical sources. For example, he rejects the Stoic idea that the *logoi* of creatures are the true eternal essences of beings, a concept which could lead to the eternal return "of worlds after their destruction." [25] Like Athanasius and Maximus, Basil remains faithful to the Biblical concept of absolute divine transcendence and freedom in the act of creation; divine providence, which gave being to the world through the *logoi,* also maintains it in existence, but not at the expense of the world's own created dynamism, which is part of the creative plan itself.

The existence of the world as dynamic "nature" (i.e., as a reality "outside of" God—for whom it is an object of love and providence), following its own order of evolutive growth and development, implies the possibility of purely objective scientific investigation of creatures by the human mind. This does not mean, however, that created nature is ontologically "autonomous." It has been created in order to "participate" in God, who is not only the prime mover and the goal of creation, but also the ultimate meaning (*logos*) of its permanence. "God is the principle, the center and the end," writes Maximus, "insofar as He *acts* without being passive. . . . He is the principle, as creator; He is the center, as providence, and He is the end, as conclusion, for *All things come from him, by him and toward him* [Rm 11:36]." [26] A scientific knowledge which would ignore this ultimate meaning of creation would, therefore, be dangerously onesided.

4. SANCTIFICATION OF NATURE

In its present, defective state, created nature fulfills its destiny quite inadequately. The Biblical, anthropocentric concept of the world is preserved in Greek patristic literature: nature suffers from the Fall of man, the "microcosm," to whom God had granted the control of nature and who, instead, preferred to be controlled by it. As a result, instead of revealing, through its internal meaning (*logos*) and purpose (*skopos*), the divine plan for creation and, through this, God Himself, nature became the domain and instrument of Satan: throughout creation, the "natural energy," which conforms to the original divine plan, is in struggle with the destructive forces of death. The dramatic character of the present existence of creation is generally taken for granted by Byzantine theologians, but it is most explicitly formulated in liturgy and spirituality.

The Byzantine rite of Baptism has inherited from Christian antiquity the strong initial emphasis on exorcism. The deliberate renunciation of Satan, the sacramental expulsion of the forces of evil from the soul of the candidate for baptism imply a passage from slavery under the "prince of this world" to freedom in Christ. Liturgical exorcisms, however, are concerned not only with the demonic forces controlling the human soul. The "Great Blessing of Water" on the Feast of the Epiphany exorcises the cosmos, whose basic element, water, is seen as a refuge of "nestling dragons." The frequent mention of the demonic forces of the universe in liturgical and patristic texts should be understood in a *theological* context, for they cannot be reduced to Biblical or medieval mythologies alone, even if they often reflect mythological beliefs. The "demonic" in nature comes from the fact that creation fell out of its original meaning and direction. God had entrusted control over the world to man—His own "image and likeness." But man chose to *be controlled* by the world and, thereby, lost his freedom. He then became subject to cosmic determinism, to which his "passions" attach him and in which ultimate power belongs to death. This is the interpretation which Gregory of Nyssa and Maximus apply to the passage of Genesis 3:21 about the "garments of skin" given to Adam and Eve after the Fall. Rejecting Origen's identification of the "garments" with material bodies—an interpretation based upon the Origenistic idea on the pre-existence of souls—Maximus describes the change in man's situation only in terms of a new *dependence* upon the animal side of the world's existence. Instead of using the potentialities of his nature to raise himself and the whole of creation to God, man submitted himself to the desires of his material senses.[27] As a result, the world which was originally created by God as "very good" became for man a prison and a constant temptation, through which the "prince of this world" establishes his reign of death.

By sanctifying water, food, and plants, as well as the results of man's own creativity, such as works of art or technology (the Byzantine liturgy is very rich in sacramental actions of sanctification, or blessing), the Church replaces them all in their original and true relation, not only to God, but also to man, who is God's "image." To proclaim God's control over the universe, as the Blessing of Epiphany does, amounts in fact to affirming that man is no longer a slave to cosmic forces:

> The immaterial powers tremble before Thee; the sun praises Thee; and the moon worships Thee; the stars are Thy servants; and light bows to Thy will; the tempests tremble and the springs adore Thee. Thou didst spread out the heavens like a tent; Thou didst set the land upon the waters. . . . [Therefore,] heeding the depth of Thy compassion, O Master, Thou couldst not bear to see humanity defeated by the devil, and so Thou didst come and didst save us. . . . Thou didst free the children of our nature. . . .

Thus, sanctification of nature implies its demystification. For a Christian, the forces of nature cannot be divine; nor can they be subject to any form of natural determinism: the resurrection of Christ, by breaking the laws of nature, has liberated man from slavery to nature, and he is called to realize his destiny as lord of nature in God's name.

Byzantine liturgy, when it proclaims the sanctification of the cosmos, frequently mentions, not only the demonic powers which have usurped authority over the world, but also the "bodiless powers of heaven" who cooperate with God and man in the restoration of the original and "natural" order in the world. Yet Byzantium has never had a universally accepted system or description of the angelic world, with the exception of the *Celestial Hierarchy* of pseudo-Dionysius, in which each of the nine orders of angels is considered as an intermediary between the highest power above it and the form of existence below. The goal of Dionysius is to preserve, inside an outwardly Christian system of thought, a hierarchical concept of the universe adopted from Neoplatonism.

In spite of its very widespread, but rather peripheral, influence, the Dionysian concept of the angelic world never succeeded in eliminating the more ancient and more Biblical ideas about the angels. Particularly striking is the opposition between the very minor role ascribed by Dionysius to the "archangels" (second rank from the bottom of the angelic hierarchy) and the concept found in Jewish apocalyptic writings, including Daniel, Jude, and Revelation, where the archangels Michael and Gabriel rank as the "chief captains" of God's celestial armies. This idea has been preserved in the liturgy, which should be considered as the main and most reliable source of Byzantine "angelology."

Involved in the struggle against the demonic powers of the cosmos, the angels represent, in a way, the ideal side of creation. According to Byzantine theologians, they were created before the visible world,[28] and their essential function is to serve God and His image, man. The scriptural idea that the angels perpetually praise God (Is 6:3; Lk 2:13) is a frequent theme of the Byzantine liturgy, especially of the Eucharistic canons, which call the faithful to join the choir of angels—i.e., to recover their original fellowship with God. This reunion of heaven and earth, anticipated in the Eucharist, is the eschatological goal of the whole of creation. The angels contribute to its preparation by participating invisibly in the life of the cosmos.

NOTES

1. Origen, *De principiis*, I, 2, 10; ed. Koetschau, pp. 41–42; trans. Butterworth, p. 23.
2. See G. Florovsky, "The Concept of Creation in Saint Athanasius," *Studia Patristica* VI, part IV, TU 81 (Berlin: Akademie Verlag, 1962), 36–37.
3. Athanasius, *Contra Arianos*, III, 60; PG 26:448–449.
4. *Contra Gentes*, 41; PG 25:81cd.
5. *Contra Arianos*, II, 31; PG 26:212b.
6. *Ibid.*, II, 2; PG 26:149c.

7. *Ibid.*, I, 20; PG 26:55A.

8. See, for example, *Thesaurus,* 15; PG 75:276B; *ibid.,* 18; PG 75:313c.

9. *De fide orth.,* I, 8; PG 94:812–813.

10. See especially Gregory of Nazianzus, *Carm. theol. IV de mundo,* V, 67–68; PG 37:421.

11. John of Damascus, *De fide orth.,* II, 2; PG 94:865.

12. *Ibid.,* I, 9; PG 94:837.

13. Maximus the Confessor, *Schol.*; PG 4:317.

14. Georges Florovsky, "The Idea of Creation in Christian Philosophy," *EChurchQ* 8 (1949), 67.

15. See Lars Thunberg, *Microcosm and Mediator,* pp. 76–84.

16. Maximus the Confessor, *Amb.* 7; PG 91:1081c.

17. *Ibid.*; PG 91:1081B.

18. Thunberg, *Microcosm and Mediator,* p. 81.

19. See S. L. Epifanovich, *Prepodobnyi Maksim Ispovednik i Vizantiiskoe bogoslovie* (Kiev, 1915), pp. 136–137.

20. See J. Meyendorff, *Christ in Eastern Christian Thought* (Washington: Corpus, 1969), pp. 100–102.

21. See Maximus the Confessor, *Ad Thal.,* 60; PG 90:621A.

22. Maximus the Confessor, *Amb.*; PG 91:1057B.

23. Milton V. Anastos, "The History of Byzantine Science: Report on the Dumbarton Oaks Symposium of 1961," *Dumbarton Oaks Papers* 16 (1962), 411.

24. Basil of Caesarea, *In Hex.,* hom. 5; PG 29:1160D.

25. *Ibid.,* 3; PG 29:73c.

26. Maximus the Confessor, *Cap. gnostica,* I, 10; PG 91:1085D–1088A.

27. See, in particular, Maximus the Confessor, *Ad Thal.* 61; PG 90:628AB.

28. Gregory Nazianzus, *Or.* 38, 9; PG 36:320c; John of Damascus, *De fide orth.,* II, 3; PG 94:873.

11

Man

THE VIEW OF MAN prevailing in the Christian East is based upon the notion of "participation" in God. Man has been created not as an autonomous, or self-sufficient, being; his very *nature* is truly itself only inasmuch as it exists "in God" or "in grace." Grace, therefore, gives man his "natural" development. This basic presupposition explains why the terms "nature" and "grace," when used by Byzantine authors, have a meaning quite different from the Western usage; rather than being in direct opposition, the terms "nature" and "grace" express a dynamic, living, and necessary relationship between God and man, different by their *natures,* but in *communion* with each other through God's energy, or grace. Yet man is the center of creation—a "microcosm"—and his free self-determination defines the ultimate destiny of the universe.

1. MAN AND GOD

According to Maximus the Confessor, God, in creating man, "communicated" to him four of His own properties: being, eternity, goodness, and wisdom.[1] Of these four *divine* properties, the first two belong to the very essence of man; the third and the fourth are merely *offered* to man's willful aptitude.

The idea that his "participation" in God is man's particular privilege is expressed in various ways, but consistently, in the Greek patristic tradition. Irenaeus, for example, writes that man is composed of three elements: body, soul, and Holy Spirit;[2] and the Cappadocian Fathers speak of an "efflux" of the Holy Spirit in man.[3] Gregory of Nyssa, in his treatise *On the Creation of Man,* in discussing man before the Fall, attributes to him the "beatitude of immortality," "justice," "purity." "God is love," writes Gregory, "and source of love. The creator of our nature has also imparted to us the character of love. . . . If love is absent, all the elements of the image are deformed."[4] Jean Daniélou's comments on this passage may, in fact, be extended to Greek patristic thought as a whole:

Gregory identifies realities which Western theology considers distinct. He ascribes to man certain traits, such as reason or freedom, which the West attributes to the [created] spirit; others such as *apatheia* or love (called *grace* by Westerners), attributed to divine life; as well as the effects of final glorification: incorruptibility and beatitude. For Gregory, the distinctions do not exist.[5]

Thus, the most important aspect of Greek patristic anthropology, which will be taken for granted by the Byzantine theologians throughout the Middle Ages, is the concept that man is not an autonomous being, that his true humanity is realized only when he lives 'in God" and possesses divine qualities. To express this idea, various authors use various terminologies—Origenistic, Neoplatonic, or Biblical; yet there is a consensus on the essential *openness* of man, a concept which does not fit into the Western categories of "nature" and "grace."

As we saw in the passage of Maximus' cited at the beginning of this section, the "natural" participation of man in God is not a static givenness; it is a challenge, and man is called to *grow* in divine life. Divine life is a gift, but also a task which is to be accomplished by a free human effort. This polarity between the "gift" and the "task" is often expressed in terms of the distinction between the concepts of "image" and "likeness." In Greek, the term *homoiōsis,* which corresponds to "likeness" in Genesis 1:26, suggests the idea of dynamic progress ("assimilation") and implies human freedom. To use an expression of Gregory Palamas': Adam, before the Fall, possessed "the ancient dignity of freedom." [6] Thus there is no opposition between freedom and grace in the Byzantine tradition: the presence in man of divine qualities, of a "grace" which is part of his nature and which makes him fully man, neither destroys his freedom, nor limits the necessity for him to become fully himself by his own effort; rather, it secures that cooperation, or synergy, between the divine will and human choice which makes possible the progress "from glory to glory" and the assimilation of man to the divine dignity for which he was created.

The understanding of man as an "open being," naturally possessing in himself a divine "spark" and dynamically oriented toward further progress in God, has direct implications for the theory of knowledge and particularly for the theory of the knowledge of God. Western Scholasticism has assumed that this knowledge is based upon revealed premises—Scripture or church magisterium—which serve as a basis for development by the human mind in conformity with the principles of Aristotelian logic. This concept of theology, which presupposes the autonomy of the human mind in defining Christian truths on the basis of Revelation, was the initial issue in the controversy between Barlaam the Calabrian and Gregory Palamas in the fourteenth century. According to Barlaam, the natural human mind could never reach divine truth itself, but only draw conclusions from revealed premisses. In cases when revealed premisses specifically affirmed a given proposition, a logical intellectual process could lead to "apodictic" conclusions, i.e., to intellectually evident truths. If a theological affirmation could not be based on revealed premisses, however, it could not be considered as "demonstrated" but only as "dialectically possible." To refute these views, Palamas developed an experiential concept of our knowledge of God, based upon the notion that God is not known through a purely intellectual process, but that man, when he is in *communion* with God (i.e., restored to his *natural* state) can, and even must, enjoy a direct knowledge and experience of his creator. This direct knowledge is possible because man, since he is not an autonomous being, but an image of God "open upward," possesses the natural property of transcending himself and of reaching the divine. This property is not simply intellectual; it implies purification of the whole being, ascetical detachment, and ethical progress: "It is impossible to possess God in oneself," writes Palamas, "or to experience God in purity, or be united with the unmixed light, unless one purify oneself through virtue, unless one get out, or rather above, oneself." [7]

Obviously, this Palamite understanding of knowledge coincides with Gregory of Nyssa's concepts of "the sense of the heart" or the "eyes of the soul," [8] and with Maximus' identification of the knowledge of God with "deification." For the entire patristic and Byzantine tradition, knowledge of God implies "participation" in God—i.e., not only intellectual knowledge, but a state of the entire human being, transformed by grace, and freely cooperating with it by the efforts of both will and mind. In the monastic tradition of Macarius, reflected, for example, in the writings of Symeon the New Theologian, this idea of "participation" is inseparable from the idea of freedom and of consciousness. A true Christian knows God through a free and conscious experience; this is precisely the friendship with God which was man's state before the Fall—the state in which God wanted man to live and which was restored in Jesus Christ.

2. MAN AND THE WORLD

The "image and likeness" of God in man implies, not only an openness of man toward God, but also a *function* and *task* of man in the whole of creation.

Against Origen, the Fathers unanimously affirmed that man is a unity of soul and body. On this point, the Biblical view decidedly overcame Platonic spiritualism; by the same token, the *visible* world and its *history* were recognized as worthy of salvation and redemption. If, in the Origenistic system, the diversity of visible phenomena was only a consequence of the Fall and of the bodily nature of man—an "engrossed" and defective mode of the soul's existence, the only true and eternal reality being spiritual and divine—the Biblical and Christian concept understood the universe in its entirety as "very good"; and this concept applied first of all to man.

According to Maximus the Confessor, body and soul are complementary and cannot exist separately.[9] If primarily directed against the Origenistic idea of the pre-existence of souls, this affirmation raises the issue of the soul's survival after death. This survival is not denied, of course, but neither is it understood as a "liberation" from the body, in a Platonic sense. The separation of body and soul at death is as contrary to "nature" as death itself, and the ultimate and eternal survival of the soul is possible only if the whole man is raised from death at the resurrection. Yet the soul's immortality is not only directed toward the resurrection of the whole man; it is also conditioned by the soul's relationship to God. The spiritual literature of the Byzantine East frequently speaks of the "death of the soul" as a consequence of rebellion against God, i.e., of sin. "After the transgression of our ancestors in Paradise," writes Gregory Palamas, ". . . sin came into life. We ourselves are dead and, before the death of the body, we suffer the death of the soul; that is to say, the separation of the soul from God." [10]

Obviously, the dual nature of man is not simply a static juxtaposition of two heterogeneous elements, a mortal body and an immortal soul: it reflects a dynamic function of man between God and creation. Describing the anthropology of Maximus, Lars Thunberg is fully justified when he writes: "Maximus seems to stress the independence of the elements [i.e., soul and body], not primarily in order to maintain the immortality of the soul in spite of its relationship to the body, but in order to underline the creative will of God as the only constitutive factor for both, as well as for their unity." [11] We are here back to the point made at the beginning of this section: man is truly man because he is the image of *God,* and the divine factor in man concerns not only his spiritual aspect—as Origen and Evagrius maintained—but the whole of man, soul and body.

This last point is the reason why a majority of Byzantine theologians describe man in terms of a trichotomist scheme: spirit (or mind), soul, body. Their trichotomism is very directly connected with the notion of participation in God as the basis of anthropology.

We have seen that this theocentrism appears in Irenaeus' use of Pauline trichotomism: Spirit, soul, body.[12] Under Origenistic influence, the Fathers of the fourth century, followed by the later Byzantine authors, prefer to speak of mind (*nous*), soul, and body. The desire to avoid ambiguity concerning the identity of the "spirit" and to affirm the created character of the human "spirit" may also have contributed to this evolution. But, even then, Origenistic and Evagrian terminology was unsatisfactory, because the concept of the *nous* was connected with the myth of eternal pre-existence, original Fall, and disincarnate restoration. Although it reflected satisfactorily the theocentric aspect of patristic anthropology, this terminology failed to emphasize the function of man in the visible world. Thus, in Maximus the Confessor, the human *mind,* though certainly understood as the element *par excellence* connecting man with God, is also seen as a created function of man's created psychosomatic unity.

The *nous,* therefore, is not so much a "part" of man as (1) the ability which man possesses to transcend himself in order to participate in God; (2) the unity of man's composite nature when it faces his ultimate destiny in God and in the world; (3) the freedom of man, which can either fully develop if it finds God or become defective if it submits itself to the body. "The spirit (*nous*) in human nature corresponds most nearly to the person," writes Vladimir Lossky.[13] The judgment of Lars Thunberg on Maximus is valid for the entire Byzantine tradition: "Maximus is able to express his conviction that there is a personal aspect in man's life, which goes, as it were, beyond his nature, and represents his inner unity, as well as his relationship to God."[14] This concept of the person or hypostasis, irreducible to nature or to any part of it, is a central notion in both theology and anthropology, as we shall see later in connection with the doctrine of the Trinity.

As image of God, man is lord of creation and "microcosm." This second concept, which was widely used in Platonism and Stoicism, was adopted by the Cappadocian Fathers and given a Christian dimension: man is a "microcosm" because (1) he unites, in his hypostatic existence, the intelligible and sensible aspects of creation; (2) he is given by God the *task* and *function* to make this unity ever more perfect, especially after the Fall, when forces of disintegration and division are also actively at work in creation. On this point, and especially in Maximus the Confessor, we find another aspect of the polarity of image–likeness: God's gift to man is also a task and a challenge.

Maximus, in a famous passage of *Ambigua* 41,[15] lists five polarities which are to be overcome by man: God and creation, the intelligible and the sensible, heaven and earth, paradise and world, man and woman. The polarities have been sharpened by sin and rendered insuperable by human capabilities alone. Only the man Jesus, because He is also God, was able to overcome them. He is the new Adam, and in Him, creation again finds communion with the creator and harmony within itself.

The central role of man in the cosmos is also reflected—better perhaps than in any system of concepts—in the Byzantine liturgy with its emphasis on the union of heaven and earth, its sacramental realism, its rites of blessing food, nature, and human life, as well as in the affirmation that, by nature, man is closer to God than are the angels themselves. The idea originates in Hebrews 1:14, and is developed by Gregory Palamas in the context of an Incarnational theology: "The Word became flesh to honor the flesh, even this mortal flesh; therefore, the proud spirits should not consider themselves, and should not be considered, worthy of greater honors than man, nor should they deify themselves on account of their incorporality and their apparent immortality." [16]

Among creatures, there is no greater glory than to be the lord of all creation: man is given this glory if he preserves in himself the image of God—i.e., if he partakes in the life and glory of the creator Himself.

3. ORIGINAL SIN

In order to understand many major theological problems which arose between East and West, both before and after the schism, the extraordinary impact upon Western thought of Augustine's polemics against Pelagius and Julian of Eclanum must be fully taken into account. In the Byzantine world, where Augustinian thought exercised practically no influence, the significance of the sin of Adam and of its consequences for mankind was understood along quite different lines.

We have seen that in the East man's relationship with God was understood as a communion of the human person with that which is *above nature*. "Nature," therefore, designates that which is, in virtue of creation, distinct from God. But nature can and must be transcended; this is the privilege and the function of the *free mind*, made "according to God's image."

Now, in Greek patristic thought, only this free, personal mind can commit sin and incur the concomitant "guilt"—a point made particularly clear by Maximus the Confessor in his distinction between "natural will" and "gnomic will." Human nature, as God's creature, always exercises its dynamic properties (which together constitute the "natural will"—a created dynamism) in accordance with the divine will which created it. But when the human person, or hypostasis, by rebelling against both God and nature misuses its freedom, it can distort the "natural will" and thus corrupt nature itself. It is able to do so because it possesses freedom, or "gnomic will," which is capable of orienting man toward the good and of "imitating God" ("God alone is good by nature," writes Maximus, "and only God's imitator is good by his *gnomē*");[17] it is also capable of sin, because "our salvation depends on our will." [18] But sin is always a personal act, never an act of nature.[19] Patriarch Photius even goes so far as to say, referring to Western doctrines, that the belief in a "sin of nature" is a heresy.[20]

From these basic ideas about the personal character of sin, it is evident that the rebellion of Adam and Eve against God could be conceived only as their personal sin; there would be no place, then, in such an anthropology for the concept of inherited guilt, or for a "sin of nature," although it admits that human nature incurs the consequences of Adam's sin.

The Greek patristic understanding of man never denies the unity of mankind or replaces it with a radical individualism. The Pauline doctrine of the two Adams ("As in Adam all men die, so also in Christ shall all be brought to life" [1 Co 15:22]), as well as the Platonic concept of the ideal man, leads Gregory of Nyssa to understand Genesis 1:27—"God created man in His own image"—to refer to the creation of mankind as a whole.[21] It is obvious, therefore, that the sin of Adam must also be related to all men, just as salvation brought by Christ is salvation for all mankind; but neither original sin nor salvation can be realized in an individual's life without involving his personal and free responsibility.

The scriptural text which played a decisive role in the polemics between Augustine and the Pelagians is found in Romans 5:12, where Paul, speaking of Adam, writes: "As sin came into the world through one man, and through sin, death, so death spread to all men *because all men have sinned* [*eph ho pantes hemarton*]." In this passage there is a major issue of translation. The last four Greek words were translated in Latin as *in quo omnes peccaverunt* ("in whom [i.e., in Adam] all men have sinned"), and this translation was used in the West to justify the doctrine of guilt inherited from Adam and spread to his descendants. But such a meaning cannot be drawn from the original Greek—the text read, of course, by the Byzantines. The form *eph ho*—a contraction of *epi* with the relative pronoun *ho*—can be translated as "because," a meaning accepted by most modern scholars of all confessional backgrounds.[22] Such a translation renders Paul's thought to mean that death, which was "the wages of sin" (Rm 6:23) for Adam, is also the punishment applied to those who, like him, sin. It presupposes a cosmic significance of the sin of Adam, but does not say that his descendants are "guilty" as he was, unless they also sin as he sinned.

A number of Byzantine authors, including Photius, understood the *eph ho* to mean "because" and saw nothing in the Pauline text beyond a moral similarity between Adam and other sinners, death being the normal retribution for sin. But there is also the consensus of the majority of Eastern Fathers, who interpret Romans 5:12 in close connection with 1 Corinthians 15:22—between Adam and his descendants there is a solidarity *in death* just as there is a solidarity *in life* between the risen Lord and the baptized.

This interpretation comes, obviously, from the literal, grammatical meaning of Romans 5:12. *Eph ho,* if it means "because," is a neuter pronoun; but it can also be masculine, referring to the immediately preceding substantive *thanatos* ("death"). The sentence then may have a meaning which seems improbable to a reader trained in Augustine, but which is indeed the meaning which most Greek Fathers accepted: "As sin came into the world through one man and death through sin, so death spread to all men; and *because of death,* all men have sinned. . . ."

Mortality, or "corruption," or simply death (understood in a personalized sense), has indeed been viewed, since Christian antiquity, as a cosmic disease which holds humanity under its sway, both spiritually and physically, and is controlled by the one who is "the murderer from the beginning"

(Jn 8:44). It is this death which makes sin inevitable, and in this sense "corrupts" nature.

For Cyril of Alexandria, humanity, after the sin of Adam, "fell sick of corruption." [23] Cyril's opponents, the theologians of the School of Antioch, agreed with him on the consequence of Adam's sin. For Theodore of Mopsuestia, "by becoming mortal, we acquired greater urge to sin." The necessity of satisfying the needs of the body—food, drink, and other bodily needs—are absent in immortal beings, but among mortals they lead to "passions," for they present unavoidable means of temporary survival.[24] Theodoret of Cyrus repeats almost literally the arguments of Theodore in his own commentary on Romans; elsewhere, he argues against the sinfulness of marriage by affirming that transmission of mortal life is not sinful in itself, in spite of Psalm 51:7 ("my mother conceived me in sin"). This verse, according to Theodoret, refers not to the sexual act but to the general sinful condition of *mortal* humanity: "Having become mortal, [Adam and Eve] conceived mortal children, and mortal beings are necessarily subject to passions and fears, to pleasures and sorrows, to anger and hatred." [25]

There is indeed a consensus in Greek patristic and Byzantine traditions in identifying the inheritance of the Fall as an inheritance essentially of mortality rather than of sinfulness, sinfulness being merely a consequence of mortality. The idea appears in Chrysostom, who specifically denies the imputation of sin to the descendants of Adam;[26] in the eleventh-century commentator Theophylact of Ohrida;[27] and in later Byzantine authors, particularly Gregory Palamas.[28] The always-more-sophisticated Maximus the Confessor, when he speaks of the consequences of the sin of Adam, identifies them mainly with the mind's submission to the flesh and finds in sexual procreation the most obvious expression of man's acquiescence in animal instincts; but as we have seen, sin remains, for Maximus, a personal act, and inherited guilt is impossible.[29] For him, as for the others, "the wrong choice made by Adam brought in passion, corruption, and mortality," [30] but not inherited guilt.

The contrast with Western tradition on this point is brought into sharp focus when Eastern authors discuss the meaning of baptism. Augustine's arguments in favor of infant baptism were taken from the text of the creeds (baptism for "the remission of sins") and from his understanding of Romans 5:12. Children are born sinful, not because they have sinned personally, but because they have sinned "in Adam"; their baptism is therefore also a baptism "for the remission of sins." At the same time, an Eastern contemporary of Augustine's, Theodoret of Cyrus, flatly denies that the creedal formula "for the remission of sins" is applicable to infant baptism. For Theodoret, in fact, the "remission of sins" is only a side effect of baptism, fully real in cases of adult baptism, which was the norm, of course, in the early Church and which indeed "remits sins." But the principal meaning of baptism is wider and more positive: "If the only meaning of baptism were the remission of sins," writes Theodoret, "why would we baptize the newborn children who have not yet tasted of sin? But the mystery [of baptism] is not limited to this; it is a promise of greater and more perfect gifts. In it are the promises of future delights; it is a type of the future resurrection, a communion with the master's passion, a participation in His resurrection, a mantle of salvation, a tunic of gladness, a garment of light, or, rather, it is light itself." [31]

Thus, the Church baptizes children, not to "remit" their yet non-existent sins, but in order to give them a new and immortal *life,* which their mortal parents are unable to communicate to them. The opposition between the two Adams is seen in terms not of guilt and forgiveness but of death and life. "The first man was from the earth, a man of dust; the second man is from heaven; as was the man of dust, so are those who are of the dust, and as is the man of heaven, so are those who are of heaven" (1 Co 15:47-48). Baptism is the paschal mystery, the "passage." All its ancient forms, and especially the Byzantine, include a renunciation of Satan, a triple immersion as type of death and resurrection, and the positive gift of new life through anointing and Eucharistic communion.

In this perspective, death and mortality are viewed, not so much as retribution for sin (although they are also a just retribution for personal sins), as means through which the fundamentally unjust "tyranny" of the devil is exercised over mankind after Adam's sin. From this, baptism is a liberation, because it gives access to the new immortal life brought into the world by Christ's Resurrection. The Resurrection delivers men from the fear of death, and, therefore, also from the necessity of struggling for existence. Only in the light of the risen Lord does the Sermon on the Mount acquire its full realism: "Do not be anxious about your life, what you shall eat or what you shall drink, nor about your body, what you shall put on. Is not life more than food, and the body more than clothing?" (Mt 6:25).

Communion in the risen body of Christ; participation in divine life; sanctification through the energy of God, which penetrates true humanity and restores it to its "natural" state, rather than justification, or remission of inherited guilt—these are at the center of Byzantine understanding of the Christian Gospel.

4. THE NEW EVE

As early as Justin and Irenaeus, primitive Christian tradition established a parallel between Genesis 2 and the Lucan account of the Annunciation, and the contrast between two virgins, Eve and Mary, to symbolize two possible uses of created freedom by man: in the first, a surrender to the devil's offer of false deification, in the second, humble acceptance of the will of God.

Although it was superseded after the Council of Ephesus by the veneration of Mary as Mother of God or *Theotokos,* the concept of the New Eve who, on behalf of all fallen humanity, was able to accept the coming of the new "dispensation" is present in the patristic tradition throughout the Byzantine period. Proclus, Patriarch of Constantinople (434–446), frequently used the idea in his homilies. The Virgin Mary is viewed as the goal of Old Testament history, which began with the children of Eve: "Among the children of Adam, God chose the admirable Seth," writes Palamas, "and so the election, which had in view, by divine foreknowledge, her who should become the Mother of God, had its origin in the children of Adam themselves, filled up in the successive generations, descended as far as the King and Prophet David. . . . When it came to the time when this election should find its fulfillment, Joachim and Anna, of the house and country of David, were chosen by God. . . . It was to them that God now promised and gave the child who would be the Mother of God." [32]

The election of the Virgin Mary is, therefore, the culminating point of Israel's progress toward reconciliation with God, but God's final response to this progress and the beginning of new life comes with the Incarnation of the Word. Salvation needed "a new root," writes Palamas in the same homily, "for no one, except God, is without sin; no one can give life; no one can remit sins." [33] This "new root" is God the Word made flesh; the Virgin Mary is His "temple."

Byzantine homiletic and hymnographical texts often praise the Virgin as "fully prepared," "cleansed," and "sanctified." But these texts are to be understood in the context of the doctrine of original sin which prevailed in the East: the inheritance from Adam is mortality, not guilt, and there was never any doubt among Byzantine theologians that Mary was indeed a *mortal* being.

The preoccupation of Western theologians to find in Byzantium ancient authorities for the doctrine of the Immaculate Conception of Mary has often used these passages out of context. And, indeed, Sophronius of Jerusalem († 638) praises Mary: "Many saints appeared before thee, but none was as filled with grace as thou. . . . No one has been purified in advance as thou hast been. . . ." [34] Andrew of Crete († 740) is even more specific, preaching on the Feast of the Virgin's Nativity: "When the Mother of Him who is beauty itself is born, [human] nature recovers in her person its ancient privileges, and is fashioned according to a perfect model, truly worthy of God. . . . In a word, the transfiguration of our nature begins today. . . ." [35] This theme, which appears in the liturgical hymns of the Feast of September 8, is further developed by Nicholas Cabasilas in the

fourteenth century: "Earth she is, because she is from earth; but she is a
new earth, since she derives in no way from her ancestors and has not
inherited the old leaven. She is . . . a new dough and has originated a
new race." [36]

Quotations can easily be multiplied, and they give clear indications that
the Mariological piety of the Byzantines would probably have led them to
accept the definition of the dogma of the Immaculate Conception of Mary
as it was defined in 1854, *if only* they had shared the Western doctrine of
original sin. But it should be remembered—especially in the context of
the poetical, emotional, or rhetorical exaggerations characteristic of Byzantine liturgical Mariology—that such concepts as "purity" and "holiness"
could easily be visualized even in the framework of pre-Christian humanity, which was considered as *mortal,* but not necessarily "guilty." In the
case of Mary, her response to the angel and her status as the "new Eve"
gave her a special relation to the "new race" born of her. Yet, never does
one read, in Byzantine authors, any statement which would imply that
she had received a special grace of *immortality.* Only such a statement
would clearly imply that her humanity did not share the common lot of the
descendants of Adam.

The only Byzantine author who definitely understood and accepted both
the Western concept of original sin and the doctrine of the Immaculate
Conception is Gennadios Scholarios († *ca.* 1472): "The grace of God
delivered her completely," Gennadios writes, "just as if she had been
conceived virginally [sic]. . . . Thence, because she was completely liberated from the ancestral guilt and punishment—a privilege which she is
the only one of the human race to have received—her soul is altogether inaccessible to the clouds of [impure] thoughts, and she became, in body
and soul, a divine sanctuary." [37] Interesting in the mouth of a convinced
Thomist, who abandons on this point the negative attitude of St. Thomas
himself, Scholarius' statement reflects the characteristically Western concept of "guilt," and anticipates later, similar utterances by Orthodox theologians, who will begin to think in the categories of Western Scholasticism.

In order to maintain a fully balanced view of Byzantine Mariology, it
is necessary to keep in mind the essentially Christological framework of the
veneration of the *Theotokos* in Byzantium (a point which will be stressed
in the next chapter). Yet the absence of any formal doctrinal definition on
Mariology as such allowed the freedom of poets and orators, as well as the
reservation of strict exegetes. They always had available in hundreds of
copies the writings of the greatest of Byzantine patristic authorities, John
Chrysostom, who found it possible to ascribe to Mary not only "original
sin," but also "agitation," "trouble," and, even, "love of honor." [38]

No one, of course, would have dared to accuse the great Chrysostom of
impiety. So the Byzantine Church, wisely preserving a scale of theological
values which always gave precedence to the *basic* fundamental truths of

the Gospel, abstained from enforcing any dogmatic formulation concerning
Mary, except that she was truly and really the *Theotokos,* "Mother of God."
No doubt, this striking title, made necessary by the logic of Cyrillian
Christology, justified her daily liturgical acclamation as "more honorable
than the Cherubim, and more glorious beyond compare than the Sera-
phim."

What greater honor could be rendered to a human being? What clearer
basis could be found for a Christian theocentric anthropology?

NOTES

1. Maximus the Confessor, *De Char.,* III, 25; PG 90:1024BC.
2. Irenaeus, *Adv. Haer.,* 5, 6, 1.
3. Gregory of Nazianzus, *Carm.;* PG 37:452.
4. Gregory of Nyssa, *De opif. hom.* 5; PG 44:137c.
5. Jean Daniélou, *Platonisme et théologie mystique* (Paris: Aubier, 1944), p. 54.
6. Gregory Palamas, *Triads,* I, 1, 9; ed. J. Meyendorff (Louvain, 1959), p. 27.
7. *Ibid.;* ed. Meyendorff, p. 203.
8. See Daniélou, *Platonisme et théologie mystique,* pp. 240–241.
9. Maximus the Confessor, *Amb.* 7; PG 91:1109CD.
10. Gregory Palamas, *Hom.* 11; PG 151:125A; see other references in J. Meyendorff,
A Study of Gregory Palamas (London: Faith Press, 1964), pp. 122–124.
11. Thunberg, *Microcosm and Mediator,* p. 103.
12. Irenaeus, *Adv. Haer.,* 5, 6, 1.
13. Vladimir Lossky, *The Mystical Theology,* p. 201.
14. Thunberg, *Microcosm and Mediator,* p. 119.
15. Maximus the Confessor, *Amb.,* 41; PG 91:1305D.
16. Gregory Palamas, *Hom.* 16; PG 157:204A.
17. *De Char.,* IV, 90; PG 90:1069c.
18. Maximus the Confessor, *Liber Asceticus*; PG 90:953B.
19. Maximus the Confessor, *Expos. or. dom.;* PG 90:905A; on this, see J. Meyendorff,
Christ, pp. 112–113.
20. Photius, *Library,* 177; ed. R. Henry (Paris: Belles Lettres, 1960), 2:177.
21. Gregory of Nyssa, *De opif. hom.* 16; PG 44:185B.
22. See Joseph A. Fitzmeyer, s.J., in *The Jerome Biblical Commentary* (Englewood
Cliffs: Prentice-Hall, 1968) 53:56–57 (II, pp. 307–308): "The meaning of the phrase
eph' hō is much disputed. The least convincing interpretations treat it as a strict rel[ative]
phrase: (1) 'in whom,' an interpretation based on the [Vulgate] translation, 'in quo,'
and commonly used in the Western Church since Ambrosiaster. This interpretation was
unknown to the G[ree]k Fathers before Theophylact. But if Paul had meant this, he
could have written *en hō* (see 1 Cor 15:22). . . . (4) 'Since, inasmuch as, because,'
. . . This interpretation, commonly used by G[ree]k patristic writers, is based on 2 Cor
5:4; Phil 3:12; 4:10, where *eph' hō* is normally translated 'because.' . . . It would thus
ascribe to all men an individual responsibility for death. . . . *all men sinned*: . . . The
verb should not be translated, 'have sinned collectively' or 'have sinned in Adam,' because these are additions to the text. Here *hēmarton* refers to personal, actual sins of men,
as Pauline usage elsewhere suggests . . . and as the G[ree]k Fathers generally understood it. . . . This clause, then, expresses a secondary—quasi-parenthetical—role the actual sins of men play in their condemnation to 'death.' However, a notion of 'Original
Sin' is already contained in the first part of the verse, as the reason why 'death' has

spread to all men. If this were not true, the rest of the paragraph would make little sense. A universal causality of Adam's sin is presupposed in 5:15a,16a,17a,18a,19a. It would be false, then, to the whole thrust of the paragraph to interpret 5:12 so as to imply that man's condition before Christ's coming was due wholly to his own personal sins."

23. Cyril of Alexandria, *In Rom.*; PG 74:789B.

24. Theodore of Mopsuestia, *In Rom.*; PG 66:801B.

25. Theodoret of Cyrus, *In Rom.*; PG 80; 1245A.

26. John Chrysostom, *In Rom.* hom. 10; PG 60:474–475.

27. Theophylact of Ohrida, *Exp. in Rom.*; PG 124:404C.

28. See J. Meyendorff, *Gregory Palamas*, pp. 121–126.

29. See Epifanovich, *Prepodobnyi Maksim Ispovednik i Vizantiiskoe bogoslovie*, p. 65n5.

30. Maximus the Confessor, *Quaest. ad Thal.*, PG 90:408BC.

31. Theodoret of Cyrus, *Haeret. fabul. compendium*, 5:18; PG 83:512.

32. Gregory Palamas, *Hom. in Present.*, 6–7; ed. Oikonomos (Athens, 1861), pp. 126–127; trans. in *EChurchQ* 10 (1954–1955), No. 8, 381–382.

33. *Ibid.*, 2; p. 122.

34. Sophronius of Jerusalem, *Oratio*, II, 25; PG 87:3248A.

35. Andrew of Crete, *Hom. I in Nativ. B. Mariae*; PG 97:812A.

36. Nicholas Cabasilas, *Hom. in Dorm.*, 4; PG 19:498.

37. Gennadios Scholarios, *Oeuvres complètes de Georges Scholarios*, edd. J. Petit and M. Jugie (Paris, 1928), II, 501.

38. John Chrysostom, *Hom. 44 in Matt.*; PG 57:464; *Hom. 21 in Jn 2*; PG 59:131.

12

Jesus Christ

BYZANTINE CHRISTOLOGY has always been dominated by the categories of thought and the terminology of the great controversies of the fifth, sixth, and seventh centuries about the person and identity of Jesus Christ. As we have shown in Part I, these controversies involved conceptual problems, as well as the theological basis of life. In the mind of Eastern Christians, the entire content of the Christian faith depends upon the way in which the question "Who is Jesus Christ?" is answered.

The five ecumenical councils which issued specific definitions on the relationship between the divine and the human natures in Christ have at times been viewed as a pendulant development: from the emphasis on the divinity of Christ, at Ephesus (431); to the reaffirmation of His full humanity, at Chalcedon (451); then back to His divinity, with the acceptance of Cyril's idea of Theopaschism, at Constantinople (553); followed by a new awareness of His human "energy" or "will," again at Constantinople (680), and of His human quality of describability in the anti-iconoclastic definition of Nicaea II (787). Still, the opinion is often expressed in Western theological literature that Byzantine Christology is crypto-Monophysite, and offered as an explanation for the lack of concern among Eastern Christians for man in his secular or social creativity. We hope that the following discussion will shed some light on these frequently recurring issues.

1. GOD AND MAN

To affirm that God became man, and that His humanity possesses all the characteristics proper to human nature, implies that the Incarnation is a cosmic event. Man was created as the master of the cosmos and called by the creator to draw all creation to God. His failure to do so was a cosmic catastrophe, which could be repaired only by the creator Himself.

Moreover, the fact of the Incarnation implies that the bond between God and man, which has been expressed in the Biblical concept of "image

and likeness," is unbreakable. The restoration of creation is a "new creation," but it does not establish a new pattern, so far as man is concerned;
it reinstates *man* in his original divine glory among creatures and in his
original responsibility for the world. It reaffirms that man is truly man
when he participates in the life of God; that he is not autonomous, either
in relation to God, or in relation to the world; that true human life can
never be "secular." In Jesus Christ, God and man are *one*; in Him, therefore, God becomes accessible not by superseding or eliminating the *humanum*, but by realizing and manifesting humanity in its purest and
most authentic form.

The Incarnation of the Logos was very consistently considered by
Byzantine theologians as having a *cosmic* significance. The cosmic dimension of the Christ-event is expressed particularly well in Byzantine hymnology: "Every creature made by Thee offers Thee thanks: the Angels
offer Thee a hymn; the heavens, a star; the Magi, gifts; the shepherds, their
wonder; the earth, its cave; the wilderness, the manger; and we offer Thee
a Virgin Mother." [1] The connection between creation and the Incarnation
is constantly emphasized in the hymns: "Man fell from the divine and
better life; though made in the image of God, through transgression he
became wholly subject to corruption and decay. But now the wise Creator
fashions him anew; for He has been glorified." [2] Similarly, the hymnology
of Good Friday stresses the involvement of creation as a whole in the
death of Christ: "The sun beholding Thee upon the Cross covered itself
with gloom; the earth trembled for fear. . . ." [3]

Thus, poetic images reflect the parallelism between Genesis 1:2 and
John 1. The coming of Christ is the Incarnation of the Logos "through
whom" all things were made: it is a new creation, but the creator is the
same. Against the Gnostics, who professed a dualism distinguishing the
God of the Old Testament from the Father of Jesus, patristic tradition
affirmed their absolute identity and, therefore, the essential "goodness" of
the original creation.

The Christ-event is a cosmic event both because Christ is the Logos—
and, therefore, in God the agent of creation—and because He is man,
since man is a "microcosm." Man's sin plunges creation into death and
decay, but man's restoration in Christ is a restoration of the cosmos to its
original beauty. Here again, Byzantine hymnology is the best witness:

> David foreseeing in spirit the sojourn with men of the Only-begotten Son
> in the flesh, called the creation to rejoice with him, and prophetically lifted
> up his voice to cry: "Tabor and Hermon shall rejoice in Thy name"
> [Ps 88:13]. For having gone up, O Christ, with Thy disciples into Mount
> Tabor, Thou wast transfigured, and hast made the nature that had grown
> dark in Adam to shine again as lightning. . . . [4]

The glorification of man, which is also the glorification of the whole of creation, should, of course, be understood eschatologically. In the person of Christ, in the sacramental reality of His Body, and in the life of the saints, the transfiguration of the entire cosmos is anticipated; but its advent in strength is still to come. This glorification, however, is indeed already a living experience available to all Christians, especially in the liturgy. This experience alone can give a goal and a meaning to human history.

The cosmic dimension of the Incarnation is implied in the Chalcedonian definition of 451, to which Byzantine theology remains faithful: Christ is "of one substance with us in His humanity, 'like unto us in all things save sin.'" He is God and man for "the distinction of natures is in no way abolished because of the union; rather, the characteristic properties of each nature are preserved." The last sentence of the definition obviously covers the creative, inventive, controlling functions of man in the cosmos. The idea is developed in the theology of Maximus the Confessor, when he argues, against the Monothelites, for the existence in Christ of a human "will," or "energy," stressing that without it authentic humanity is inconceivable. If Christ's manhood is identical with ours in all things except sin (and unless one classifies as "sin" every human "motion," "creativity," or "dynamism"), one must admit that Christ, who is man in His body, in His soul, and in His mind, was indeed acting with all these functions of true humanity. As Maximus fully understood, Christ's human energy or will was not superseded by His divine will, but accepted conformity with it. "The two natural wills [of Christ] are not contrary to each other, . . . but the human will follows [the divine]." [5] This conformity of the *humanum* with the *divinum* in Christ is, therefore, not a diminution of humanity, but its restoration: "Christ restores nature to conformity with itself. . . . Becoming man, He keeps His free will in impassibility and peace with nature." [6] "Participation" in God—as we have shown—is the very nature of man, not its abolition. This is the key to Eastern Christian understanding of the God–man relationship.

In Christ, the union of the two natures is hypostatic: they "concur into one person [*prosōpon*] and one hypostasis," according to the Fathers of Chalcedon. The controversies which arose from the Chalcedonian formula led to further definitions of the meaning of the term hypostasis. While Chalcedon had insisted that Christ was indeed one in His personal identity, it did not clearly specify that the term hypostasis, used to designate this identity, also designated the hypostasis of the pre-existing Logos. The anti-Chalcedonian opposition in the East so built its entire argument around this point that Byzantine Christology of the age of Justinian committed itself very strongly to excluding that interpretation of Chalcedon which would have considered the "*prosōpon,* or hypostasis," mentioned in the definition as simply the "*prosōpon* of union" of the old Antiochian School

—i.e., the new synthetic reality resulting from the union of the two natures. It affirmed, on the contrary, following Cyril of Alexandria, that Christ's unique hypostasis is the pre-existing hypostasis of the Logos; that is, that the term is used in Christology with exactly the same meaning as in the Trinitarian theology of the Cappadocian Fathers: one of the three eternal hypostases of the Trinity "took flesh," while remaining essentially the same in its divinity. The hypostasis of Christ, therefore, *pre-existed* in its divinity, but it *acquired* humanity by the Virgin Mary.

This fundamental position has two important implications. (*a*) There is no absolute symmetry between divinity and humanity in Christ because the unique hypostasis is only divine and because the human will *follows* the divine. It is precisely a "symmetrical" Christology which was rejected as Nestorian in Ephesus (431). This "assymetry" of Orthodox Christology reflects an idea which Athanasius and Cyril of Alexandria stressed so strongly: only God can *save,* while humanity can only cooperate with the saving acts and will of God. However, as we emphasized earlier, in the patristic concept of man, "theocentricity" is a *natural* character of humanity; thus assymetry does not prevent the fact that Christ was fully and "actively" man.

(*b*) The human nature of Christ is not personalized into a separate human hypostasis, which means that the concept of hypostasis is not an expression of natural existence, either in God or in man, but it designates *personal* existence. Post-Chalcedonian Christology postulates that Christ was fully man and also that He was a human *individual,* but it rejects the Nestorian view that He was a human hypostasis, or person. A fully human individual life was en-hypostasized in the hypostasis of the Logos, without losing any of its human characteristics. The theory, associated with the name of Apollinaris of Laodicea, and according to which the Logos, in Jesus, had taken the place of the human soul, was systematically rejected by Byzantine theologians since it implied that the humanity of Christ was not complete. Cyril's celebrated formula—wrongly attributed to Athanasius and, in fact, uttered by Apollinaris—"one nature incarnate of God the Word" was accepted only in a Chalcedonian context. Divine nature and human nature could never merge, or be confused, or become complementary to each other, but, in Christ, they were united in the single, divine hypostasis of the Logos: the divine model matched the human image.

The fact that the notion of hypostasis is irreducible to the concepts of "particular nature," or to the notion of "individuality," is crucially important not only in Christology but also in Trinitarian theology. Hypostasis is the personal, "acting" *source* of natural life; but it is not "nature," or life itself. In the hypostasis, the two natures of Christ accomplish a union without confusion. They retain their natural characteristics; but, because they share a common hypostatic life, there is a "communication of idioms," or *perichoresis,* which, for example, enables some of Christ's human actions —words or gestures—to carry consequences which only God could have provoked. The clay made out of His spittle, for example, restores sight to the blind man.

> Christ is one [writes John of Damascus]. Therefore the glory which naturally comes from the divinity has become common [to both natures] thanks to the identity of hypostasis; and, through the flesh, humility has also become common [to both natures] . . . , [but] it is the divinity which communicates its privileges to the body, remaining itself outside the passions of the flesh.[7]

The hypostatic union implies also that the Logos made humanity *His own* in its totality; thus the Second Person of the Trinity was indeed the subject, or agent, of the *human* experiences, or acts, of Jesus. The controversy between Cyril of Alexandria and Nestorius concerning the term *Theotokos,* applied to the Virgin Mary, concerned essentially this very problem. Was there, in Jesus, a human person whose mother could have been Mary? Cyril's answer—emphatically negative—was, in fact, a Christological option of great importance. In Christ, there was only one Son, the Son of God, and Mary could not have been the Mother of anyone else. She was, therefore, indeed the "Mother of God." Exactly the same problem arose in connection with the death of Christ: impassibility and immortality were indeed characteristics of the divine nature. How, then, asked the theologians of Antioch, could the Son of God *die*? Obviously, the "subject" of Christ's death was only His humanity. Against this point of view, and following Cyril, the Fifth Council (553) affirms: "If anyone does not confess that our Lord Jesus Christ who was crucified in the flesh is true God and the Lord of Glory and one of the Holy Trinity, let him be anathema." [8] This conciliar text, which paraphrases 1 Corinthians 2:8 ("If they had understood, they would never have crucified the Lord of glory"), inspired the hymn "The Only-begotten Son," attributed to Emperor Justinian and sung at every Byzantine Eucharistic liturgy: "One of the Holy Trinity, you were crucified for us."

"Theopaschism"—the acceptance of formulae which affirm that the "Son of God died in the flesh"—illustrates how distinct the concepts of "hypostasis" and "nature" or "essence" really are. The distinction is stressed by one of the main Chalcedonian theologians of the age of Justinian, Leontius of Jerusalem: "The Logos," writes Leontius, "is said to have suffered according to the hypostasis, for within His hypostasis He assumed a passible [human] essence besides His own impassible essence, and what can be asserted of the [human] essence can be asserted of the hypostasis." [9] What this implies is that the characteristics of the divine essence—impassibility, immutability, etc.—are not absolutely binding upon the *per-*

sonal, or hypostatic, existence of God. Later we shall see the importance of this fact for the patristic and Byzantine understanding of God. Meanwhile, on the level of soteriology, the affirmation that the Son of God indeed "died in the flesh" reflects, better than any other Christological formula, the boundlessness of God's love for man, the reality of the "appropriation" by the Logos of fallen and mortal humanity—i.e., the very mystery of salvation.

An often-recurring criticism of Byzantine Christology, as it was defined by the Fifth Council, is that it, in fact, had betrayed Chalcedon by assuring the posthumous triumph of the one-sided views of Alexandrian Christology. Assumed by the divine hypostasis of the Logos, the humanity of Christ, according to these critics, would have been deprived of an authentically human character. "In Alexandrian Christology," writes Marcel Richard, "there will never be any place for a true psychology of Christ, for a real cult of the Savior's humanity, even if the assumption by the Word of a human soul is expressively recognized." [10] And Charles Moeller also maintains: "The tendency of the East to see Christ more and more as God (a tendency which is so marked in its liturgy) betrays a certain exclusivism which will increase after the schism." [11] This "neo-Chalcedonism" of the Byzantines is thus opposed to true Chalcedonian Christology and branded as a crypto-Monophysitism; it consists essentially in an understanding of the hypostatic union which would so modify the human properties of Jesus that He would no longer be fully man.[12]

It is undoubtedly true that Byzantine theology and spirituality are very conscious of the uniqueness of the personality of Jesus and are reluctant to investigate His human "psychology." A balanced judgment on this subject, however, can be attained only if one keeps in mind, not only the doctrine of the hypostatic union, but also the prevailing Eastern view of what "natural" man is. For, in Jesus, the new Adam, "natural" humanity has been restored. As we have seen, "natural" man was considered as participating in the glory of God. Such a man, undoubtedly, would no longer be fully subject to the laws of "fallen" psychology. These laws, however, were not simply denied in Jesus, but seen in the light of soteriology.

The full dimension of the problem was never directly discussed by Byzantine theologians, but there are indications which can help us to understand their position: (*a*) their interpretation of such passages as Luke 2:52 ("He progressed in age and wisdom"); (*b*) their attitude toward the heresy of Aphthartodocetism; and (*c*) the stand of the Orthodox defenders of the images against the iconoclasts.

(*a*) The idea of "progress in wisdom" implies a degree of ignorance in Jesus, which is confirmed by other well-known passages of the Gospels (Mk 13:32, for example). Byzantine thought on this subject may often have been confused by the Evagrian idea that "essential knowledge" is the very characteristic of humanity before the Fall. Evagrius also thought that Jesus was precisely a created "intellect" which has preserved this original "knowledge." The search for *gnosis* was indeed conceived, in the Evagrian spiritual tradition, which remained alive in the Christian East, as the very content of spiritual life. This may have contributed to the fact that a majority of Byzantine authors deny any "ignorance" in Jesus Himself. John of Damascus, for example, can write:

> One must know that the Word assumed *the ignorant and subjected nature,*
> [but,] thanks to the identity of the hypostasis and the indissoluble union,
> the Lord's soul was enriched with the knowledge of things to come and
> other divine signs; similarly, the flesh of human beings is not by nature
> life-giving, while the Lord's flesh, *without ceasing to be mortal by nature,*
> became life-giving, thanks to its hypostatic union with the Word.[13]

This text certainly represents a clear case of a representative Byzantine author's affirming that the hypostatic union—in virtue of the "communication of idioms"—modifies the character of human nature. But this modification is clearly seen in the framework of a dynamic and soteriological Christology; the humanity of Christ is "paschal," in the sense that in it man *passes* from death to life, from ignorance to knowledge, and from sin to righteousness. However, in many less-justifiable cases, the ignorance of Jesus, as described in the Gospel texts, is simply interpreted as a pedagogical device or "appearance" on the part of Christ to show His "condescension." This obviously unsatisfactory solution is rejected by other authors who affirm Christ's real, human ignorance. "Most Fathers admitted," writes the anonymous author of the *De sectis,* "that Christ was ignorant of certain things; since He is in all things consubstantial with us, and since we ourselves are ignorant of certain things, it is clear that Christ also suffered ignorance. Scripture says about Christ: 'He progressed in age and wisdom' [Lk 2:52]; this means that 'He was learning what He did not previously know." [14] Obviously, Byzantine theologians are authentically concerned about recognizing in Christ *our fallen humanity,* but their minds are less clear about the moment when, in Jesus, this humanity became the transfigured, perfect, and "natural" humanity of the New Man.

(*b*) The heresy of the *Aphthartodocetae,* whose leader was the sixth-century theologian Julian of Halicarnassus, conceived Christ's humanity as incorruptible, and they were accused of a docetic understanding of the Incarnation. As R. Draguet has shown, the issue was not so much the connection between hypostatic union and corruptibility, but the very nature of man. Is man *naturally* corruptible (as he is naturally ignorant), or did corruptibility come with sin? The *Aphthartodocetae* denied that man by nature was corruptible. Since Christ is the New Adam and the truly "natural" man, His humanity was indeed incorruptible. In rejecting Aphthartodocetism, the Orthodox affirmed (1) that the inheritance of mortality from Adam was not an inheritance of guilt, and (2) that the Logos voluntarily assumed, not an abstract ideal manhood, but our fallen humanity, with all the consequences of sin, including corruptibility. Opposition to Aphthartodocetism certainly contributed to preserving a clearer notion of Christ's real and full human nature.

(c) Iconoclasm was certainly another way of denying that Christ is man in a concrete and individual manner. Patriarch Nicephorus, one of the leading Orthodox polemicists, called it *Agraptodocetism* because iconoclasts considered Jesus as "undescribable." [15] In order to justify the possibility of painting an image of Christ, John of Damascus, and even more explicitly Theodore the Studite, insisted upon His individual human characteristics: "An indescribable Christ," writes Theodore, "would also be an incorporeal Christ; but Isaiah [8:3] describes this as a male being, and only the forms of the body can make man and woman distinct from one another." [16] Nicephorus, in order to defend the use of images, stresses very forcibly the human limitations of Jesus, His experience of tiredness, hunger, thirst:[17] "He acted, desired, was ignorant, and suffered as man." [18] This means that He was man like all of us, and can be represented on an image.

As interpreted by the Orthodox theologians of the eighth and ninth centuries who struggled against iconoclasm, the icon of Christ becomes a confession of faith in the Incarnation:

> The Inconceivable is conceived in the womb of a Virgin [writes Theodore the Studite]; the Unmeasurable becomes three cubits high, the Unqualifiable acquires a quality; the Undefinable stands up, sits down, and lies down; He who is everywhere is put into a crib; He who is above time gradually reaches the age of twelve; He who is formless appears with the shape of a man, and the Incorporeal enters into a body. . . . Therefore, He is describable and indescribable.[19]

For Theodore the icon of Christ is the best possible illustration of what is meant by the hypostatic union. What appears on the image is the very hypostasis of God the Word in the flesh. In the Byzantine tradition the inscription around the halo surrounding the head of Jesus says "The One who is," the equivalent of the sacred name YHWE, the name of God, whose person is revealed, but whose essence is inaccessible. It is neither God's indescribable divinity nor His human nature alone which is represented on an icon, but the person of God the Son who took flesh: "Every portrait," writes Theodore, "is the portrait of an hypostasis, and not of a nature." [20]

To paint an image of the divine essence or of God before His incarnation is obviously impossible; just as it is impossible to represent human nature as such, other than symbolically. Thus, symbolic images of Old Testament theophanies are not yet "icons" in a true sense. But the icon of Christ is different. With bodily eyes, the hypostasis of the Logos could be seen in the flesh, although its divine essence remained hidden; it is this mystery of the Incarnation which makes possible the sacred icons and requires their veneration.

The defense of images forced Byzantine thought to reaffirm the full concrete humanity of Christ. If an additional doctrinal stand against Monophysitism was necessary, it was taken by the Byzantine Church in the eighth and ninth centuries. But it is important to recognize that this stand was made neither at the expense of the doctrine of the hypostatic union nor at that of the Cyrillian understanding of the hypostatic identity of the incarnate Logos, but in the light of the former Christological formulations. The victory over iconoclasm was a reaffirmation of Chalcedonian and post-Chalcedonian Christology.

2. REDEMPTION AND DEIFICATION

The Chalcedonian definition proclaimed that Christ is consubstantial, not only with His Father, but also "with us." Though fully man, Christ does not possess a human hypostasis, for the hypostasis of His two natures is the divine hypostasis of the Logos. Each human individual, fully "consubstantial" with his fellow men, is, nonetheless, radically *distinct* from them in his unique, unrepeatable, and unassimilable personality or hypostasis: no man can fully be *in* another man. But Jesus' hypostasis has a fundamental affinity with all human personalities: that of being their *model*. For indeed all men are created according to the image of God, i.e., according to the image of the Logos. When the Logos became incarnate, the divine stamp matched all its imprints: God assumed humanity in a way which did not exclude any human hypostasis, but which opened to all of them the possibility of restoring their unity in Himself. He became, indeed, the "new Adam," in whom every man finds his own nature realized perfectly and fully, without the limitations which would have been inevitable if Jesus were only a human personality.

It is this concept of Christ which Maximus the Confessor had in mind when he re-emphasized the old Pauline image of "recapitulation" in reference to the incarnate Logos,[21] and saw in Him the victory over the disintegrating separations in humanity. As man, Christ "accomplishes in all truth the true human destiny that He Himself had predetermined as God, and from which man had turned: He unites man to God." [22] Thus Chalcedonian and post-Chalcedonian Christology would be meaningless speculation were it not oriented toward the notion of redemption. "The whole history of christological dogma was determined by this basic idea: the Incarnation of the Word, as Salvation." [23]

Byzantine theology did not produce any significant elaboration of the Pauline doctrine of justification expressed in Romans and Galatians. The Greek patristic commentaries on such passages as Galatians 3:13 ("Christ redeemed us from the curse of the Law, having become a curse for us") generally interpret the idea of redemption by substitution in the wider context of victory over death and of sanctification. They never develop the idea in the direction of an Anselmian theory of "satisfaction." The voluntary assumption of human mortality by the Logos was an act of God's "condescension" by which He united to Himself the whole of humanity; for, as Gregory of Nazianzus wrote, "what is not assumed is not healed, and what is united to God is saved";[24] therefore, "we needed a God made flesh and put to death in order that we could live again." [25]

The death of "One of the Holy Trinity in the flesh" was a voluntary act, a voluntary assumption by God of the entire dimension of human tragedy. "There is nothing in Him by compulsion or necessity; everything is free: willingly He was hungry, willingly thirsty, willingly He was frightened, and willingly He died." [26] But—and this is the essential difference between the Orthodox and the *Aphthartodocetae*—this *divine* freedom of the hypostasis of the Logos did not limit the reality of His human condition: the Lord assumed a *mortal* humanity at the very moment of the Incarnation, at which time the free divine decision to die had already been made. "He takes a body, a body which is not different from ours," writes Athanasius; "He takes from us a nature similar to ours and, since we all are subject to corruption and death, He delivers His body to death for us." [27]

The idea that the cross was the purpose of the Incarnation itself is vividly suggested by the Byzantine liturgical texts of the Nativity. The hymnology of the pre-feast (December 20 to 24) is structured according to that of Holy Week, and the humility of Bethlehem is viewed as leading toward Golgotha: "The kings, first fruits of the Gentiles, bring Thee gifts. . . . By myrrh they point to Thy death. . . ." "Born now in the flesh, Thou shalt in the flesh undergo burial and death, and Thou shalt rise again on the third day." [28]

The question whether the Incarnation would have taken place, had there not been a Fall, never stood at the center of attention in Byzantium: Byzantine theologians envisaged rather the concrete fact of human mortality: a cosmic tragedy in which God through the Incarnation undertook to become personally—rather, *hypostatically*—involved. The major, and, apparently, the only, exception to this general view is given by Maximus the Confessor, for whom the Incarnation and "recapitulation" of all things in Christ is the true "goal" and "aim" of creation; the Incarnation, therefore, was foreseen and foreordained independently of man's tragic misuse of his own freedom.[29] This view fits in exactly with Maximus' idea of created "nature" as a dynamic process oriented toward an eschatological goal—Christ the incarnate Logos. As creator, the Logos stands as the "beginning" of creation, and as incarnate, He is also its "end" when all things will exist not only "through Him," but "in Him." In order to be "in Christ," creation had to be assumed by God, made "His own"; the Incarnation, therefore, is a precondition of the final glorification of man independent of man's sinfulness and corruption.

Given the fallen state of man, the redemptive death of Christ makes this final restoration possible. But the death of Christ is truly redemptive and "life-giving" precisely because it is the death of the Son of God in the flesh (i.e., in virtue of the hypostatic union). In the East, the cross is envisaged not so much as the punishment of the just one, which "satisfies" a transcendent Justice requiring a retribution for man's sins. As Georges Florovsky rightly puts it: "the death of the Cross was effective, not as a death of an Innocent One, but as the death of the Incarnate Lord." [30] The point was not to satisfy a legal requirement, but to vanquish the frightful cosmic reality of death, which held humanity under its usurped control and pushed it into the vicious circle of sin and corruption. And, as Athanasius of Alexandria has shown in his polemics against Arianism, God alone is able to vanquish death, because He "alone has immortality" (1 Tm 6:16). Just as original sin did not consist in an inherited guilt, so redemption was not primarily a justification, but a victory over death. Byzantine liturgy, following Gregory of Nyssa, uses the image of the devil swallowing a hook, hidden by the body of Emmanuel; the same idea is found in a pseudo-Chrysostomic sermon, read during the liturgy of the paschal night: "Hell received a body, and encountered God; it received mortal dust, and met Heaven face to face."

Summarizing this patristic concept of death and resurrection, in the light of the Christological statements of the fifth and sixth centuries, John of Damascus writes:

> Although Christ died as man, and His holy soul was separated from His most pure body, His divinity remained with both the soul and the body, and continued inseparable from either. Thus the one hypostasis was not divided into two hypostases, for from the beginning both body and soul existed in the hypostasis of the Word. Although at the hour of death body and soul were separated from each other, yet each of them was preserved, having the one hypostasis of the Word. Therefore, the one hypostasis of the Word was an hypostasis as of the Word; so also of the body and of the soul. For neither the body nor the soul ever had any proper hypostasis other than that of the Word. The hypostasis, then, of the Word is ever one, and there were never two hypostases of the Word. Accordingly, the hypostasis of Christ is ever one. And though the soul is separated from the body in space, yet they remain hypostatically united through the Word.[31]

The triduum of Easter—the three days when Christ's humanity suffered the common fate of man, yet remained mysteriously en-hypostasized in the one divine hypostasis of the Logos—is graphically expressed in the traditional Byzantine iconography of the Resurrection: Christ trampling down the gates of Sheol and lifting Adam and Eve back to life. Better than any conceptual language, and better also than the image of any particular event or aspect of the mystery—such as the empty tomb, or even the crucifixion itself—this icon points to the dynamic, soteriological dimension of Christ's death: God's intrusion into the domain usurped by the devil and the breaking up of his control over humanity. The same mystery of hypostatic unity, which remained unbroken in death itself, is expressed in the Byzantine liturgy of Holy Week; on Good Friday, at vespers, at the very moment when Christ gave up the spirit, the first hymns of the Resurrection are beginning to resound: "Myrrh is fitting for the dead, but Christ has shown Himself free from corruption." The hidden, yet decisive, triumph over death permeates the liturgical celebration of Holy Saturday: "Though the temple of Thy body was destroyed in the hour of the passion, yet even then one was the hypostasis of Thy Divinity and Thy flesh." [32] One discovers in these texts the ultimate, soteriological reason why Cyril's theopaschite formula became a criterion of orthodoxy in sixth-century Byzantine theology: death was vanquished precisely because God Himself had tasted of it hypostatically in the humanity which He had assumed. This is the paschal message of Christianity.

In connection with our discussion of the Greek patristic view of original sin as inherited mortality, we mentioned the concomitant understanding of the Resurrection as the foundation of Christian ethics and spirituality. For the Resurrection of Christ means indeed that death has ceased to be the controlling element of man's existence and that, therefore, man is also free from slavery to sin. Death certainly remains as a physical phenomenon, but it does not *dominate* man as an unavoidable and ultimate fate: "As in Adam all die, so also in Christ shall all be made alive" (1 Co 15:22). And Athanasius writes: "Henceforth we are dissolved for a time only, according to our bodies' mortal nature, in order the better to receive resurrection; like seeds cast into the earth, we do not perish, but sown in the earth we shall rise again, since death has been brought to nought by the grace of the Savior." [33] And Chrysostom: "It is true, we still die as before, but we do not remain in death; and this is not to die. The power and the very reality of death are just this, that a dead man has no possibility of returning to life. But if after death he is to be quickened and, moreover, to be given a better life, then this is no longer death, but a falling asleep." [34] Since death has ceased to be the only possible end of existence, man is free from fear, and sin, based on the instinct of self-preservation, is no longer unavoidable. The vicious circle was broken on Easter Sunday and is broken each time "the death of Christ is announced and His resurrection is confessed."

But what does "being in Christ" mean concretely? The last quotation—from the Byzantine Eucharistic canon of St. Basil—suggests the answer: through baptism, chrismation, and the Eucharist, man freely becomes a member of the risen Body of Christ.

This element of *freedom*—and even of "consciousness"—is essential to the doctrine of salvation as understood by the Byzantine patristic, sacramental, and liturgical tradition. On the one hand, there are emphatic affirmations of the universality of redemption. Gregory of Nyssa, for example, assures us that

> As the principle of death took its rise in one person and passed on in succession through the whole of the human nature, so the principle of the Resurrection extends from one person to the whole of humanity. . . . This is the mystery of God's plan with regard to His death and His resurrection from the dead,[35]

and his thoughts on the universality of redemption and "recapitulation" are echoed by Maximus the Confessor. On the other hand, the new life in Christ implies personal and free commitment. On the last day the Resurrection will indeed be universal, but blessedness will be given only to those who longed for it. Nicholas Cabasilas tells us that baptismal "resurrection of nature" is a free gift from God, given even to children who do not express consent; but "the Kingdom, the contemplation of God, and common life with Christ belong to free will." [36]

Byzantine theologians seldom devote much explicit attention to speculation about the exact fate of souls after death. The fact that the Logos assumed human nature as such implied the universal validity of redemption, but not the *apokatastasis,* or universal salvation, a doctrine which in 553 was formally condemned as Origenistic. Freedom must remain an inalienable element of every man, and no one is to be forced into the Kingdom of God against his own free choice; the *apokatastasis* had to be rejected precisely because it presupposes an ultimate limitation of human freedom—the freedom to remain outside of God.

But by rejecting God, human freedom, in fact, destroys itself. Outside of God, man ceases to be authentically and fully human. He is enslaved to the devil through death. This idea, which is central to Maximian thought and which made him profess so strongly the existence of a human, created will in Christ, serves as the basis of the Byzantine understanding of the destiny of man: participation in God, or "deification" (*theōsis*), as the goal of human existence.

En-hypostasized in the Logos, Christ's humanity, in virtue of the "communication of idioms," is penetrated with divine "energy." It is, therefore, a *deified* humanity, which, however, does not in any way lose its human characteristics. Quite to the contrary. These characteristics become even more real and authentic by contact with the divine model according to which they were created. In this deified humanity of Christ's, man is called to participate, and to share in its deification. This is the meaning of sacramental life and the basis of Christian spirituality. The Christian is called not to an "imitation" of Jesus—a purely extrinsic and moral act— but, as Nicholas Cabasilas puts it, to "life *in* Christ" through baptism, chrismation, and the Eucharist.

Deification is described by Maximus as a participation of the "whole man" in the "whole God":

> In the same way in which the soul and the body are united, God should become accessible for participation by the soul and, through the soul's intermediary, by the body, in order that the soul might receive an unchanging character, and the body, immortality; and finally that the whole man should become God, deified by the grace of God-become-man, becoming whole man, soul and body, by nature, and becoming whole God, soul and body, by grace.[37]

"Thus for Maximus the doctrinal basis of man's deification is clearly to be found in hypostatic unity between the divine and the human nature in Christ." [38] The man Jesus is God hypostatically, and, therefore, in Him there is a "communication" (*perichōrēsis—circumincessio*) of the "energies" divine and human. This "communication" also reaches those who are "in Christ." But they, of course, are human hypostases, and are united to God not hypostatically but only "by grace" or "by energy." "A man who becomes obedient to God in all things hears God saying: 'I said: you are gods' [Jn 10:34]; he then is God and is called 'God' not by nature or by relation but by [divine] decree and grace." [39] It is not through his own activity or "energy" that man can be deified—this would be Pelagianism—but by divine "energy," to which his human activity is "obedient"; between the two there is a "synergy," of which the relation of the two energies in Christ is the ontological basis. But there is no confusion of natures, just as there cannot be any participation in divine essence by man. This is the theology of deification which we will also find in Gregory Palamas: "God in His completeness deifies those who are worthy of this, by uniting Himself with them, not hypostatically—that belonged to Christ alone—nor essentially, but through a small part of the uncreated *energies* and the uncreated divinity . . . while yet being entirely present in each." [40] Actually, the Byzantine Council of 1351, which confirmed the theology of Palamas, defined it as a "development" of the decrees of the Sixth Ecumenical Council (680) on the two wills or "energies" of Christ.[41]

In "deification," man achieves the supreme goal for which he was created. This goal, already realized in Christ by a unilateral action of God's love, represents both the meaning of human history and a judgment over man. It is open to man's response and free effort.

3. THE THEOTOKOS

The only doctrinal definition on Mary to which the Byzantine Church was formally committed is the decree of the Council of Ephesus which called her the *Theotokos,* or "Mother of God." Obviously Christological, and not Mariological, the decree nevertheless corresponds to the Mariological theme of the "New Eve," which has appeared in Christian theological literature since the second century and which testifies, in the light of the Eastern view on the Adamic inheritance, to a concept of human freedom more optimistic than that which prevailed in the West.

But it is the theology of Cyril of Alexandria, affirming the personal, hypostatic identity of Jesus with the pre-existent Logos, as it was endorsed in Ephesus, which served as the Christological basis for the tremendous development of piety centered on the person of Mary after the fifth century. God became our Savior by becoming man; but this "humanization" of God came about through Mary, who is thus inseparable from the person and work of her Son. Since in Jesus there is no human hypostasis, and since a mother can be mother only of "someone," not of something, Mary is indeed the mother of the incarnate Logos, the "Mother of God." And since the deification of man takes place "in Christ," she is also—in a sense just as real as man's participation "in Christ"—the mother of the whole body of the Church.

This closeness of Mary with Christ led to an increasing popularity, in the East, of those apocryphal traditions which reported her bodily glorification after her death. These traditions found a place in the hymnographical poetry of the Feast of the Dormition (*Koimesis,* August 15), but were never the object of theological speculation or doctrinal definition. The tradition of Mary's bodily "assumption" was treated by poets and preachers as an eschatological sign, a follow-up of the resurrection of Christ, an anticipation of the general resurrection. The texts speak very explicitly of the Virgin's natural death, excluding any possible connection with a doctrine of Immaculate Conception, which would attribute immortality to her and which would be totally incomprehensible in the light of the Eastern view of original sin as inherited mortality.[42] Thus, the boundless expressions of Marian piety and devotion in the Byzantine liturgy are nothing other than an illustration of the doctrine of hypostatic union in Christ of divinity and humanity. In a sense, they represent a legitimate and organic way of placing the somewhat abstract concepts of fifth- and sixth-century Christology on the level of the simple faithful.

NOTES

1. Dec. 24, Vespers; *The Festal Menaion,* trans. Mother Mary and K. Ware (London: Faber, 1969), p. 254.

2. Dec. 25, Matins; *Ibid.,* p. 269.

3. Holy and Great Friday, Vespers.

4. Aug. 6, Transfiguration, Vespers; *Festal Menaion,* pp. 476–477.

5. Council of Constantinople, 680; Denz. 291.

6. Maximus the Confessor, *Expos. orat. domin.*; PG 90:877D.

7. John of Damascus, *De fide orth.,* III, 15; PG 94:1057BC.

8. Denz. 222; Anathema 10 of Council of 553.

9. Leontius of Jerusalem, *Adv. Nest.,* VIII, 9; PG 86:1768A.

10. Marcel Richard, "St. Athanase et la psychologie du Christ selon les Ariens," *Mel Sci Rel* 4 (1947), 54.

11. Charles Moeller, "Le chalcédonisme et le néo-chalcédonisme en Orient de 451 à la fin du VI° siècle," in Grillmeier–Bacht, I, 717.

12. See *ibid.,* pp. 715–716.

13. John of Damascus, *De fide orth.,* III, 21; PG 94:1084B–1085A.

14. Anonymous, *De sectis*; PG 86:1264A.

15. Patriarch Nicephorus, *Antirrh.,* I; PG 100:268A.

16. Theodore the Studite, *Antirrh.,* III; PG 99:409C.

17. Nicephorus, *Antirrh.,* I; PG 100:272B.

18. *Ibid.*; PG 100:328BD.

19. Theodore the Studite, *Antirrh.* III; PG 99:396B.

20. *Ibid.,* III; PG 99:405A.

21. See especially Maximus the Confessor, *Amb.*; PG 90:1308D, 1312A.

22. J. Meyendorff, *Christ,* p. 108.

23. Georges Florovsky, "The Lamb of God," *Scottish Journal of Theology* (March 1961), 16.

24. Gregory of Nazianzus, *Ep. 101 ad Cledonium*; PG 37:181C–184A.

25. Gregory of Nazianzus, *Hom. 45*; PG 36:661C.

26. John of Damascus, *De fide orth.,* IV, 1; PG 94:1101A.

27. Athanasius, *De incarn.,* 8; PG 25:109C.

28. Dec. 24, Compline, Canon, odes 5 and 6; *Festal Menaion,* pp. 206–207.

29. Maximus the Confessor, *Ad Thal.,* 60; PG 90:621AC.

30. Florovsky, "The Lamb of God," p. 24.

31. John of Damascus, *De fide orth.,* III, 27; PG 94:1097AB.

32. Holy Saturday, Matins, Canon, ode 6.

33. Athanasius, *De incarn.,* 21; PG 25:129D.

34. John Chrysostom, *In Haebr.,* hom. 17:2; PG 63:129.

35. Gregory of Nyssa, *Catechetical Oration,* 16; ed. J. H. Srawley (Cambridge: Harvard University Press, 1956), pp. 71–72.

36. Nicholas Cabasilas, *The Life in Christ,* II; PG 150:541C.

37. Maximus the Confessor, *Amb.,* PG 91:1088C.

38. Thunberg, *Microcosm and Mediator,* p. 457.

39. Maximus the Confessor, *Amb.*; PG 91:1237AB.

40. Gregory Palamas, *Against Akindynos,* V, 26; edd. A. Kontogiannes and V. Phanourgakes, in P. Khrestov, *Gregoriou tou Palama Syggrammata* III (Thessaloniki, 1970), p. 371.

41. Tome of 1351; PG 151:722B.

42. I do not imply here that the Western doctrine of the Immaculate Conception necessarily implies Mary's immortality, although some Roman Catholic theologians have suggested this implication (for example, M. Jugie, *l'Immaculée Conception dans l'Ecriture sainte et dans la Tradition orientale*, Bibliotheca Immaculatae Conceptionis, 3 [Rome, 1952]).

13

The Holy Spirit

THE EARLY CHRISTIAN UNDERSTANDING of creation and of man's ultimate destiny is inseparable from pneumatology; but the doctrine of the Holy Spirit in the New Testament and in the early Fathers cannot easily be reduced to a system of concepts. The fourth-century discussions on the divinity of the Spirit remained in a soteriological, existential context. Since the action of the Spirit gives life "in Christ," He cannot be a creature; He is indeed consubstantial with the Father and the Son. This argument was used both by Athanasius in his *Letters to Serapion* and by Basil in his famous treatise *On the Holy Spirit*. These two patristic writings remained, throughout the Byzantine period, the standard authorities in pneumatology. Except in the controversy around the *Filioque*—a debate about the nature of God rather than about the Spirit specifically—there was little conceptual development of pneumatology in the Byzantine Middle Ages. This does not mean, however, that the *experience* of the Spirit was not emphasized with greater strength than in the West, especially in hymnology, in sacramental theology, and in spiritual literature.

"As he who grasps one end of a chain pulls along with it the other end to himself, so he who draws the Spirit draws both the Son and the Father along with It," Basil writes.[1] This passage, quite representative of Cappadocian thought, implies first that all major acts of God are Trinitarian acts, and secondly that the particular role of the Spirit is to make the "first contact," which is then followed—existentially, but not chronologically—by a revelation of the Son and, through Him, of the Father. The personal being of the Spirit remains mysteriously hidden, even if He is active at every great step of divine activity: creation, redemption, ultimate fulfillment. His function is not to reveal Himself, but to reveal the Son "through whom all things were made" and who is also personally known in His humanity as Jesus Christ. "It is impossible to give a precise definition of the hypostasis of the Holy Spirit and we must simply resist errors concerning Him which come from various sides."[2] The personal existence of the Holy Spirit thus remains a mystery. It is a "kenotic" existence whose fulfillment consists in manifesting the kingship of the Logos in creation and in salvation history.

1. THE SPIRIT IN CREATION

For the Cappadocian Fathers, the Trinitarian interpretation of all the acts of God implies the participation of the Spirit in the act of creation. When Genesis mentions "the Spirit of God moving upon the face of the waters" (Gn 1:2), patristic tradition interprets the passage in the sense of a primeval maintenance of all things by the Spirit, which made possible the subsequent appearance of a created logical order through the Word of God. No chronological sequence is implied here, of course; and the action of the Spirit is part of the continuous creative action of God in the world: "The principle of all things is one," writes Basil, "which creates through the Son and perfects in the Spirit." [3]

Basil identifies this function of "perfecting" creation as "sanctification," and implies that not only man, but nature as a whole, is perfectly itself only when it is in communion with God and when it is "filled" with the Spirit. The "secular" is always imperfect, or rather it exists only as a fallen and defective state of creation. This is particularly true of man, whose nature consists precisely in his being "theocentric." He received this "theocentricity," which the Greek Fathers always understood as a real "participation" in the life of God, when he was created and when God "breathed into his nostrils the breath of life" (Gn 2:7). This "breath" of God's life, identified with the Holy Spirit on the basis of the Septuagint version, is what made man to be "God's image." "A being taken from the earth," writes Cyril of Alexandria, "could not be seen as an image of the Most High, if he had not received this [breath]." [4] Thus the "perfecting" action of the Spirit does not belong to the category of the "miraculous," but forms a part of the original and natural plan of God. It assumes, inspires, and vivifies everything which is still fundamentally good and beautiful, in spite of the Fall, and maintains in creation the first fruits of the eschatological transfiguration. In this sense, the Spirit is the very content of the Kingdom of God. Gregory of Nyssa reports the ancient variant for the text of the Lord's prayer, "Thy Kingdom come," in Luke 11:2, as "May Thy Holy Spirit come upon us and cleanse us." [5] And the Byzantine liturgical tradition maintains the same tradition when it starts every single office with an eschatological invocation of the Spirit, addressing Him as "Heavenly King."

The liturgical offices of Pentecost, though centered mainly on the role of the Spirit in redemption and salvation, also glorify the Spirit as "the One who rules all things, who is Lord of all, and who preserves creation from falling apart." [6] Popular Byzantine customs associated with Pentecost suggest that the outpouring of the Spirit is indeed an anticipation of cosmic transfiguration; the traditional decoration of churches with greens and flowers on that day reflects the experience of new creation. The same idea dominates the "Great Blessing of Water," celebrated with great solemnity on the Feast of the Epiphany (January 6). Water, the primeval cosmic element, is sanctified "by the power, effectual operation ["energy"], and descent of the Holy Spirit" (Great Litany of the Day). Since, after the Fall, the cosmic elements are controlled by the "prince of this world," the action of the Spirit must have a purifying function: "Thou didst hallow the streams of Jordan," says the priest, "in that Thou didst send down from heaven Thy Holy Spirit, and didst crush the heads of serpents which lurked there."

The full significance of this rite of exorcism becomes evident when one recalls that, in Biblical categories, water is a source of life for the entire cosmos, over which man is called to rule. Only through the Fall did nature become subject to Satan. But the Spirit liberates man from dependence upon nature. Instead of being a source of demonic power, nature receives "the grace of redemption, the blessing of Jordan," and becomes a "fountain of immortality, a gift of sanctification, a remission of sins, a healing of infirmities, a destruction of demons." [7] Instead of dominating man, nature becomes his servant, since he is the image of God. The original paradisaic relationship between God, man, and the cosmos is proclaimed again: the descent of the Spirit anticipates the ultimate fulfillment when God will be "all in all."

This anticipation, however, is not a magical operation occurring in the material universe. The universe does not change in its empirical existence. The change is seen only by the eyes of faith—i.e., because *man* has received in his heart the Spirit which cries: "Abba, Father" (Ga 4:6), he is able to experience, in the mystery of faith, the paradisaic reality of nature serving him and to recognize that this experience is not a subjective fancy, but one which reveals the ultimate truth about nature and creation as a whole. By the power of the Spirit, the true and natural relationship is restored between God, man, and creation.

2. THE SPIRIT AND MAN'S REDEMPTION

In the "economy" of salvation, the Son and the Spirit are inseparable: "When the Word dwelt upon the holy Virgin Mary," Athanasius writes, "the Spirit, together with the Word, entered her; in the Spirit, the Word fashioned a body for Himself, making it in conformity with Himself, in His will to bring all creation to the Father through Himself." [8] The main argument, in favor of the consubstantiality of the Spirit with the Son and the Father, used by Athanasius, by Cyril of Alexandria, and by the Cappadocian Fathers, is the unity of the creative and redemptive action of God, which is always Trinitarian: "The Father does all things by the Word in the Holy Spirit." [9]

But the essential difference between the action of the Logos and that of the Spirit is that the Logos, and not the Spirit, became man, and thus could be directly *seen* as the concrete person and hypostasis of Jesus Christ, while the personal existence of the Holy Spirit remained covered by divine incognoscibility. The Spirit, in His action, reveals not Himself but the Son; when He indwells in Mary, the Word is being conceived; when He reposes on the Son at the baptism in Jordan, He reveals the Father's good will toward the Son. This is the Biblical and theological basis of the very current notion, found in the Fathers, and in the liturgical texts, of the Spirit as image of the Son.[10] It is impossible to *see* the Spirit, but in Him one sees the Son, while the Son Himself is the image of the Father. In the context of a dynamic and soteriological thought, the static Hellenic concept of image reflects a living relationship between the divine persons, into which, through the incarnation of the Son, mankind is introduced.

We have already seen that, in Greek patristic and Byzantine thought, salvation is understood essentially in terms of *participation* in and *communion* with the deified humanity of the incarnate Logos, the New Adam. When the Fathers call the Spirit the "image of the Son," they imply that He is the main agent which makes this communion a reality. The Son has given us "the first fruits of the Spirit," writes Athanasius, "so that we may be transformed into sons of God, according to the image of the Son of God." [11] Thus, if it is through the Spirit that the Logos became man, it is also only through the Spirit that true life reaches all men. "What is the effect and the result of the sufferings and works and teaching of Christ?" asks Nicholas Cabasilas. "Considered in relation to ourselves, it is nothing other than the descent of the Holy Spirit upon the Church." [12]

The Spirit transforms the Christian community into the "Body of Christ." In Byzantine hymns for the day of Pentecost, the Spirit is sometimes called the "glory of Christ" granted to the disciples after the Ascension,[13] and at each Eucharist, the congregation after communion chants: "We have seen the true light; we have received the heavenly Spirit; we have found the true faith; we worship the undivided Trinity, for it has saved us." Pentecost, the birthday of the Church, is the moment when the true meaning of Christ's cross and Resurrection becomes manifest, when a new mankind enters back into divine fellowship, when a new knowledge is granted to "fishermen." This is the main theme of the feast of Pentecost in the Byzantine tradition, and, curiously, it matches the awareness of many modern students of Christian origins that full understanding of Christ's teaching is indeed a "post-Resurrection" experience of the early Church: "The Spirit, through His appearance in tongues of fire, firmly plants the memory of those man-saving words, which Christ told the

Apostles, having received them from the Father." [14] But the "knowledge" or "memory" granted by the Spirit is not an intellectual function; it implies an "illumination" of human life as a whole. The theme of "light," which, through Origen and Gregory of Nyssa, permitted the association of the Biblical theophanies with Greek Neoplatonic mysticism, also permeates the liturgical hymnography of Pentecost. "The Father is light, the Word is light, and the Holy Spirit is light, which was sent to the Apostles as tongues of fire, and through which the whole world is illumined and venerates the Holy Trinity" (solemn hymn, called *exaposteilarion*). For indeed, the Holy Spirit is the "glory" of Christ, which not only transfigures the body of the historical Jesus, as was the case at the Transfiguration, but glorifies as well His wider "Body," i.e., all those who believe in Him. In fact, a comparison of the Byzantine liturgical texts of Pentecost with those appointed for the Feast of the Transfiguration (August 6)—and it is always important to remember that, for the Byzantines, the liturgy was the highest expression of their faith and Christian experience—shows that the miracle of Pentecost was considered as an expanded form of the mystery of Tabor. On Mount Tabor the divine light was shown to a restricted circle of disciples, but at Pentecost Christ "by sending the Spirit, has shone forth as the light of the world," [15] because the Spirit "enlightens the disciples and has initiated them into the heavenly mysteries." [16]

Examples can be easily multiplied, which show that the Byzantine theological tradition is constantly aware that in the "economy" of creation and salvation the Son and the Spirit are accomplishing one single divine act—without, however, being subordinated to one another in their hypostatic or personal existence. The "head" of the new, redeemed humanity is, of course, Christ, but the Spirit is not only Christ's agent; He is, in the words of John of Damascus (which are paraphrased in the hymns of Pentecost), "Spirit of God, direct, ruling; the fountain of wisdom, life and holiness; God existing and addressed along with the Father and Son; uncreated, full, creative, all-ruling, all-effecting, all-powerful, of infinite power, Lord of all creation and not subject to any; deifying, not deified; filling, not filled; shared in, not sharing in; sanctifying, not sanctified." [17]

This personal "independence" of the Spirit is connected, as Vladimir Lossky points out, with the whole mystery of redemption, which is both a unification (or "recapitulation") of mankind in the one divine–human hypostasis of Christ, the new Adam, and a mysterious personal encounter between *each man* and God. The unification of human nature is a free divine gift, but the personal encounter depends upon human freedom: "Christ becomes the sole image appropriate to the common nature of humanity. The Holy Spirit grants to each person created in the image of God the possibility of fulfilling the likeness in the common nature. The one lends His hypostasis to the nature, the other gives His divinity to the persons." [18] There is, of course, one divinity and one divine action, or "energy," leading mankind to the one eschatological goal of deification; but the personal, hypostatic functions of the Son and of the Spirit are not identical. Divine grace and divine life are a single reality, but God is Trinity, and not an impersonal essence into which humanity would be called to merge. Thus, here, as we have seen above, Byzantine Christian tradition requires the distinction in God, between the One unapproachable Essence, the three hypostases, and the grace, or energy, through which God enters into communion with creatures.

The mystery of Pentecost is not an incarnation of the Spirit, but the bestowing of these gifts. The Spirit does not reveal His Person, as the Son does in Jesus, and does not en-hypostasize human nature as a whole; He communicates His uncreated grace to each human person, to each member of the Body of Christ. New humanity is realized in the hypostasis of the Son incarnate, but it receives only the *gifts* of the Spirit. The distinction between the Person of the Spirit and His gifts will receive great emphasis in Byzantine theology in connection with the theological controversies of the thirteenth and fourteenth centuries. Gregory of Cyprus and Gregory Palamas will insist, in different contexts, that at Pentecost the Apostles received the eternal gifts or "energies" of the Spirit, but that there was no new hypostatic union between the Spirit and humanity.[19]

Thus, the theology of the Holy Spirit implies a crucial polarity, which concerns the nature of the Christian faith itself. Pentecost saw the birth of the Church—a community, which will acquire structures, and will presuppose continuity and authority—and was an outpouring of spiritual gifts, *liberating* man from servitude, giving him freedom and personal experience of God. Byzantine Christianity will remain aware of an unavoidable tension between these two aspects of faith: faith as doctrinal continuity and authority, and faith as the personal experience of saints. It will generally understand that an exaggerated emphasis on one aspect or the other destroys the very meaning of the Christian Gospel. The Spirit gives a structure to the community of the Church and authenticates the ministries which possess the authority to preserve the structure, to lead, and to teach; but the same Spirit also maintains in the Church prophetic functions and reveals the whole truth to each member of Christ's body, if only he is able and worthy to "receive" it. The life of the Church, because it is created by the Spirit, cannot be reduced to either the "institution" or the "event," to either authority or freedom. It is a "new" community created by the Spirit in Christ, where true freedom is recovered in the spiritual communion of the Body of Christ.

3. THE SPIRIT AND THE CHURCH

In Byzantine liturgical language, the term *koinonia* ("communion") is the specific expression designating the presence of the Holy Spirit in the

Eucharistic community, and one of the key notions in Basil's treatise on the Holy Spirit.[20] This observation is important inasmuch as it emphasizes that the "communion" of the Father, the Son, and the Spirit, as divine Trinity, the "communion of the Holy Spirit" which introduces man into divine life, and the "communion" or "community" which is then created between men in Christ, not only are designated with the same term, but, ultimately, represent the same spiritual experience and reality. The Church is not simply a society of human beings, associated with each other by common beliefs and goals; it is a *koinonia* in God and with God. And if God Himself were not a Trinitarian *koinonia,* if He were not three Persons, the Church could never be an association of persons, irreducible to each other in their personal identity. Participation in divine life would be nothing more than a Neoplatonic or Buddhist integration into an impersonal "One."

The very specific "oneness" realized in the Eucharistic *koinonia,* is, *par excellence,* a gift of the Spirit.

One of the recurring themes in the Byzantine hymnography of Pentecost is a parallel drawn between the "confusion" of Babel and the "union" and "symphony" effected by the descent of the Spirit in tongues of fire: "When the Most High came down and confused the tongues, He divided the nations; but when He distributed the tongues of fire, He called all to unity. Therefore, with one voice, we glorify the all-holy Spirit." [21] The Spirit does not suppress the pluralism and variety of creation; nor, more particularly, does He exclude the truly personal experience of God, accessible to each man; He overcomes division, contradiction, and corruption. He Himself is the "symphony" of creation, which will be fully realized in the eschatological fulfillment. The Church's function is to render this fulfillment accessible by anticipation through its role of "sanctification," effected by the Spirit.

"Creation is sanctified," Basil writes, "and the Spirit is the Sanctifier. In the same manner, the angels, the archangels and all the supercelestial powers receive their sanctity from the Spirit. But the Spirit Himself possesses sanctity by nature. He does not receive it by grace, but essentially; hence, He is distinctively called Holy. Thus He is holy by nature, as the Father and the Son are holy by nature." [22] The mysterious, but overwhelming, role of the Spirit in the "economy" of salvation cannot be expressed fully other than by this suggestive tautology: the Holy Spirit "sanctifies," i.e., He creates a *koinonia* of man with God, and, hence, of men between themselves as a "community of saints." It is best expressed in the "anaphora of St. Basil," celebrated ten times each year in the Byzantine Church, at the most solemn moment of the epiclesis:

> We pray Thee and call upon Thee, O Holy of Holies, that, by the favor of
> Thy goodness, Thy Holy Spirit may come upon us and upon the gifts

now offered, to bless, to hallow, and to show this bread to be the precious Body of our Lord and God and Savior Jesus Christ, and this cup to be the precious Blood of our Lord and God and Savior Jesus Christ, shed for the life of the world, and [that the Spirit may] unite all of us to one another who become partakers of the one Bread and Cup in the communion [koinonia] of the Holy Spirit.

Each one individually having been baptized "in the death of Christ" and having received the "seal of the gift of the Holy Spirit" in the sacrament of chrismation, the faithful participate together in the mystery of the Eucharist. The existence of their *koinonia* is both a *condition* of the Eucharistic miracle—the Spirit is being invoked not only on the "gifts" but *"upon us* and upon the gifts"—and its consequence: the Spirit sanctifies the gifts so that the *koinonia* may become an always-renewed reality.

The role of the Spirit in transforming a community of sinners into the "Church of God" is distinct, but not essentially different, from His role in creation; for the "new Adam," being a "new creation," is also an anticipation of the universal transfiguration of the world, which is the ultimate intent and goal of God's creative activity. Byzantine liturgy and theology are always aware of the fact that "by the Holy Spirit, every living thing receives life," [23] and that, therefore, as the new temple of the Spirit, the Church is invested with a divine mission to the world. It does not receive the Spirit for its own sake, but in order to accomplish God's purpose in human history and in the whole cosmos. The parallelism as well as the difference between the "first" and the "new" creation is well expressed by Nicholas Cabasilas: "[God] does not create anew out of the same matter which He created in the beginning. Then He made use of the dust of the earth; today He calls upon His own body. He restores life to us, not by forming anew a vital principle which He formerly maintained in the natural order, but by shedding His blood in the hearts of communicants so that He may cause His own life to spring in them. Of old He breathed a breath of life; now He imparts to us His own Spirit." [24]

"New creation" implies mission to the world; hence the Church is always "apostolic," i.e., not only founded on the faith of those who saw the risen Lord, but assuming their function of "being sent" to announce and establish the Kingdom of God. And this mission receives its authenticity from the Spirit. The Byzantine hymns for Pentecost glorify Christ "who has made the fishermen most wise by sending down upon them the Holy Spirit, and through them did draw the world into His net." [25]

The Spirit has bestowed upon the Church its "apostolicity," since the day of Pentecost; and only through the Spirit can the Church preserve consistency and continuity with the original Christian Gospel. The various ministries, created by the Spirit in the Christian *koinonia,* and more particularly that of the episcopate, are meant to maintain and structure this continuity, thus assuring the purity and effectiveness of the Church's mission in the world.

4. THE SPIRIT AND MAN'S FREEDOM

We have seen in Chapter 11 that man was not understood, in the Greek patristic tradition, as an autonomous being; participation in divine life was seen as an integral part of his *nature*. But since man is created free, it is obvious that there cannot be, as in Western theology, any opposition between "grace" and freedom. Quite to the contrary. Man can be authentically free only "in God," when, through the Holy Spirit, he has been liberated from the determinism of created and fallen existence and has received the power to share in God's lordship over creation.

This approach to freedom has crucial implications for man's attitude toward the Church, as well as for his social and personal ethics. On the one hand, it presupposes that nowhere, except in the sacramental community of the Church, is it possible to achieve the truly liberating divine life. On the other hand, the whole approach to man's salvation remains based on a personal, responsible, and free experience of God. This paradox, irreducible to a rational scheme, corresponds to an essential element of pneumatology: the Spirit simultaneously guarantees the continuity and authenticity of the Church's sacramental institutions and bestows upon each human person a possibility of free divine experience and, therefore, a full responsibility for both personal salvation and corporate continuity of the Church in the divine truth. Between the corporate and the sacramental on the one hand, and the personal, on the other, there is, therefore, a necessary tension in the spiritual life of the Christian and in his ethical behavior. The Kingdom to come is already realized in the sacraments, but each individual Christian is called to grow into it, by exercising his own efforts and by using his own God-given freedom with the cooperation of the Spirit.

In the Byzantine tradition, there has never been any strong tendency to build systems of Christian ethics, and the Church has never been viewed as the source of authoritative and detailed statements on Christian behavior. Church authority was certainly often called upon to solve concrete cases, and its decisions were seen as authoritative criteria for future judgments; but the creative mainstream of Byzantine spirituality was a call to "perfection" and to "holiness," and not a propositional system of ethics. It is the mystical, eschatological, and, therefore, maximalistic character of this call to holiness which gives it its essential difference from the legalism of medieval Roman Catholicism, the puritanical moralism of other Western trends, and the relativism of modern "situation ethics." Whenever they searched for models of Christian behavior, Byzantine Christians looked rather at saints and "athletes of the faith," especially the monks. Monastic literature is the source *par excellence* for our own understanding of Byzantine spirituality, and it is dominated by a "quest" of the Spirit.

Especially associated with the tradition of Macarius, this quest is particularly evident in the flowery hymns of Symeon the New Theologian, addressed to the Holy Spirit:

> I give thanks to Thee for this, that Thou, divine Being above all things, makest Thyself a single spirit with me—without confusion, without change —and that Thou didst become all in all for me, ineffable nourishment, freely distributed, which falls from the lips of my soul, which flows abundantly from the source of my heart; the resplendent vesture which covers me and protects me and which destroys the demons; the purification which washes from me every stain through these holy and perpetual tears which Thy presence accords to those whom Thou visitest. I give thanks to Thee for Thy being which was revealed to me as the day without twilight, as the sun which does not set. O Thou who hast no place where Thou hidest Thyself, for Thou dost never shun us, never hast Thou disdained anyone; it is we, on the contrary, who hide ourselves, not wishing to go toward Thee.[26]

The conscious and personal experience of the Holy Spirit is, therefore, the supreme goal of Christian life in the Byzantine tradition, an experience which presupposes constant growth and ascent. This experience is not opposed to an essentially Christocentric understanding of the Gospel, for it itself is possible only "in Christ," i.e., through communion in the deified humanity of Jesus; nor is it contradictory to practical ethical requirements, for it remains impossible unless these requirements are fulfilled. But, obviously, such experience reflects a basically personalistic understanding of Christianity. To a degree larger than in the West, then, the Byzantine Church will see in the saint or in the mystic the guardian of the faith, and will trust him more than any permanent institution; and it will not develop legal or canonical guarantees for an independent Christian action in the world, hoping rather that, if they are needed, prophets will arise to preserve the identity of the Gospel; this hope will indeed be fulfilled in the irreducible non-conformity of monastic personalities and communities throughout Byzantine history.

Obviously, however, Byzantine Christianity will also be faced with temptations inherent in its personalistic outlook. Spiritualistic and dualistic sects will often prosper in the Byzantine, and post-Byzantine, world, side by side with Orthodox spirituality. Between the fourth and the fourteenth centuries, various forms of Messalianism—"the Pelagianism of the East" [27] —will promote an anti-social, non-sacramental, and dualistic interpretation of the monastic ideal. They will be followed by the Russian *Strigol'niki* and other sects. Their influence, under the form of an exaggerated anti-institutionalism, will always be felt inside the canonical boundaries of the Orthodox Church itself.

The Church, of course, has never admitted that spiritualistic individualism and "enthusiasm" be erected as an ecclesiological system, but maintained its sacramental structure and canonical discipline. Conscious of the fact that in the Kingdom of God there are no laws other than those of the Spirit, it has also remembered that the Kingdom, already accessible as a true and direct experience, has not yet come in strength, and remains hidden under the sacramental veils. In the present *aion*, structures, laws, canons, and institutions are unavoidable, as *means* toward a fuller realization of the Kingdom. In practice, the Byzantine world recognized that the Christian empire had a legitimate role to play in codifying practical Christian ethics and in supervising their application. The standard code of Christian behavior was the *Nomocanon,* a collection of Church rules and of state laws concerning religion. Even there, however, the basic personalism of Byzantine Christianity was preserved in the fact that a *person,* not an institution, was invested with direct responsibilities in the Christian world: the Christian emperor, "elect of God." Historically, the perpetuation of the empire in the East played a role in preventing the Byzantine Church from assuming the direct role of ruling society politically, and thus keeping more strictly to its function as a signpost of the Kingdom to come—a Kingdom fundamentally different from all political systems of this age.

Whatever the obvious ambiguity and the hypocrisy which, at times, was evident in the Byzantine state, it thus served as an historical framework for a tradition which maintained the *eschatological* character of Christianity. In general, whether in the lands of Islam, or in modern secular societies of Eastern Europe, the Orthodox settled for a ghetto life: the closed liturgical community, with its experience of the heavenly, served both as a refuge and as a school. It demonstrated a remarkable capacity for survival and also, as for example in nineteenth- and twentieth-century Russia, for influencing intellectual development. Its emphasis on the free experience of the Spirit, as the liberating goal of human life, may be even better appreciated among those who today are looking for alternatives to the over-institutionalized ecclesiasticism of Western Christianity.

NOTES

1. Letter 38, 4; PG 32:332c; trans. R. J. Deferrari (London: Heinemann, 1961), p. 211.
2. *Cat.* 16, 11; PG 33:932c.
3. *De Spir. S.,* 16, 38; PG 32:136B.
4. *In Joh.* XI, 10; PG 74:541c.

5. See R. Leaney, "The Lucan text of the Lord's Prayer (in Gregory of Nyssa)," *Novum Testamentum* 1 (1956), 103–111.

6. *Apodeipnon,* canon, ode 5.

7. Great Blessing of Water.

8. *Ad Serap.* 1, 31; PG 26:605A.

9. *Ibid.,* 1, 28; PG 26:596A.

10. See for example Basil, *De Spirit. S.,* 9, 23, PG 32:109B.

11. *On the Incarnation* and *Against the Arians,* 8; PG 26:997A.

12. *A Commentary on the Divine Liturgy,* 37, 3, SC 4 bis, p. 229; trans. J. M. Hussey and P. A. McNulty (London: SPCK, 1960), p. 90.

13. *Kathisma,* after the Polyeleon.

14. Canon 2, ode 8.

15. Canon 1, ode 1.

16. *Kathisma* 1.

17. *De fide orth.* I, 8; PG 94:821BC.

18. Lossky, *Mystical Theology,* pp. 166–167.

19. Cf. J. Meyendorff, *Gregory Palamas,* pp. 14–15, 231.

20. Boris Bobrinskoy, "Liturgie et ecclésiologie trinitaire de St. Basile," *Etudes patristiques: le traité sur le Saint-Esprit de Saint Basile,* Foi et Constitution, 1969, pp. 89–90; also in *Verbum Caro,* 23, No. 88.

21. *Kontakion* of Pentecost.

22. Letter 159, 2; PG 32:621AB; ed. Deferrari, p. 396.

23. Sunday Matins, Antiphon, tone 4.

24. *On the Life in Christ,* IV; PG 150:617B.

25. *Troparion.*

26. PG 120:509BC.

27. I. Hausherr, "L'erreur fondamentale et la logique du messalianisme," *OCP* 1 (1955), 328–360.

The Triune God

"When I say *God,* I mean Father, Son, and Holy Spirit," writes Gregory of Nazianzus.[1] Far from being a form of abstract speculation, the doctrine of the Trinity was always, for the Greek patristic tradition, a matter of religious experience—liturgical, mystical, and, often, poetical:

> No sooner do I conceive of the one than I am illumined by the splendor of the three; no sooner do I distinguish them than I am carried back to the one. When I think of any one of the three, I think of Him as the whole, and my eyes are filled, and the greater part of what I am thinking escapes me.[2]

The basis of this Trinitarian theology, which was formulated by the Cappadocian Fathers in the fourth century at the conclusion of the Arian controversies, and which remained standard throughout the Byzantine period, is found in soteriology: the Fathers were actually preoccupied, not with speculation, but with man's salvation. The Nicaean doctrine of consubstantiality meant "the confession of the fullness of divinity in Christ and implied that the Incarnation was essential to the redemptive act of Christ"; and maintained, similarly, that if "the Spirit is not fully God, He is unable to bestow sanctification."[3] In itself, the Cappadocian doctrine of the Trinity remains totally meaningless unless one remember that its goal is to maintain the Christological and pneumatological presuppositions developed in the last two chapters: the incarnate Logos and the Holy Spirit are met and experienced first as *divine agents of salvation,* and only then are they also discovered to be essentially one God. It is well known that, during the theological debates of the fourth century, the Cappadocian Fathers were accused of tritheism, so that Gregory of Nyssa was even obliged to issue his famous apologetic treatise proving that "there are not three gods."[4] It remains debatable, however, whether he succeeded in proving his point *philosophically.* The doctrine of the three hypostases, adopted by the Cappadocian Fathers to designate the three divine Persons, had definite Plotinian and Origenistic associations, which normally implied *substantial* differentiation. The Fathers, however, remained faithful to the terminology they had adopted, in spite of all difficulties and criticism—both from the "old Nicaeans" faithful to Athanasius and from the theologians of the Latin West—because they saw no other means of preserving the Biblical experience of salvation in the fully identifiable and distinct persons of Christ and the Spirit, an experience which could never enter the categories of philosophical essentialism.

The Latin West adopted a different approach to Trinitarian theology, and the contrast has been well expressed by Théodore de Régnon: "Latin philosophy considers the nature in itself first and proceeds to the agent; Greek philosophy considers the agent first and passes through it to find the nature. The Latins think of personality as a mode of nature; the Greeks think of nature as the content of the person." [5] Practically speaking, the difference of emphasis means that in both the *lex orandi* and the *lex credendi* of Byzantine Christianity, the Trinity remained a primary and concrete experience; the unity of God's nature was an article of faith, coupled always with an insistence on the absolute unknowability of the divine essence. In the West, however, especially since the time of Augustine, the unity of the divine being served as the starting point of Trinitarian theology. Obviously, as long as the two schools of thought remained open to dialogue and mutual understanding, they could have developed in a complementary way. Unfortunately, the bitter polemics on the *Filioque* issue led to a stiffening of positions and became one of the major causes of the schism. The modern crisis of deism, the increasing difficulty faced by modern theologians in explaining and justifying the being of God as a philosophically definable entity, may prove helpful, not only in solving the medieval controversy between East and West, but also in the revival of a more authentic Trinitarianism. "It would seem that in our time," writes Théodore de Régnon, "the dogma of the divine unity had, as it were, absorbed the dogma of the Trinity of which one only speaks as a memory." [6] But the "dogma of the divine unity" is being challenged by that of the "death of God"; hence, there is a return to an existential and experiential approach to the doctrine of God, seen in the context of salvation history: "Without our experience of Father, Son, and Spirit in salvation history," writes Karl Rahner, "we would ultimately be unable to conceive at all of their subsisting distinctly as the one God." [7]

These modern concerns meet directly the consistent position of Byzantine theology.

1. UNITY AND TRINITY

The Cappadocian Fathers adopted the formulation which would remain the criterion of Orthodox Trinitarian theology in the East: God is one essence in three hypostases. This Cappadocian settlement, given the circumstances of the fourth century, never pretended to be anything more than the best possible *description* of the divine mystery, not the solution of a philosophical process, similar to the Plotinian "Trinity of hypostases." The Fathers always affirmed that we cannot know *what* God is, only *that He is,* because He has revealed Himself—in salvation history—as Father, Son, and Spirit. God is Trinity, "and this fact can be deduced from no principle nor explained by any sufficient reason for there are neither principles nor causes anterior to the Trinity." [8]

Why then are *this* description and this terminology preferable to others? Mainly because all the options then available seemed inadequate from the start. The formula "one essence, three *prosopa,*" for example, was not able to exclude a modalistic Trinity, since the term *prosopon,* although commonly used to designate "person," could also mean "mask" or "appearance." The Cappadocian Fathers, meanwhile, wanted to affirm simultaneously that God is one object and three objects, that both His unity and His trinity are full realities. "When I speak of God," writes Gregory of Nazianzus, "you must be illumined at once by one flash of light and by three. Three in properties, in hypostases or Persons, if any prefer so to call them, for we will not quarrel about names so long as the syllables amount to the same meaning; but one in respect of the *ousia,* that is, the Godhead." [9]

There is no claim here for philosophical consistency, although an effort is made to use current philosophical terms. The ultimate meaning of the terms, however, is clearly different from their meaning in Greek philosophy, and their inadequacy is frankly recognized.

This is particularly true of hypostasis, a term crucial in Trinitarian theology, and in Christology. Neither in Aristotelianism nor in Neoplatonism was the term intended to designate a *person* in the Christian (and modern) sense, an *agent,* "possessing" his own nature and "acting" accordingly, a *unique subject,* whose absolute identity can in no way be duplicated. Against the "old Nicaeans," the Cappadocian Fathers wanted to emphasize that the Nicaean *homoousion* ("consubstantial") does not identify the Son with the Father on the personal level, but only on the level of the *ousia.* "Neither is the Son Father, for the Father is one, but He is what the Father is; nor is the Spirit Son because He is of God, for the Only-begotten is one, but He is what the Son is." [10] Thus, in God, the "what" is one, but the three hypostases are personal identities, irreducible to each other in their personal being. They "possess divinity" [11] and divinity is "in them." [12]

One recognizes the hypostatic character [of the Spirit] in that He is revealed after the Son and with the Son, and in that He receives His subsistence from the Father. And the Son, in Himself and with Himself re-

vealing the Spirit, who proceeds from the Father, shines alone with the unbegotten light and has nothing in common with the Father and the Spirit
in the identity of His particularities, but is revealed alone in the characters proper to His hypostasis. And the Father possesses the particular
hypostatic character of being the Father and of being independent from
all causality. . . .[13]

The same personalistic emphasis appears in the Greek Fathers' insistence
on the "monarchy" of the Father. Contrary to the concept which prevailed
in the post-Augustinian West and in Latin Scholasticism, Greek theology
attributes the *origin* of hypostatic "subsistence" to the *hypostasis* of the
Father—not to the common essence. The Father is the "cause" (*aitia*)
and the "principle" (*archē*) of the divine nature, which is in the Son and
in the Spirit. What is even more striking is the fact that this "monarchy"
of the Father is constantly used by the Cappadocian Fathers against those
who accuse them of "tritheism": "God is one," writes Basil, "because the
Father is one." [14] And the same thought is found in Gregory of Nazianzus:
"God is the common nature of the three, but the Father is their union
[*henōsis*]." [15] Pseudo-Dionysius also speaks of the Father as the "source
of Divinity," [16] and John of Damascus in his *Exact Exposition of the
Orthodox Faith* also affirms the essential dependence of the Son and the
Spirit upon the *Person* of the Father:

Whatsoever the Son has from the Father, the Spirit also has, including His
very being. And if the Father does not exist, then neither does the Son and
the Spirit; and if the Father does not have something, then neither has the
Son or the Spirit. Furthermore, because of the Father, that is, because of
the fact that the Father is, the Son and the Spirit are; and because of the
Father, the Son and the Spirit have everything that they have.[17]

By accepting Nicaea, the Cappadocian Fathers eliminated the ontological
subordinationism of Origen and Arius, but they preserved indeed, together
with their understanding of hypostatic life, a Biblical and Orthodox subordinationism, maintaining the personal identity of the Father as the ultimate origin of all divine being and action: "The three [are] one God
when contemplated together; each [is] God because [they are] consubstantial; the three [are] one God because of the monarchy [of the Fa-
ther]." [18] Developing his well-known doctrine of the divine image in man,
Gregory of Nyssa defines one aspect of human personal existence which is
clearly *different* from that of God: *each* human person possesses the power
of reproducing himself, while, in God, there is only "one and the same
Person of the Father from whom the Son is born and the Spirit proceeds." [19]
Thus, the human race is in a constant process of fragmentation, and can
recover its unity only through *adoption* by the Father in Christ—i.e., by
becoming children of the one single hypostasis which generates without

fragmenting, or multiplying. The origin of unity in the Trinity, the Father restores the unity of creation by adopting humanity in His Son, the New Adam, in whom humanity is "recapitulated" through the activity of the Spirit.

Not an abstract intellectual speculation, the doctrine of the Trinity stands at the very center of Byzantine religious experience: the immanent Trinity manifests itself as the "economic" Trinity, i.e., the saving revelation of God in history. This is made particularly clear in the liturgy, especially in the Eucharistic canon. As a solemn prayer to the Father by the adopted human community, united in the incarnate Son and invoking the Spirit, the Eucharist is indeed the sacrament of divine unity being bestowed upon men. The same Trinitarian reality is expressed in innumerable hymns, scattered throughout the Byzantine liturgical cycles. Here is a solemn hymn of Pentecost, attributed to the emperor-poet Leo VI (886–912), and constituting a variation on the famous *Trisagion*:

Come, O peoples, let us venerate the tri-hypostatic Deity,
The Son in the Father, with the Holy Spirit.
For before time the Father generated a Son, sharing His eternity and His
   Throne;
And the Holy Spirit was in the Father, glorified together with the Son.
One Power, One Essence, One Deity, whom we all venerate and say:
Holy God, who created all things through the Son, with the cooperation of
   the Holy Spirit;
Holy Mighty, through whom we knew the Father and the Holy Spirit
   dwelt in the world;
Holy Immortal, the Spirit Comforter, who proceeds from the Father and
   abides in the Son,
Holy Trinity, glory to Thee.[20]

In the classical Latin Trinitarian doctrine, "Father, Son, and Spirit are only 'relatively' distinct." [21] Whatever the interpretation given to the idea of "relation" implied in this statement, it is clear that Western thought recognized the ontological primacy of essential *unity* over personal diversity in God; that is, that God is essentially one, except in the divine *Persons,* who are defined in terms of *relations*. In Byzantine thought, however—to use an expression from Maximus the Confessor—"God is identically monad and triad," [22] and there is probably a tendency in both worship and philosophical formulations (as distinct from doctrinal statements) to give a certain pre-eminence to the personal diversity over essential unity. A reference to the Nicaean "consubstantial" was the Byzantine response to the accusation of "tritheism."

This reference, however, could not be decisive in itself, simply because Greek patristic thought, and particularly that of the Cappadocians, always presupposed the starting point of apophatic theology: that God's being and, consequently, the ultimate meaning of hypostatic relations were understood to be totally above comprehension, definition, or argument. The very notion of God's being both Unity and Trinity was a *revelation* illustrating this incomprehensibility; for no reality, accessible to the mind, could be both "one" and "three." As Vladimir Lossky puts it: "the Incomprehensible reveals Himself in the very fact of His being incomprehensible, for His incomprehensibility is rooted in the fact that God is not only Nature but also Three Persons." [23]

The knowledge of God is therefore possible only inasmuch as He reveals Himself, inasmuch as the immanent Trinity manifests itself in the "economy" of salvation, inasmuch as the transcendent *acts* on the immanent level. It is in the fundamental oneness of these "acts" or "energies" of God that the Greek Fathers, particularly Basil and Gregory of Nyssa, discover the decisive and existential sign of the unity of God's essence. Basil's well-known argument in favor of the divinity of the Spirit is that He has the same "energy" as the Father and the Son. Similarly, Gregory of Nyssa proves the essential unity of Father, Son, and Spirit from the unity of their operation.[24] This argument also fits into the context of the Cappadocians' polemics against Eunomius, who affirmed the possibility of knowing God's essence; no knowledge concerning God, they asserted, was possible, except from His "energies." The "economic" Trinity, revealed in God's action in the world, is, therefore, the only possible basis for affirming that God is indeed, paradoxically and incomprehensibly, a transcendent and immanent Trinity. Gregory of Nyssa's doctrine of the "energies" is well described by G. L. Prestige:

> In men . . . , in spite of the solidarity of the whole race, each individual acts separately, so that it is proper to regard them as many. This is not so . . . with God. The Father never acts independently of the Son, nor the Son of the Spirit. Divine action . . . always begins from the Father, proceeds through the Son, and is completed in the Holy Spirit; there is no such thing as a separate individual operation of any Person; the energy invariably passes through the three, though the effect is not three actions but one.[25]

In fact, the Aristotelian principle according to which each "nature" (*physis*) has an "energy" (*energeia*)—i.e., an existentially perceivable manifestation—provides the terminological background for the patristic concept of "energy." (We find this terminology used, as well, in Christology, where Maximus the Confessor, for example, will maintain that the two natures of Christ presuppose two "energies" or wills.) However, significantly, the Aristotelian dyad, nature–energy, was not considered sufficient in itself when applied to God, because in God's nature, the decisive *acting* factor is hypostatic; hence, divine "energy" is not only unique but tri-hypostatic, since the "energy" reflects the common life of the three Persons. The personal aspects of the divine subsistence do not disappear in the one "energy," and it is indeed the Trinitarian life of God which is communicated and participated in in the "energy": through the "energy," therefore, the divine hypostases appear in their co-inherence (*perichōrēsis*):[26] "I am in the Father and the Father in me" (Jn 14:11). Human persons, though also one in nature and substance, act disjointly and often in conflict with each other; in God, however, the *perichōrēsis* expresses the perfect love, and, therefore, the perfect unity of "energy," of the three hypostases, without, however, any mingling or coalescence. The "energy," because it is always Trinitarian, is always an expression and a communication of love: "As the Father has loved me, so I have loved you: abide in my love" (Jn 15:9).

It is probably in the context of the doctrine of the *perichōrēsis* that one should understand a unique passage in Palamas, where he seems inspired by the Augustinian "psychological" image of the Trinity.[27] Palamas writes: "This Spirit of the Word from on high is like the mysterious love of the Father toward the Word mysteriously begotten; it is that possessed by the Word, the beloved Son, toward the Father who begat Him; this the Son does insofar as He comes from the Father conjointly with this love, and this love rests naturally upon him." [28] Since the whole approach to the Trinity in Palamas is different from Augustine's, it is certainly the result of the personalistic interpretation, which can be given to the "psychological" image being used here to suggest the Trinitarian mystery: love unites the three divine hypostases, and pours out, through their common divine "energy" or "action," upon those worthy to receive it.

2. HYPOSTASIS, ESSENCE, AND ENERGY

The distinction—a *real* distinction—between divine "essence" and divine "energy" is made unavoidable in the context of the doctrine of "deification," which implies a "participation" of created man in the uncreated life of God, whose essence remains transcendent and totally unparticipable. All these aspects of the doctrine of God will, in fact, be faced simultaneously during the controversies between Gregory Palamas and his adversaries in the fourteenth century. His conclusion, necessarily, is that "three elements belong to God: essence, energy, and the triad of the divine hypostases." [29]

This triple distinction is rendered inescapable, as soon as one rejects the Augustinian option of Trinitarianism in favor of the Cappadocian. For, indeed, if the Persons are only relations internal to the essence, the revelation of God, if any, is a revelation either of the "essence" or of "analogous" created symbols; the "energies," then, are either the "essence" of God or created signs, and there is no real distinction *in God*. But if, on the contrary, the Persons are distinct from the essence, which is common to

them but transcendent and inaccessible to man, and if in Christ man meets
God "face to face," so that there is a real "participation" in divine existence,
this participated divine existence can only be a free gift from God, which
safeguards the inaccessible character of the essence and the transcendence
of God. This God-giving-Himself is the divine "energy"; a living and personal God is indeed an *acting* God.

We have seen that the doctrine of the "energies" in the Byzantine tradition is central both to the understanding of creation and to Christology.
Refusing to reduce the being of God to the philosophical concept of simple
"essence," Byzantine thought affirms the full and distinct reality of the
Triune hypostatic life of God *ad intra*, as well as His "multiplication" as
creator *ad extra*. These two "multiplicities" do not, however, coincide. The
terminology which the doctrine of energies received, in its relation to the
three hypostases, was stabilized in the Palamite synthesis of the fourteenth
century:

> The proper appellations of the divine hypostases are common to the
> energies; whereas appellations common to the hypostases are particular to
> each of the divine energies. Thus *life* is a common appellation of the Father,
> the Son and the Spirit, but *foreknowledge* is not called *life*, nor is *sim-
> plicity*, nor *unchangeableness*, nor any other energy. Thus each of the
> realities which we have enumerated belongs at the same time to the Father,
> the Son, and the Spirit; but they only belong to one energy, and not to all;
> each reality in fact has only one signification. Inversely, *Father* is the
> proper appellation of one sole hypostasis, but it is manifest in all the ener-
> gies. . . . And the same is true of the appellations Son and Spirit. . . .
> Thus since God in His wholeness is wholly incarnate, He has unchange-
> ably united to the whole of me . . . the divine nature and all its power
> and energy in one of the divine hypostases. Thus, also, through each of His
> energies one shares in the whole of God . . . the Father, the Son and the
> Holy Spirit. . . .[30]

The triple distinction—essence, hypostasis, energy—is not a division of
God's being; it reflects the mysterious life of the "One-who-is"—transcendent, tri-personal, and present to His creation.

The Palamite formulations of the fourteenth century were preceded by
theological developments which dealt with the same triple distinction. In
1156 and 1157, two local councils held in Constantinople debated the problem whether the sacrifice of Christ, in both its historical and its Eucharistic
dimensions, was offered to the Father alone, or to the Holy Trinity. Soterichos, a theologian, was condemned because he held that the acts of offering
and of receiving constituted the *hypostatic characteristics* of the Son and the
Father respectively, an opinion the councils considered to be a confusion
between the "immanent" and the "economic" Trinity, or between the hypostatic characteristics and "energies." And, indeed, the Byzantine liturgies of

Basil and of John Chrysostom include, at the offertory, a prayer addressed
to Christ: "For it is you who offer and are offered, who receive and are
yourself received." The mystery of the hypostatic life, as it is revealed in
the Incarnation and in the act of redemption, is also expressed in a Byzantine Easter *troparion* (repeated by the priest during the offertory, at the
Eucharist): "O Christ undescribable! You filled all things: bodily in the
grave, in Hades with your soul as God, in Paradise with the thief; you also
sat on the divine throne with the Father and the Spirit."

Therefore, even if the Father alone is the addressee of the Eucharistic
prayer, the act of "receiving" the sacrifice is a Trinitarian act, as are all the
divine acts *ad extra*.[31] The mystery of the Incarnation, however, consists
in the fact that the divine hypostasis of the Logos assumed *also* the role of
offering, bringing humanity with itself to the throne of the Father. The
Eucharistic sacrifice is precisely this offering, accomplished in the body of
Christ, where human nature is penetrated with divine energy, assumed as
it is by the hypostasis of the Logos.

The hypostatic, personal existence implies an "openness," which makes
it possible for the incarnate Logos to "offer" and to "receive," to be man
and God, and to remain, with the Father and the Spirit, the "actor" of
the "energies" characterizing divine nature.

3. THE LIVING GOD

"God, when He was speaking with Moses, did not say: 'I am the essence,'
but 'I am who am' [Ex 3:14]. It is therefore not He-who-is who comes from
the essence, but it is the essence which comes from He-who-is, for He-
who-is embraces in Himself all being." [32] When Palamas, in the passage
just quoted, explicitly refers to the Biblical doctrine of the living God, or
when he refuses to identify the being of God with the philosophical notion
of essence—"The essence is necessarily being, but being is not necessarily
essence" [33]—he expresses the very content of his quarrel with Barlaam and
Akindynos, but also maintains the *theologia* of the Cappadocian Fathers.

We have already noted that the conflict within Byzantine society which
set the monks against the "humanists" involved an understanding of man's
destiny based on the Bible as opposed to one based on Platonic spiritualism.
A similar problem developed on the level of "theology" proper, i.e., the
doctrine of God. The issue was complicated by the fact that Latin Scholasticism provided the Byzantine anti-Palamites with a truly "Greek" interpretation of the divine being, and they readily turned into *Latinophrones*.
For indeed the *real* significance of the *Filioque* quarrel consisted in the fact
that the two sides held to a different approach to God. The East refused
to identify God's being with the concept of "simple essence," while the
West admitted this identification on the basis of Greek philosophical presuppositions. The issue certainly could not be solved by collections of

scriptural and patristic "proof texts," even if agreement was obviously possible on the canonical level (unilateral interpolation of the universal creed by the Latins) and in the terminology (procession "from both" could be admitted by the Easterns on the level of the "economy"). The controversy was really concerned, as Vladimir Lossky puts it, with the fact that

> by the dogma of the *Filioque* the God of the philosophers and savants is introduced into the place of the Living God. . . . The Unknowable Essence of the Father, the Son, and the Holy Spirit receives positive qualifications. It becomes the subject of a Natural Theology, concerned with "God in general," who may be the God of Descartes, or the God of Leibniz, or even perhaps, to some extent, the God of Voltaire and the dechristianized Deists of the eighteenth century.[34]

This conclusion may appear to some as an overstatement. It is both characteristic and refreshing, however, that precisely those modern theologians of the West who are most concerned with making Christian theology again as kerygmatic and appealing as it was in another age are suggesting a return to the pre-Augustinian concepts of God, "where the three hypostases were seen first of all in their personal, irreducible functions." [35] "Without our experience of Father, Son, and Spirit in salvation history, we would ultimately be unable to conceive at all of their subsisting distinctly as the one God." [36]

NOTES

1. *Oratio* 45, 4; PG 36:628c.
2. *Oratio* 40, 41; PG 36:417BC.
3. Both quotations from Georges Florovsky, *Vostochnye Ottsy* (Paris: YMCA Press, 1931), p. 23.
4. The treatise is addressed *To Ablabius*, ed. F. Mueller (Leiden, 1958), pp. 37–57.
5. Théodore de Régnon, *Etudes de théologie positive sur la Sainte Trinité* (Paris, 1892), I, 433. See also G. L. Prestige, *God in Patristic Thought* (London: SPCK, 1952), pp. 233–241, and J. N. D. Kelly, *Early Christian Doctrines* (London: Black, 1958), pp. 253–279.
6. De Régnon, *Etudes*, I, 365.
7. Karl Rahner, *The Trinity*, trans. Joseph Donceel, s.j. (London: Burns & Oates, 1969), pp. 110–111.
8. Lossky, *Mystical Theology*, p. 47.
9. *Oratio* 39, 11; PG 36:345CD.
10. Gregory of Nazianzus, *Oratio*, 31, 9; PG 36:144A.
11. Gregory of Nazianzus, *Poem. Dogm.* 20,3; PG 37:414A.
12. Gregory of Nazianzus, *Oratio* 31, 41; PG 36:149A.
13. Basil, *Ep.* 38, 4; PG 32:329CD.
14. Basil, *Contra Sab.*, 3; PG 31:605A.
15. *Oratio* 42, 15; PG 36:476B.
16. Pseudo-Dionysius, *De div. nom.* 2, 7; PG 3:645B.

17. *De fide orthodoxa* 1, 8; PG 94:324B; trans. F. H. Chase, *Fathers of the Church* 37 (New York, 1958), p. 184.

18. Gregory of Nazianzus, *Oratio* 40, 41; PG 36:417B.

19. *Adv. Graecos*; PG 45:180.

20. *Pentekostarion* (Athens: Phos, 1960), p. 218.

21. K. Rahner, *op. cit.*, p. 68.

22. *Capita theol. et oecon.* II, 1; PG 90:1125A.

23. *Op. cit.*, p. 64.

24. See G. L. Prestige, *op. cit.*, pp. 257–260.

25. *Op. cit.*, p. 260.

26. The term was first used in Christology (see Prestige, *God in Patristic Thought,* pp. 291–299); it began to be applied to the hypostatic relations by pseudo-Cyril and by John of Damascus.

27. St. Augustine's *De Trinitate* had been translated into Greek by Maximus Planudes in the thirteenth century, and could have been known by Palamas.

28. *Cap. phys.* 36; PG 151:1144D–1145A.

29. *Cap. phys.* 75; PG 151:1173B.

30. *Against Akindynos*, V, 27; edd. Kontogiannes and Phanourgakes, pp. 373–374.

31. On the councils of 1156 and 1157, see J. Meyendorff, *Christ*, pp. 152–154.

32. Gregory Palamas, *Triads* III, 2, 12; ed J. Meyendorff, in *Spicilegium Sacrum Lovaniense*, 31 (Louvain, 1959); Palamas is paraphrasing Gregory of Nazianzus, *Oratio* 45, 3; PG 36:625c.

33. *Against Akindynos* III, 10; edd. Kontogiannes and Phanourgakes, p. 184.

34. "The procession of the Holy Spirit in the Orthodox Triadology" in *Eastern Churches Quarterly*. Supplemental issue *Concerning the Holy Spirit* (1948), p. 46. See also the debate on the *Filioque* between Orthodox (Bishop Cassian, Meyendorff, Verhovskoy, and others) and Roman Catholic (Camelot, Bouyer, Henry, Dubarle, Dondaine, and others) theologians published in *Russie et Chrétienté* (1950), No. 3–4.

35. Cf. J. Meyendorff, *Christ*, p. 166.

36. K. Rahner, *op. cit.*, p. 111.

Sacramental Theology:
The Cycle of Life

In his book on *The Life in Christ*—a commentary on baptism, confirmation, and communion—Nicholas Cabasilas writes: "It is possible for the saints in this present world, not only to be disposed and prepared for [eternal] life [in Christ], but also even now to live and act according to it." [1] The Kingdom of God, an anticipation of the eschatological fulfillment, is already accessible in the Body of Christ: this possibility of "being in Christ," of "participating" in divine life—the "natural" state of humanity—is, for the Byzantines, essentially manifested in the sacraments, or *mysteria,* of the Church. These sacraments are understood less as isolated acts through which a "particular" grace is bestowed upon individuals by properly appointed ministers acting with the proper intention, and more as the aspects of a unique mystery of the Church, in which God shares divine life with humanity, redeeming man from sin and death and bestowing upon him the glory of immortality.

1. NUMBER OF SACRAMENTS

Byzantine theology ignores the Western distinction between "sacraments" and "sacramentals," and never formally committed itself to any strict limitation of the number of sacraments. In the patristic period there was no technical term to designate "sacraments" as a specific category of church acts: the term *mysterion* was used primarily in the wider and general sense of "mystery of salvation," [2] and only in a subsidiary manner to designate the particular *actions* which bestow salvation. In this second sense, it was used concurrently with such terms as "rites" or "sanctifications." [3] Theodore the Studite in the ninth century gives a list of six sacraments: the holy "illumination" (baptism), the "synaxis" (Eucharist), the holy chrism, ordination, monastic tonsure, and the service of burial. [4] The doctrine of the "seven sacraments" appears for the first time—very characteristically—in the Profession of Faith required from Emperor Michael Paleologus by Pope Clement IV in 1267.[5] The Profession had been prepared, of course, by Latin theologians.

The obviously Western origin of this strict numbering of the sacraments did not prevent it from being widely accepted among Eastern Christians after the thirteenth century, even among those who fiercely rejected union with Rome. It seems that this acceptance resulted not so much from the influence of Latin theology as from the peculiarly medieval and Byzantine fascination with symbolic numbers: the number seven, in particular, evoked an association with the seven gifts of the Spirit in Isaiah 11:2–4. But among Byzantine authors who accept the "seven sacraments," we find different competing lists. The monk Job (thirteenth century), author of a dissertation on the sacraments, includes monastic tonsure in the list, as did Theodore the Studite, but combines as one sacrament penance and the anointing of the sick.[6] Symeon of Thessalonica (fifteenth century) also admits the sacramental character of the monastic tonsure, but classifies it together with penance,[7] considering the anointing as a separate sacrament. Meanwhile, Joasaph, Metropolitan of Ephesus, a contemporary of Symeon's, declares: "I believe that the sacraments of the Church are not seven, but more," and he gives a list of ten, which includes the consecration of a church, the funeral service, and the monastic tonsure.[8]

Obviously, the Byzantine Church never committed itself formally to any specific list; many authors accept the standard series of seven sacraments—baptism, confirmation, Eucharist, holy orders, matrimony, penance, and the anointing of the sick—while others give a longer list, and still others emphasize the exclusive and prominent importance of baptism and the Eucharist, the basic Christian initiation into "new life." Thus, Gregory Palamas proclaims that "in these two [sacraments], our whole salvation is rooted, since the entire economy of the God–man is recapitulated in them."[9] And Nicholas Cabasilas composes his famous book on *The Life in Christ* as a commentary on baptism, chrismation, and the Eucharist.

2. BAPTISM AND CHRISMATION

In the Eastern Church, baptism and confirmation (the latter being effected through anointment with "holy chrism" blessed by the bishop) are normally celebrated together. Immediately after receiving baptism and confirmation, the child is admitted to Eucharistic communion. There is, therefore, no practical difference between admitting a child or an adult to membership in the Church; in both cases, a human being who belonged to the "old Adam" through his natural birth is introduced to "new life" by partaking of baptism, chrismation, and holy communion. Christian initiation is one single and indivisible act: "If one does not receive the chrism one is not perfectly baptized," writes Symeon of Thessalonica.[10]

As we have seen, the patristic doctrine of salvation is based, not on the idea of guilt inherited from Adam and from which man is relieved in Christ, but on a more existential understanding of both "fallen" and "redeemed" humanity. From the "old Adam," through his natural birth, man inherits a defective form of life—bound by mortality, inevitably sinful, lacking fundamental freedom from the "prince of this world." The alternative to this "fallen" state is "life in Christ," which is true and "natural" human life, the gift of God bestowed in the mystery of the Church. "Baptism," writes Nicholas Cabasilas, "is nothing else but to be born according to Christ and to receive our very being and nature." [11]

The emphasis, in both the rite of baptism and the theological commentaries of the Byzantine period, is on the *positive* meaning of baptism as "new birth." "The salutary day of Baptism," Cabasilas continues, "becomes a name day to Christians, because then they are formed and shaped, and our shapeless and undefined life receives shape and definition." [12] Again according to Cabasilas all the scriptural and traditional designations of baptism point to the same *positive* meaning: " 'Birth' and 'new birth,' 'refashioning' and 'seal,' as well as 'baptism' and 'clothing' and 'anointing,' 'gift,' 'enlightening,' and 'washing'—all signify this one thing: that the rite is the beginning of existence for those who are and live in accordance with God." [13]

Considering baptism as "new birth" implies also that it is a free gift from God, and is in no sense dependent upon human choice, consent, or even consciousness: "Just as in the case of physical birth we do not even contribute willingness to all the blessings derived from baptism." [14] In the East, therefore, there was never any serious doubt or controversy about the legitimacy of infant baptism. This legitimacy was based, not on the idea of a "sin" which would make even the infant guilty in the eyes of God and in need of baptism as justification, but on the fact that, at all stages of life, including infancy, man needs to be "born anew"—i.e. to begin a new and eternal life in Christ. The ultimate eschatological goal of new life cannot be fully comprehended even by the "conscious adult."

> Just as it is not possible to understand the power of the eyes or the grace of color without light, or for those who sleep to learn the affairs of those who stay awake while they are yet asleep, in the same way in this life it is not possible to understand the new members and their faculties which are directed solely to the life to come. . . . Yet we are members of Christ, and this is the result of baptism. The splendor and beauty of the members consists in the Head, for the members would not appear to be beautiful unless they are attached to the Head. Of these members the Head is hidden in the present life, but will be clearly apparent when they shine forth together with the Head.[15]

Since he is a member of the Body of Christ through baptism, man again becomes "theocentric"—that is, he recovers his original destiny, which is eschatological and mysterious, because it participates in the very mystery of God. As a divine gift, whether bestowed upon an adult or an infant, baptism is the beginning of new life. As Theodoret of Cyrus writes:

> If the only meaning of baptism were remission of sins, why would we bap-tize newborn children who have not yet tasted of sin? But the mystery of baptism is not limited to this; it is a promise of greater and more perfect gifts. In it are the promises of future delights; it is the type of the future resurrection, a communion with the master's Passion, a participation in His Resurrection, a mantle of salvation, a tunic of gladness, a garment of light, or rather it is light itself.[16]

As a "beginning" and a promise of new life, baptism implies free self-determination and growth. It does not suppress human freedom, but re-stores it to its original and "natural" form. In the case of infant baptism, this restoration is, of course, only potential, but the sacrament always im-plies a *call* to freedom. In the Byzantine tradition, the formula of baptism is not pronounced, as in the West, in the name of the minister who per-forms the sacrament ("I baptize you"), but is a solemn declaration on behalf of the baptized: "The servant of God, *N.,* is baptized in the name of the Father, and of the Son, and of the Holy Spirit." "This," writes Symeon of Thessalonica, "signifies the freedom of the baptized." [17] After baptism, the way toward God is a "synergy" of God's power and free hu-man effort. It is also a liberation from the bonds of Satan—the tyrant and the usurper—signified by the exorcisms which precede the sacrament of baptism itself.[18]

The Byzantine tradition has retained the ancient Christian practice of baptism through triple immersion. Actually, immersion was sometimes considered essential to the validity of the sacrament, and some extreme anti-Latin polemicists questioned the effectiveness of Western baptism on the grounds that it was performed by sprinkling. Immersion is indeed the very sign of what baptism means: "The water destroys the one life, but shows forth the other; it drowns the old man and raises the new," writes Cabasilas.[19] "Drowning" cannot be meaningfully signified other than through immersion.

To the man liberated through baptism from servitude to Satan, the Spirit bestows the faculty of "being active in spiritual energies," according to another expression of Cabasilas'.[20] We have already seen that Byzantine patristic theology recognized a connection between the gifts of the Spirit and human freedom; redemption of humanity implies that not only human "nature" but also *each man,* freely and personally, will find his place in the new creation, "recapitulated" in Christ. The gift of the Spirit in chrismation is the main sacramental sign of this particular dimension of salvation, which is, according to the liturgical norm, inseparable from baptism. Thus the "life in Christ" and "life in the Spirit" are not two separate forms of spirituality; they are complementary aspects of the same road, leading toward eschatological "deification."

Normally united with baptism in a single rite of Christian initiation, chrismation is celebrated separately only in cases of reconciliation to the Church of certain categories of heretics and schismatics, enumerated in Canon 95 of the Council *in Trullo*. Its significance, then, is to validate, through "the seal of the gift of the Holy Spirit" (the formula pronounced by the priest during the anointing), a Christian baptism performed in irregular circumstances—i.e., outside the canonical boundaries of the Church.

3. PENANCE

Sacramental penance—i.e., reconciliation to the Church after sins committed after baptism—has had a parallel development in East and West. Originally a public act, required from sinners who either had been officially excommunicated or had performed acts liable to excommunication, penance, gradually and especially after the fourth century, took the form of private confession, followed by a prayer of absolution pronounced by a priest. It then identified itself almost completely with the practice of private spiritual direction, especially widespread in monastic communities.

The development of penitential practice and theology in the Byzantine world was distinct from its Western counterpart in that it never knew the influence of legalistic interpretations of salvation, such as the Anselmian doctrine of "satisfaction," and never faced a crisis comparable to the Western Reformation and Counter-Reformation, with the latter's stress on clerical authority.

Patristic and Byzantine literature on repentance is almost entirely ascetical and moral. Very few authors of ascetical treatises on repentance specifically mention sacramental absolution as a formal requirement. This silence does not imply that sacramental repentance did not exist; except in cases of formal excommunication, which had to be followed by an equally formal reconciliation, it was only encouraged, but not required. In his innumerable calls to repentance, Chrysostom frequently mentions "confession," i.e., an opening of one's conscience before a witness or "the Church"; but regular sacramental confession does not seem to be meant. In his nine sermons specifically dealing with "repentance," only once does he refer to the Church as a direct recourse: "Did you commit sin? Enter the Church and repent for your sin. . . . You are an old man, and still you commit sin? Enter [the Church], repent; for here is the physician, not the judge; here one is not investigated, one receives remission of sins." [21]

A French ecclesiastical historian is probably correct when he writes: "The Byzantines seldom go to confession, at least in the secular world, for in the monasteries . . . confession is regularly practiced. But is this confession, or is it a direction of conscience of simple laymen by their spiritual fathers? Both practices exist and, in the monasteries, are indistinguishable from one another." [22]

Ascetical and canonical literature frequently mentions penitential requirements—periods of excommunication, prostrations, and charitable works required as retribution for sins committed and confessed; but, except in case of "mortal" sins—murder, apostasy, adultery—followed by formal excommunication, it is nowhere evident that a priest's absolution is necessary to seal the act of repentance. On the contrary, numerous sources describe absolutions given by non-ordained monks,[23] a practice which has survived in Eastern monasteries until our own day.

The various forms of absolution found in Byzantine *euchologia* and penitentials[24] all have the form of *prayer*: "In the East," writes A. Almazov, "it was always understood that absolution is expressed through prayer, and, even if a declaratory formula is being used, it implies that remission of sins is attributed to God Himself." [25] Declaratory formulas ("I, an unworthy priest . . . , forgive and absolve . . .") which crept into some *euchologia,* Greek and Slavic, are all of post-Scholastic Latin origin and were adopted within the framework of a general Latinization of the Byzantine rite.

Byzantine theologians themselves were hesitant about the exact status of penance among the *mysteria* of the Church, and often listed it with either monastic tonsure or anointing of the sick. By the fifteenth century, however, private confession to a priest, followed by a prayer of remission, was a generally accepted practice among laymen, with confession to lay monks existing as an alternative in monasteries. This lack of clarity in both theology and practice has a positive implication: confession and penance were interpreted primarily as a form of spiritual healing. For sin itself in Eastern Christian anthropology is primarily a disease, "passion." Without denying the Petrine privilege of the keys transmitted to all the bishops, or the apostolic power to remit sins, of which the Church is bearer, Byzantine theologians never succumbed to the temptation of reducing sin to the notion of a legal crime, which is to be sentenced, punished, or forgiven; yet they were aware that the sinner is primarily a prisoner of Satan and, as such, mortally sick. For this reason, confession and penance, at least ideally, preserved the character of liberation and healing rather than that of judgment; hence, the great variety of forms and practices, and the impossibility of confining them within static theological categories.

4. MARRIAGE

The Byzantine theological, liturgical, and canonical tradition unanimously stresses the absolute uniqueness of Christian marriage, and bases this emphasis upon the teaching of Ephesians 5. As a sacrament, or *mysterion,* marriage reflects the union between Christ and the Church, between Yahweh and Israel, and as such can be only *one*—an eternal bond, which death itself does not destroy. In its sacramental nature, marriage transfigures and transcends both fleshly union and contractual legal association: human love is being projected into the eternal Kingdom of God.

Only this basic understanding of Christian marriage can explain the fact that until the tenth century no second marriage, whether of those widowed or of those divorced, was blessed in church. Referring to the custom of "crowning" the bridal pair—a feature of the Byzantine rite of marriage—a canon attributed to Nicephorus the Confessor (806–815) specifies: "Those who enter a second marriage are not crowned and are not admitted to receive the most pure mysteries for two years; those who enter a third marriage are excommunicated for five years." [26] This text, which merely repeats the earlier prescriptions of the canons of Basil,[27] presupposes that second and third marriages of those widowed or divorced can be concluded as civil contracts only. Actually, since the marriage blessing was normally given at a Eucharist, where the bridal pair received communion, the required temporary excommunication excluded the Church's participation or blessing in cases when marriage was repeated.

Absolute uniqueness, as the *norm* of Christian marriage, is also affirmed in the fact that in Byzantine canon law it is strictly required from clergy; a man who was married twice, or was married to a widow or a divorcée, is not eligible for ordination to the diaconate or to the priesthood.[28] But laymen, after a period of penitence and abstention from the sacraments, are re-admitted to full communion with the Church, even after a second or third marriage; understanding and toleration is extended to them, when they cannot agree to remaining single, or would like to have a second chance to build up a true Christian marriage. Obviously, Byzantine tradition approaches the problem of remarriage—after widowhood or divorce —in terms of penitential discipline. Marriage, as a sacrament, implies the bestowing of God's grace; but this grace, to be effective, requires human cooperation ("synergy"). This is true of all the sacraments, but particularly of baptism, whose fruits can be dispersed through sin and then restored through repentance. In the case of marriage, which presupposes personal understanding and psychological adjustment, Byzantine tradition accepts the possibility of an initial mistake, as well as the fact that single life, in cases of death or the simple absence of the partner, is a greater evil than remarriage for those who cannot "bear" it.

The possibility of divorce remained an integral part of Byzantine civil legislation at all times. In the framework of the "symphony" between Church and state, it was never challenged, a fact which cannot be explained simply by reference to caesaropapism. The Byzantine Church never lacked saints who were ready to castigate imperial despotism, social injustice, and other evils contrary to the Gospel. John Chrysostom (398–404), Theodore the Studite († 820), or Patriarch Polyeuktos (956–970) were able to challenge the power of the state without fear; none of them, however, protested against the legislation concerning divorce. Obviously, they considered it as an inevitable factor of human life in the fallen world, where man can accept grace and refuse it; where sin is inevitable, but repentance always accessible; where the Church's function is never to compromise the norms of the Gospel, but to show compassion and mercy to human weakness.

This attitude of the Byzantine Church was clearly maintained as long as the primary function of the Church (to make the Kingdom of God present in man's life) and that of the state (to manage fallen humanity by choosing the lesser evil and maintaining order through legal means) remained clearly distinct. In the question of marriage, this essential distinction disappeared (at least in practice) when Emperor Leo vi († 912) published his *Novella* 89, formally giving the Church the legal obligation to validate all marriages.[29] Civil marriage disappeared as a legal possibility for free citizens; and soon, quite logically, Alexis i Comnenus would also make church marriage an obligation for slaves. By these imperial acts the Church theoretically gained formal control over the marriage discipline of all citizens. In fact, however, it began to be directly responsible for all the inevitable compromises, which had been solved so far by the possibility of civil marriage and divorce, and lost the possibility of applying its early penitential discipline. If the Church now gave legal authority to marriage, it had also to resolve the legal difficulties involved in this new responsibility. Indeed, it began to "grant divorces" (which were previously granted by secular courts alone) and to allow "remarriage" in church; because, without such "remarriages," second and third unions were legally invalid. It succeeded in making a fourth marriage totally illegal (Council of 920),[30] but had to compromise on many other counts.

It maintained, however, at least in principle, an essential distinction between the first and the following marriages: a special service was introduced for the latter, dissociated from the Eucharist and penitential in character. It was understood, therefore, that second and third marriages were not the norm, and as such were deficient sacramentally. The most striking difference between the Byzantine theology of marriage and its medieval Latin counterpart is that the Byzantines strongly emphasized the *unicity* of Christian marriage and the *eternity* of the marriage bond; they never considered that Christian marriage was a legal contract, automatically dissolved by the death of one of the partners. Remarriage of the widowed was only tolerated by them, as was the remarriage of the divorced. But this "toleration" did not mean approval. It implied repentance, and remarriage was allowed only to those men or women whose previous marriages could be considered as non-existent in practice (the various imperial codes listed the cases). Meanwhile, the Latin West became legalistically intolerant toward divorce, while admitting, without limitation, any number of remarriages after widowhood. Guided in its practice by the legal notion of contract, indissoluble as long as both parties were alive, the West seemed to ignore the idea that marriage, if it is a sacrament, has to be projected as an eternal bond into the Kingdom of God; that like all sacraments marriage requires a free response and implies the possibility of human rejection and human mistake; and that, after such a sinful rejection or human mistake, repentance always allows a new beginning. This is the theological basis for the toleration of divorce in the early Christian Church, as well as in Byzantium.

5. HEALING AND DEATH

Frequently associated with penance as a single sacrament, the office of "holy unction" did not evolve—except in some areas of the Christian East after the sixteenth century—into "extreme unction," a sacrament reserved for the dying. In Byzantium it involved the concelebration of several priests, usually seven, in accordance with James 5:14, a text considered to be the scriptural foundation of the sacrament. It was composed of scriptural readings and prayers of healing, the texts of which definitely exclude the possibility of giving a magic interpretation to the rite; healing is requested only in a framework of repentance and spiritual salvation, and not as an end in itself. Whatever the outcome of the disease, the anointing symbolized divine pardon and liberation from the vicious cycle of sin, suffering, and death, in which fallen humanity is held captive. Compassionate to human suffering, assembled together to pray for its suffering member, the Church through its presbyters asks for relief, forgiveness, and eternal freedom. This is the meaning of holy unction.

The funeral service, also considered a "sacrament" by some Byzantine authors, has no different significance. Even in death the Christian remains a member of the living and resurrected Body of Christ, into which he has been incorporated through baptism and the Eucharist. Through the funeral service, the Church gathers to bear witness to this fact, visible only to the eyes of faith, but already experienced by every Christian who possesses the awesome privilege of living, by anticipation, in the future Kingdom.

NOTES

1. Cabasilas, *De vita in Christo*, I, 3; PG 150:496D.
2. See, for example, Chrysostom, *Hom. 7, 1 in 1 Cor.*; PG 61:55.
3. Chrysostom, *Catechèses baptismales*, ed. A. Wenger, *Sources Chrétiennes* 50 (Paris: Cerf, 1957), II, 17, p. 143.

4. *Ep.* II, 165; PG 99:1524B.

5. G. M. Jugie, *Theologia dogmatica Christianorum orientalium*, III (Paris, 1930), p. 16.

6. Quoted by M. Jugie, *ibid.*, pp. 17–18.

7. *De sacramentis*, 52; PG 155:197A.

8. *Responsa canonica*, ed. A. I. Almazov (Odessa, 1903), p. 38.

9. *Hom. 60*, ed. S. Oikonomos (Athens, 1860), p. 250.

10. *De sacramentis*, 43; PG 155:188A.

11. *De vita in Christo*, II, 3; PG 150:524A.

12. *Ibid.*, 4, 525A.

13. *Ibid.*, 524C.

14. *Ibid.*, 5, 525D.

15. *Ibid.*, 22:548BC.

16. *Haeret. fabul. compendium* 5, 18; PG 83:512.

17. *De sacramentis*, 64; PG 155:228D–229B. See also Manuel of Corinth, *Apology* 7; PG 140:480.

18. Nicholas Cabasilas, *loc. cit.*, 6:528B.

19. *Ibid.*, 9:532B.

20. *Ibid.*, III, 1; 569A.

21. *De penitentia*, III, 1; PG 49:292.

22. J. Pargoire, *L'Eglise byzantine de 527 à 847* (Paris: Lecoffre, 1932), p. 347.

23. *Ibid.*, p. 348.

24. The earliest available manuscripts are of the tenth century. By far the best collection of penitential rites, in Greek and Slavic versions, is found in A. Almazov, *Tainaia Ispoved' v pravoslavnoi vostochnoi tserkvi* III (Odessa, 1894).

25. *Op. cit.*, I, pp. 149–150.

26. Canon 2, in *Syntagma Canonum* IV, edd. G. Rhalles and M. Potles (Athens, 1854), p. 457. On the discipline of marriage in the Byzantine Church, see mainly J. Zhishman, *Das Eherecht der orientalischen Kirche* (Vienna, 1864); K. Ritzer, *Le mariage dans les églises Chrétiennes du I*^{er} *au XI*^e *siècle* (Paris: Cerf, 1970), pp. 163–213; and J. Meyendorff, *Marriage: An Orthodox Perspective* (New York: St. Vladimir's Seminary Press, 1971).

27. Particularly canons 4 and 50 in Rhalles-Potles, *op. cit.*, pp. 102 and 203.

28. Quinisext Council, canon 3, *ibid.*, II, pp. 312–314.

29. *Les novelles de Leon VI, le Sage*, ed. A. Dain (Paris: Belles Lettres, 1944), pp. 294–297.

30. Rhalles-Potles, *op. cit.*, V, pp. 4–10.

16

The Eucharist

FORMAL CONSERVATISM was one of the predominant features of Byzantine civilization, affecting both the secular and the sacred aspects of life, and the forms of the liturgy in particular. But if the avowed intention was to preserve things as they were, if the basic structures of the Eucharistic liturgy have not been modified since the early centuries of Christianity and even today retain the forms which they acquired in the ninth century, the *interpretation* of words and gestures was subject to substantial change and evolution. Thus, Byzantine ritual conservatism was instrumental in preserving the original Christian *lex orandi,* otherwise often reinterpreted in the context of a Platonizing or moralizing symbolism, though it also allowed in due time—especially with Nicholas Cabasilas and the Hesychast theologians of the fourteenth century—a strong reaffirmation of the original sacramental realism in liturgical theology.

1. SYMBOLS, IMAGES, AND REALITY

Early Christianity and the patristic tradition understood the Eucharist as a mystery of true and real communion with Christ. Speaking of the Eucharist, Chrysostom insists that "Christ even now is present, even now operates";[1] and Gregory of Nyssa, in spite of the Platonizing tendencies of his thought, otherwise stands for the same view of the Eucharist as a mystery of real "participation" in the glorified Body of Christ, the seed of immortality.

> By dispensation of His grace, He disseminates Himself in every believer through that flesh, whose existence comes from bread and wine, blending Himself with the bodies of believers, to secure that, by this union with the Immortal, man, too, may be a sharer in incorruption. He gives these gifts by virtue of the benediction through which He "trans-elements" [*metastoicheiōsis*] the natural quality of these visible things to that immortal thing.[2]

Participation in these sources of immortality and unity is a constant concern for every Christian:

> It is good and beneficial to communicate every day [Basil writes,] and to partake of the holy body and blood of Christ. For He distinctly says, "He that eats my flesh and drinks my blood has eternal life" [Jn 6:55]. And who doubts that to share frequently in life is the same thing as to have manifold life? I indeed communicate four times a week, on the Lord's day, on Wednesday, on Friday, and on the Sabbath, and on the other days if there is a commemoration of any saint.[3]

This realistic and existential theology of the Eucharist was, as we have seen,[4] challenged by pastoral needs in the post-Constantinian Church: large congregations in large churches caused a lessening of participation by the laity.

It may be argued that the pastoral considerations which prompted this evolution were at least partially justified; the eschatological meaning of the Eucharist implied a withdrawal from the "world," a "closed" community of committed participants. Now that in the empire of Constantine and Justinian, the Church and the world had become indistinguishable as a single society, the Eucharist had to be protected from the "crowd," which had ceased to be the "people of God." More questionable, however, was the theological rationalization of this new situation, which was endorsed by some commentators on the liturgy who began to explain the Eucharist as a system of *symbols* to be "contemplated"; sacramental participation was thus gradually replaced with intellectual *vision*. Needless to say, this new attitude was perfectly suited to the Origenistic and Evagrian understanding of religion as an ascent of the *mind* to God, of which liturgical action was a symbol.

Most influential in promoting this symbolic understanding of the Eucharist were the writings of pseudo-Dionysius. Reducing the Eucharistic synaxis to a moral appeal, the Areopagite calls his readers to a "higher" contemplation:

> Let us leave to the imperfect these signs which, as I said, are magnificently painted in the vestibules of the sanctuaries; they will be sufficient to feed their contemplation. As far as we are concerned: let us turn back, in considering the holy synaxis, from the effects to their causes, and, thanks to the lights which Jesus will give us, we shall be able to contemplate harmoniously the intelligible realities in which are clearly reflected the blessed goodness of the models.[5]

Thus, the Eucharist is only the visible "effect" of an invisible "model"; and the celebrant "by offering Jesus Christ to our eyes, shows us in a tangible way and, as in an image, our intelligible life." [6] Thus, for Dionysius, "the loftiest sense of the Eucharistic rites and of sacramental communion itself is in symbolizing the union of our minds with God and with Christ. . . . Dionysius never formally presents Eucharistic communion as a participation in the Body and Blood of Christ." [7]

Dionysius' symbolism only superficially affected the Eucharistic rites themselves, but it became quite popular among commentators on the liturgy. Thus, the great Maximus the Confessor, whose use of the concept of "symbol" is probably more realistic than Dionysius', nevertheless systematically applies the terms "symbol" or "image" to the Eucharistic liturgy in general and to the elements of bread and wine in particular.[8]

In the eighth century, this symbolism led to a serious theological debate concerning the Eucharist—the only one Byzantium ever knew. The iconoclastic council of 754, in condemning the use of religious images, proclaimed that the only admissible "image" of Christ is the one established by Christ Himself, the Eucharistic Body and Blood.[9] This radical and clear contention, based upon a long-standing tradition, was a real challenge to the Orthodox party; the ambiguity of the Areopagite was evidenced once more, and a clarification of symbolism made necessary.

Thus, the defenders of the images, especially Theodore the Studite and Patriarch Nicephorus, firmly rejected it. For Theodore, the Eucharist is not "type," but the very "truth"; it is the "mystery which recapitulates the whole of the [divine] dispensation." [10] According to Nicephorus, it is the "flesh of God," "one and the same thing" with the Body and Blood of Christ,[11] who came to save the very reality of human flesh by becoming and remaining "flesh," even after His glorification; thus, in the Eucharist, "what is the matter of the sacrament, if the flesh is not real, so that we see it being perfected by the Spirit?" [12]

As a result of the iconoclastic controversy, Byzantine "Eucharistic realism," clearly departing from Dionysian terminology, was redirected along Christological and soteriological lines; in the Eucharist, man participates in the glorified humanity of Christ, which is not the "essence of God," [13] but a humanity still consubstantial to man and available to him as food and drink. In his treatise *Against Eusebius and Epiphanius,* Patriarch Nicephorus is particularly emphatic in condemning the Origenist idea that in the Eucharist man contemplates or participates in the "essence" of God.[14] For him, as also for later Byzantine theologians, the Eucharist is Christ's transfigured, life-giving, but still human, body, en-hypostasized in the Logos and penetrated with divine "energies." Characteristically, one never finds the category of "essence" (*ousia*) used by Byzantine theologians in a Eucharistic context. They would consider a term like "transubstantiation" (*metousiōsis*) improper to designate the Eucharistic mystery, and generally use the concept of *metabole,* found in the canon of John Chrysostom, or such dynamic terms as "trans-elementation" (*metastoicheiōsis*) or "re-ordination" (*metarrhythmisis*). Transubstantiation (*metousiōsis*) appears only in the writings of the *Latinophrones* of the thirteenth century, and is nothing but a straight translation from the Latin. The first Orthodox author to use it is Gennadios Scholarios;[15] but, in his case as well, direct Latin influence is obvious. The Eucharist is neither a symbol to be "contemplated" from outside nor an "essence" distinct from humanity, but Jesus Himself, the risen Lord, "made known through the breaking of bread" (Lk 24:35); Byzantine theologians rarely speculated beyond this realistic and soteriological affirmation of the Eucharistic presence as that of the glorified humanity of Christ.

The rejection of the concept of the Eucharist as "image" or "symbol" is, on the other hand, very significant for the understanding of the entire Eucharistic "perception" of the Byzantines; the Eucharist for them always remained fundamentally a mystery to be received as food and drink, and not to be "seen" through physical eyes. The elements remain covered, except during the prayers of consecration and during communion; and, in contrast with Western medieval piety, were never "venerated" outside the framework of the Eucharistic liturgy itself. The Eucharist cannot reveal anything to the sense of vision; it is only the bread of heaven. Vision is offered another channel of revelation—the icons: hence, the revelatory program of the Byzantine iconostasis, with the figures of Christ and the saints exposed precisely in order to be *seen* and venerated. "Christ is not shown in the Holy Gifts," writes Leonid Ouspensky; "He is given. He is shown in the icons. The visible side of the reality of the Eucharist is an image which can never be replaced either by imagination or by looking at the Holy Gifts." [16]

As a result of the iconoclastic controversy, Byzantine Eucharistic theology retained and re-emphasized the mystery and hiddenness of this central liturgical action of the Church. But it also reaffirmed that the Eucharist was essentially a *meal* which could be partaken of only through eating and drinking, because God had assumed the fullness of our humanity, with all its psychic and physical functions, in order to lead it to resurrection.

Byzantine theologians had an opportunity to make the same point in connection with their anti-Latin polemics against the use of unleavened bread in the Eucharist. The discussion on the azymes, which started in the eleventh century, was generally entangled in arguments of purely symbolic nature (the Greeks maintained, for example, that the Eucharistic bread had to be leavened in order to symbolize the *animated* humanity of Christ, while the Latin use of azymes implied Apollinarianism, i.e., the denial that Jesus had a human soul), but the controversy also recognized that the Byzantines understood the Eucharistic bread to be necessarily *consubstantial* with humanity, while Latin medieval piety emphasized its "supersubstantiality," its otherworldliness. The use of ordinary bread, identical with the bread used as everyday food, was the sign of true Incarnation: "What is the daily bread [of the Lord's prayer]," asks Nicetas

Stethatos, "if it is not consubstantial with us? And the bread consubstantial with us is none other than the Body of Christ, who became consubstantial with us through the flesh of His humanity." [17]

The Byzantines did not see the substance of the bread somehow changed in the Eucharistic mystery into another substance—the Body of Christ—but viewed this bread as the "type" of humanity: our humanity changed into the transfigured humanity of Christ.[18] For this reason, Eucharistic theology played such a prominent role in the theological debates of the fourteenth century, when the basic issue was a confrontation between an autonomous concept of man and the Hesychast defense of "deification." The great Nicholas Cabasilas, though still bound to the old Dionysian symbolism, overcomes the dangers of Nominalism; clearly, for him as also for Gregory Palamas, the Eucharist is the mystery which not only "represents" the life of Christ and offers it to our "contemplation"; it is the moment and the place, in which Christ's deified humanity becomes ours.

> He not merely clothed Himself in a body. He also took a soul and mind and will and everything human, so that He might be able to be united to the whole of us, penetrate through the whole of us, and resolve us into Himself, having in every respect joined His own to that which is ours. . . . For since it was not possible for us to ascend and participate in that which is His, He comes down to us and participates in that which is ours. And so precisely does He conform to the things which He assumed that, in giving those things to us which He has received from us, He gives Himself to us. Partaking of the body and blood of His humanity, we receive God Himself in our souls—the Body and Blood of God, and the soul, mind, and will of God—no less than His humanity.[19]

The last word on the Eucharist, in Byzantine theology, is thus an anthropological and soteriological understanding of the mystery. "In approaching the Eucharist, the Byzantines began not with bread *qua* bread, but with bread *qua* man." [20] Bread and wine are offered only because the Logos has assumed humanity, and they are being *changed* and deified by the operation of the Spirit because Christ's humanity has been transformed into glory through the cross and Resurrection. This is the thought of Cabasilas, as just quoted, and the meaning of the canon of John Chrysostom: "Send down Thy Holy Spirit *upon us and upon these gifts,* and make this bread the precious Body of Thy Christ, and that which is in this cup the precious Blood of Thy Christ, so that, for those who partake, they may be a purification of soul, a remission of sins, the communion of Thy Holy Spirit, the fullness of the Kingdom of heaven. . . ."

The sacrament of new humanity *par excellence*, the Eucharist, for Cabasilas "alone of the mysteries perfects the other sacraments . . . , since they cannot fulfill the initiation without it." [21] Christians partake of it "continually," for "it is the perfect sacrament for all purposes, and there is nothing of which those who partake thereof stand in need which it does not supply in an eminent way." [22] The Eucharist is also "the much praised marriage according to which the most holy Bridegroom espouses the Church as a bride";[23] that is, the Eucharist is the very sacrament which truly transforms a human community into "the Church of God," and is, therefore, as we will see later, the ultimate criterion and basis of ecclesial structure.

2. EUCHARIST AND CHURCH

The ecclesiological significance of the Eucharist, though challenged by the Hellenistic world-view which tended to interpret it as a system of "symbols" visually contemplated by the individual, was always maintained by the Byzantine *lex orandi* and reaffirmed by those who followed the mainstream of traditional theology. In the controversy on the azymes, the implication on the Byzantine side was that the Eucharist is indeed a paschal mystery, in which our fallen humanity is transformed into the glorified humanity of the New Adam, Christ: this glorified humanity is realized in the Body of the Church.

These anthropological presuppositions of Byzantine Eucharistic theology necessarily had to include the concepts of "synergy" and of the unity of mankind.

It is against the background of the Greek patristic doctrine of "synergy" that one can really understand the significance of the Byzantine insistence on the epiclesis in the Eucharistic liturgy, another issue debated in the fourteenth and fifteenth centuries by Greek and Latin theologians. The text of the epiclesis, as it appears in the canon of John Chrysostom and in other Eastern liturgies, implies that the mystery is accomplished through a prayer of the entire Church ("We ask Thee . . .")—a concept which does not necessarily exclude the idea that the bishop or priest pronouncing the words of institution acts *in persona Christi,* as Latin theology insists, but which deprives this notion of its exclusivity by interpreting the ministerial sacerdotal "power" to perform the sacraments as a function of the entire worshipping Body of the Church.

In well-known passages of his *Commentary on the Liturgy,* Cabasilas, defending the epiclesis, rightly recalls that all sacraments are accomplished through prayer. Specifically, he quotes the consecration of the chrism, the prayers of ordination, of absolution, and of the anointing of the sick.[24] Thus, he writes, "it is the tradition of the Fathers, who received this teaching from the Apostles and from their successors, that the sacraments are rendered effective through prayer; all the sacraments, as I have said, and particularly the holy Eucharist." [25] This "deprecatory" form of sacramental rites does not imply, however, a doctrine of validity *ex opere operantis,* i.e., dependent upon the worthiness of the celebrant. "He who celebrates the sacrifice daily," Cabasilas continues, "is but the minister of the grace. He brings to it nothing of his own; he would not dare to do or say anything according to his own judgment and reason. . . . Grace works all; the priest is only a minister, and that very ministry comes to him by grace; he does not hold it on his own account." [26]

The mystery of the Church, fully realized in the Eucharist, overcomes the dilemma of prayer and response, of nature and grace, of the divine as opposed to the human, because the Church, as the Body of Christ, is precisely a communion of God and man, not only where God is present and active, but where humanity becomes fully "acceptable to God," fully adequate to the original divine plan; prayer itself then becomes an act of communion, where there cannot be any question of its not being heard by God. The conflict, the "question," the separateness, and the sinfulness are still present in each individual member of the Church, but only inasmuch as he has not fully appropriated the divine presence and refuses to conform to it; the presence itself, however, is the "new testament in my Blood" (Lk 22:20), and God will not take it away. Thus, all Christians—including the bishop, or the priest—are individually nothing more than sinners, whose prayers are not necessarily heard, but *when gathered together in the name of Christ*, as the "Church of God," they are a part in the New Testament, to which God has eternally committed Himself through His Son and the Spirit.

As a divine–human communion and "synergy," the Eucharist is a prayer addressed "in Christ" to the Father, and accomplished through the descent of the Holy Spirit. The epiclesis, therefore, is the fulfillment of the Eucharistic action, just as Pentecost is the fulfillment of a divine "economy" of salvation; salvation is always a Trinitarian action. The pneumatological dimension of the Eucharist is also presupposed in the very notion of "synergy"; it is the Spirit which makes Christ present in the age between His two comings: when divine action is not imposing itself on humanity, but offering itself for acceptance by human freedom and, by communicating itself to man, making him authentically free.

At all times, Byzantine theologians understood the Eucharist as the center of a soteriological and triadological mystery, not simply as a change of bread and wine. Those who followed Dionysian symbolism approached the Eucharist in the context of a Hellenistic hierarchical cosmos, and understood it as the center of salvific action through mystical "contemplation," which still involved the whole destiny of humanity and the world. Those who held a more Biblical view of man and a more Christocentric understanding of history approached the Eucharist as the key to ecclesiology; the Church, for them, was primarily the place where God and man met in the Eucharist, and the Eucharist became the criterion of ecclesial structure and the inspiration of all Christian action and responsibility in the world. In both cases the Eucharist was understood in a cosmological and ecclesiological dimension affirmed in the formula of the Byzantine oblation: "Thine own of thine own, we offer unto Thee in behalf of all and for all."

One of the ideas which constantly appears in Byzantine "symbolic" interpretations of the Eucharist is that the temple in which the Eucharistic liturgy is celebrated is an image of the "new," transfigured cosmos. The idea is found in several early Christian writers, and reappears in Maximus the Confessor[27] and, later, in Symeon of Thessalonica.[28] Undoubtedly, it inspired the Byzantine architects who built Hagia Sophia in Constantinople, the model of all temples of the East, with the *circle* as its central geometrical theme. In the Neoplatonic tradition, the circle, the symbol of plenitude, is the standard image of God; God is reflected in His creatures, once they are restored to their original design: "He circumscribes their expansion in a circle and sets Himself as the pattern of the beings which He has created," writes Maximus, adding immediately that "The holy Church is an image of God, since it effects the union of the faithful, as God does." [29] The Church, as community and as building, is, therefore, a sign of the new age, the eschatological anticipation of the new creation, the created cosmos restored in its original wholeness. Clearly, a theologian like Maximus uses the models and categories of his age to describe the fullness of the world to come. His interpretation of the Eucharistic liturgy is "less an initiation into the mystery of the liturgy than an introduction to the mystery with the liturgy as a starting point";[30] but the very idea that the Eucharist is an anticipation of the eschatological fulfillment is affirmed in the canon of the Byzantine liturgy itself, which recalls the second coming of Christ as an event which *has already occurred*: "Remembering this saving commandment and all the things which have come to pass for us, the cross, the tomb, the Resurrection on the third day, the ascension into heaven, and the second and glorious coming, we offer unto Thee . . ."

This eschatological character of the Eucharistic mystery, strongly expressed in the liturgy, in the religious art which served as its framework, and in the theological commentaries, whatever their school of thought, explains why the Byzantines always believed that in the Eucharist the Church is fully "the Church," and that the Eucharist is the ultimate criterion and seal of all the other sacraments. Following pseudo-Dionysius, who spoke of the Eucharist as the "sacrament of sacraments," [31] as the "focal point" of each particular sacrament,[32] Byzantine theologians affirm the absolute centrality of the Eucharist in the life of the Church: "It is the final sacrament," writes Cabasilas, "because it is not possible to proceed further and to add anything to it." [33] "The Eucharist alone of the mysteries brings perfection to the other sacraments . . . , since they cannot complete the initiation without it." [34] Symeon of Thessalonica applies this idea concretely to individual sacraments. Concerning marriage, for example, he writes that the bridal pair "must be ready to receive communion, so that their crowning be a worthy one and their marriage valid"; and he specifies that communion is not given to those whose marriage is defective from the point of view of Church discipline, and is, therefore, not fully the sacrament, but simply a "good fellowship." [35]

Any local church where the "divine liturgy" of the Eucharist is celebrated possesses, therefore, the "marks" of the true Church of God: unity, holiness, catholicity, and apostolicity. These marks cannot belong to any human gathering; they are the eschatological signs given to a community through the Spirit of God. Inasmuch as a local church is built upon and around the Eucharist, it is not simply a "part" of the universal people of God; it *is the fullness* of the Kingdom which is anticipated in the Eucharist, and the Kingdom can never be "partially" one or "partially" catholic. "Partiality" belongs only to the individual appropriation of the given fullness by the members, who are limited by belonging to the "old Adam"; it does not exist in the Body of Christ, indivisible, divine, and glorious.

Liturgical discipline and Byzantine canon law try to protect this unifying and catholic character of the Eucharist. They require that on each altar no more than one Eucharist be celebrated each day; similarly, a priest, or bishop, is not allowed to celebrate twice on the same day. Whatever the practical inconveniences, these rules aim at preserving the Eucharist at least nominally as the gathering "of all together at the same place" (Ac 2:1); *all* should be together at the same altar, around the same bishop, at the same time, because there is only one Christ, one Church, and one Eucharist. The idea that the Eucharist is the sacrament uniting the whole Church remained alive in the East and prevented the multiplication of Masses of intention and of low Masses. The Eucharistic liturgy always remained a festal event in Byzantium, a celebration involving, at least in principle, the whole Church.

As a manifestation of the Church's unity and wholeness, the Eucharist served also as the ultimate theological norm for ecclesiastical structure: the local church where the Eucharist is celebrated was always considered to be not merely a "part" of a universal organization, but the *whole* Body of Christ manifested sacramentally and including the entire "communion of saints," living or departed. Such a manifestation was seen as a necessary basis for the geographical expansion of Christianity, but it was not identical with it. Theologically, the *sacrament* is the sign and reality of the eschatological anticipation of the Kingdom of God, and the episcopate—necessary center of this reality—is envisaged primarily in its sacramental function, with the other aspects of its ministry (pastorate, teaching) based on this "high priestly" function in the local community, rather than on the idea of a co-optation into a universal apostolic college. The bishop was, first of all, the image of Christ in the Eucharistic mystery. "O Lord our God," says the prayer of episcopal ordination, "who in Thy providence hast instituted for us teachers of like nature with ourselves, to maintain

Thine Altar, that they may offer unto Thee sacrifice and oblation for all
Thy people; do Thou, the same Lord, make this man also, who has been
proclaimed a steward of the episcopal grace, to be an imitator of Thee,
the true Shepherd. . . ." [36]

Thus, according to pseudo-Dionysius, the "high priest" (*archiereys*)
possesses the "first" and the "last" order of hierarchy and "fulfills every
hierarchic consecration." [37] Symeon of Thessalonica also defines the episcopal dignity in terms of its sacramental functions; the bishop for him
is the one who performs all sacraments—baptism, chrismation, Eucharist,
ordination; he is the one "through whom all ecclesiastical acts are perfected." [38] The Eucharist is, indeed, the *ultimate* manifestation of God
in Christ; and there cannot be, therefore, any ministry higher and more
decisive than that which presides over the Eucharist. The centrality of the
Eucharist, the awareness that the fullness of Christ's Body abides in it and
that the episcopal function is the highest in the Church will be the principal foundation of the Byzantine opposition to any theological interpretation of supra-episcopal primacies: there cannot be, according to them, any
authority "by divine right" over the Eucharist and the bishop who heads
the Eucharistic assembly.

The practice of the Byzantine Church was not always consistent with
the inner logic of this Eucharistic ecclesiology. The historical development
of the episcopal function—which, on the one hand, after the fourth century delegated the celebration of the Eucharist to presbyters on a permanent basis, and, on the other, became *de facto* a part of wider administrative structures (provinces, patriarchates)—lost some of its exclusive
and direct connections with the sacramental aspect of the life of the Church.
But the essential theological and ecclesiological norms were reaffirmed
whenever they were directly challenged, and thus remained an essential
part of what, for the Byzantines, was the tradition of the Catholic Church.[39]

NOTES

1. *Hom. in II Tim.* 2, 4; PG 62:612.
2. *Catechetical oration,* 37, ed. Strawley, p. 152.
3. Letter 93, ed. Deferrari, II, 145.
4. See Chapter 1. For a good historical review of Byzantine Eucharistic theologies and
practices (with earlier bibliography), see H. J. Schulz, *Die byzantinische Liturgie—vom
Werden ihrer Symbolgestalt* (Freiburg: Lambertus-Verlag, 1964).
5. *Eccl. Hier.,* III, 3, 1–2; PG 3:428AC.
6. *Ibid.,* III, 13; 444c; see our comments on these texts in *Christ,* pp. 79–80.
7. R. Roques, *L'univers dionysien. Structure hiérarchique du monde selon le pseudo-
Denys* (Paris: Aubier, 1954), pp. 267, 269.
8. See particularly *Quaestiones et dubia* 41; PG 90:820A. On the liturgical theology of
Maximus, see R. Bornert, *Les commentaires byzantins de la divine liturgie du VIIe au*

XVe siècle, Archives de l'Orient chrétien, 9 (Paris: Institut français d'études byzantines, 1966), pp. 82–124.

9. Mansi, XIII, 261D–264C.

10. *Antirrh.* I; PG 99:340AC.

11. *Antirrh.* II; PG 100:336B–337A.

12. *Contra Eusebium,* ed. J. B. Pitra, *Spicilegium Solesmense,* I (Paris, 1852), pp. 440–442.

13. Nicephorus, *ibid.,* p. 446.

14. *Ibid.,* pp. 468–469.

15. *De sacramentali corpore Christi,* edd. L. Petit and M. Jugie, I (Paris: Bonne Presse, 1928), pp. 126, 134.

16. "The Problem of the Iconostasis," *St. Vladimir's Seminary Quarterly* 8 (1964), No. 4, 215.

17. *Dialexis et antidialogus,* ed. A. Michel, *Humbert und Kerullarios* II (Paderborn: Quellen und Forschungen, 1930), pp. 322–323.

18. This aspect of the controversy on the azymes is brilliantly shown in J. H. Erickson, "Leavened and Unleavened: Some Theological Implications of the Schism of 1054," *St. Vladimir's Theological Quarterly* 14 (1970), No. 3, 155–176.

19. *De vita in Christo,* IV, 9: PG 150:592D–593A.

20. Erickson, *op. cit.,* p. 165.

21. *De vita in Christo,* IV, 4, 585B. See also Gregory Palamas, *Confession of Faith;* PG 151:765, trans. A. Papadakis, "Gregory Palamas at the Council of Blachernae, 1351," *Greek, Roman, and Byzantine Studies* 10 (1969), 340.

22. *Ibid.,* 11; 596C.

23. *Ibid.,* 10; 593.

24. *Commentary on the Divine Liturgy,* 29, edd. R. Bornert, J. Gouillard, and P. Perichon, *Sources Chrétiennes,* 4 bis (Paris: Cerf, 1967), pp. 185–187; trans. Hussey and McNulty (London: SPCK, 1960), pp. 74–75.

25. *Ibid.,* p. 190; tr. pp. 75–76.

26. *Ed. cit.,* 46, p. 262; tr. pp. 104–105.

27. See the references in R. Bornert, *op. cit.,* pp. 93–94.

28. *De sacro templo,* 131, 139, 152; PG 155:337D, 348C, 357A.

29. *Mystagogia,* 1; PG 91:668B.

30. R. Bornert, *op. cit.,* p. 92.

31. *Eccl. Hier.,* III, 1; PG 3:424C.

32. *Ibid.,* col. 444D.

33. *De vita in Christo,* IV, 1; PG 150:581B.

34. *Ibid.,* IV, 4; 585B.

35. *De sacro templo,* 282; PG 155:512D–513A.

36. Jacobus Goar, *Euchologion sive Rituale Graecorum* (Venice, 1730; repr. Graz: Akademische Druck- und Verlagsanstalt, 1960), p. 251; trans. *Service Book of the Holy Orthodox Catholic Apostolic Church,* ed. I. F. Hapgood (New York: Association Press, 1922), p. 330.

37. *Hier. Eccl.* V, 5; PG 3:505A, 6:505C, etc.

38. *De sacris ordinationibus* 157; PG 155:364B.

39. *De vita in Christo,* IV, 8; PG 150:604B.

The Church in the World

Christians were Christians only because Christianity brought to them liberation from death. If one would penetrate to the heart of Eastern Christianity one must be present on the night when the Easter liturgy is celebrated: of this liturgy all other rites are but reflections or figures. The three words of the Easter troparion—the Easter hymn—repeated a thousand times in tones ever more and more triumphant, repeated to the point of ecstasy and of an overflowing mystic joy—"By His death He has trodden death beneath His feet"—here is the great message of the Byzantine Church: the joy of Easter, the banishing of that ancient terror which beset the life of man, this it is which has won and kept the allegiance of the masses; it is this creed of triumph which has been translated into all the languages of the Orient, and yet has never lost its virtue; this is the faith which found its material expression in the icon, so that even when the originality of the artist fell short, man's shortcoming could not veil the meaning of that joyous Mystery.[1]

THESE WORDS of a secular historian reflect quite adequately what we have tried to suggest about Byzantine Christianity as *experience*. Whether he was a theologian, a monk, or an average layman, the Byzantine Christian knew that his Christian faith was not an obedient acceptance of intellectual propositions, issued by an appropriate authority, but on *evidence*, accessible to him personally in the liturgical and sacramental life of the Church, and also in the life of prayer and contemplation, the one being inseparable from the other. Not physical, or emotional, or intellectual, this experience is described as *gnosis,* or as "spiritual senses," or as inner "certainty." To affirm that it was impossible for any Christian to achieve this knowledge was considered as the greatest "heresy" by Symeon the New Theologian.

Whether one considers with Vladimir Lossky that "in a certain sense all theology is mystical,"[2] or whether one looks down skeptically upon Byzantine "obligatory mysticism," it is obvious that the definition of Christianity as "experience" raises the issue of its witness to the world in terms of verbal expressions, or definitions, and in terms of action, of behavior, and of practical responsibility. In the eyes of Western Christians, the Eastern Church often appears as quite other-worldly, and, indeed, the West has traditionally been much more concerned than the East with organizing human society, with defining the Christian truth in terms which could be readily understood, with giving man concrete normative formulae of behavior and conduct. To attempt a critical description of this problem in Byzantine theology is to raise one of the basic theological and anthropological issues of Christian life: the relation between the absolute divine truth and the relative faculties of perception and action possessed by created and fallen man.

1. CHURCH AND SOCIETY

The great dream of Byzantine civilization was a universal Christian society administered by the emperor and spiritually guided by the Church. This idea obviously combined Roman and Christian universalisms in one single socio-political program. It was also based upon the theological presuppositions concerning man which were developed above:[3] man, by nature, is God-centered in *all* aspects of his life, and he is responsible for the fate of the *entire* creation. As long as Christianity was persecuted, this Biblical assertion could be nothing more than an article of faith, to be realized at the end of history and anticipated in the sacraments. With the "conversion" of Constantine, however, it suddenly appeared as a concrete and reachable goal. The original enthusiasm with which the Christian Church accepted imperial protection was never corrected by any systematic reflection on the nature and role of the state or of secular societies in the life of *fallen* humanity. There lies the tragedy of the Byzantine system: it assumed that the state, as such, could become intrinsically Christian.

The official version of the Byzantine social ideal is expressed in the famous text of Justinian's Sixth *Novella*:

> There are two greatest gifts which God, in his love for man, has granted from on high: the priesthood and the imperial dignity. The first serves divine things, the second directs and administers human affairs; both, however, proceed from the same origin and adorn the life of mankind. Hence, nothing should be such a source of care to the emperors as the dignity of the priests, since it is for the [imperial] welfare that they constantly implore God. For if the priesthood is in every way free from blame and possesses access to God, and if the emperors administer equitably and judiciously the state entrusted to their care, general harmony will result, and whatever is beneficial will be bestowed upon the human race.[4]

In the thought of Justinian, the "symphony" between "divine things" and "human affairs" was based upon the Incarnation, which united the divine and human natures, so that the person of Christ is the unique source of the two—the civil and ecclesiastical hierarchies. The fundamental mistake of this approach was to assume that the ideal humanity which was manifested, through the Incarnation, in the person of Jesus Christ could also find an adequate manifestation in the Roman Empire. Byzantine theocratic thought was, in fact, based upon a form of "realized eschatology," as if the Kingdom of God had already appeared "in power" and as if the empire were the manifestation of this power in the world and in history. Byzantine Christian thought of course recognized the reality of evil, both personal and social, but it presumed, at least in the official philosophy of imperial legislation, that such evil could be adequately controlled by subduing the whole "inhabited earth" to the power of the one emperor and to the spiritual authority of the one Orthodox priesthood.

The providential significance of the one world-empire was exalted, not only in imperial laws, but also in ecclesiastical hymnography. A Christmas hymn, ascribed to the ninth-century nun Kassia, proclaims a direct connection between the world-empire of Rome and the "recapitulation" of humanity in Christ. *Pax Romana* is thus made to coincide with *Pax Christiana*:

When Augustus reigned alone upon earth, the many kingdoms of man came
        to end:
And when Thou wast made man of the pure Virgin, the many gods of
        idolatry were destroyed.
The cities of the world passed under one single rule;
And the nations came to believe in one sovereign Godhead.
The peoples were enrolled by the decree of Caesar;
And we, the faithful, were enrolled in the Name of the Godhead,
        When Thou, our God, wast made man.
        Great is Thy mercy: glory to Thee.[5]

As late as 1397, when he had almost reached the nadir of political misery, the Byzantine still understood the universal empire as the necessary support of Christian universalism. Solicited by Prince Basil of Moscow on the issue whether the Russians could omit the liturgical commemoration of the emperor, while continuing to mention the patriarch, Patriarch Anthony IV replied: "It is not possible for Christians to have the Church and not to have the Empire; for Church and Empire form a great unity and community; it is not possible for them to be separated from one another." [6]

The idea of the Christian and universal empire presupposed that the emperor had obligations, both as guardian of the faith and as witness of God's mercy for man. According to the ninth-century *Epanagogē*, "The purpose of the emperor is to do good, and therefore he is called benefactor, and when he fails in this obligation to do good, he forsakes his imperial dignity." [7] The system was an authentic attempt to view human life in

Christ as a whole: it did not admit any dichotomy between the spiritual and the material, the sacred and the secular, the individual and the social, or the doctrinal and the ethical, but recognized a certain polarity between "divine things"—essentially the sacramental communion of man with God —and "human affairs." Yet between the two, there had to be a "symphony" in the framework of a single Christian "society" in which both Church and state cooperated in preserving the faith and in building a society based on charity and humaneness.[8]

This wholeness of the Byzantine concept of the Christian mission in the world reflects the fundamental Chalcedonian belief in the total assumption of humanity by the Son of God in the Incarnation. The Christian faith, therefore, is understood to lead to the transfiguration and "deification" of the *entire man*; and, as we have seen, this "deification" is indeed accessible, as a living experience, *even now,* and not merely in a future kingdom. Byzantine ecclesiology and Byzantine political philosophy both assume that baptism endows man with that experience, which transforms not only the "soul" but the whole man, and makes him, already in this present life, a citizen of the Kingdom of God.

One can actually see that the main characteristic of Eastern Christianity, in its ethical and social attitudes, is to consider man as already redeemed and glorified in Christ; by contrast, Western Christendom has traditionally understood the present state of humanity in both a more realistic and a more pessimistic way: though redeemed and "justified" in the eyes of God by the sacrifice of the cross, man remains a sinner. The primary function of the Church, therefore, is to provide him with criteria of thought and a discipline of behavior, which would allow him to overcome his sinful condition and direct him to good works. On this assumption, the Church is understood primarily as an institution established *in the world,* serving the world and freely using the means available in the world, and appropriate for dealing with sinful humanity, particularly the concepts of law, authority, and administrative power. The contrast between the structures built by the medieval papacy and the eschatological, experiential, and "other-worldly" concepts which prevailed in the ecclesiological thinking of the Byzantine East helps us to understand the historical fate of East and West. In the West, the Church developed as a powerful institution; in the East, it was seen primarily as a sacramental (or "mystical") organism, in charge of "divine things" and endowed with only limited institutional structures. The structures (patriarchates, metropolitanates, and other officialdom) themselves were shaped by the empire (except for the fundamental tripartite hierarchy—bishop, priest, deacon—in each local church) and were not considered to be of divine origin.

This partial surrender on the "institutional" side of Christianity to the empire contributed to the preservation of a sacramental and eschatological understanding of the Church, but it was not without serious dangers. In its later history the Eastern Church experienced the fact that the state did not always deserve its confidence, and often assumed a clearly demonic face.

Throughout the Byzantine period proper, however, the Justianian "symphony" worked better than one could expect. The mystical and otherworldly character of Byzantine Christianity was largely responsible for some major characteristics of the state itself. The emperor's personal power, for example, was understood as a form of charismatic ministry: the sovereign was chosen by God, not by men; hence the absence, in Byzantium, of any legally defined process of imperial succession. Both strict legitimism and democratic election were felt to be limitations to God's freedom in selecting His appointee.

This charismatic understanding of the state obviously lacked political realism and efficiency. "Providential usurpations" were quite frequent, and political stability an exception. In political terms, the Byzantine imperial system was indeed a utopia. Conceived as a universal counterpart of a universal Church, the empire never achieved universality; understood as a reflection of the heavenly kingdom of God, it has a history of bloody revolutions, of wars, and—like all medieval states—of social injustice. As always and everywhere, the ideals of Christianity proved unapplicable in legal and institutional terms; they only gave hope to individual heroes of the faith and impulse to those who were striving to draw man closer to the ideal of the "life in Christ" which had become accessible to man. The Byzantines recognized this fact, at least implicitly, when they paid such great veneration to the saints, in whom they saw the divine light shining in a "world" which was theoretically Christianized, but which in fact had changed little after the establishment of Christianity. The permanent presence, in the midst of Byzantine society, of innumerable monastic communities, which—at least the best among them—were withdrawing from the world in order to manifest that the Kingdom was *not yet* there, was another reminder that there could not be any real and permanent "symphony" between God and the world, only an unstable and dynamic polarity.

This polarity was, in fact, nothing else than the opposition between the "old" and the "new" Adam in man. In terms of social ethics, it excluded clear-cut formulae and legal absolutes, and prevented the Church from being fully identified with an institution defined in terms of politics, or sociology; but, at times, it was also interpreted as a Platonic or Manichaean dualism, and it then meant total withdrawal from social responsibility. Occasionally this attitude led to a takeover by the state of the Church's mission, leaving the monks alone in their witness to the inevitable conflict and polarity between the Kingdom of God and the kingdom of Caesar.

2. THE MISSION OF THE CHURCH

The Byzantine concept according to which the empire and the Church were allied in the leadership of a single universal Christian *oikoumene* implied their cooperation in the field of mission. The designation of "equal-to-the-Apostles" (*isapostolos*) was applied to Constantine the Great precisely because of his contribution to the conversion of the *oikoumene* to Christ. The emperors of Constantinople, his successors, were normally buried in the Church of the Holy Apostles. Their missionary responsibility was stressed in court ceremonial. The emperor was expected to propagate the Christian faith and to maintain Christian ethics and behavior, and to achieve these goals through both legislation and support given to the Church's missionary and charitable activities.

Outside the imperial borders, the Church–state alliance frequently led to a *de facto* identification, in the eyes of the non-Christians, of the political interests of the empire with the fate of Orthodox Christianity. Non-Christian rulers of Persia and Arab caliphs often persecuted Christians, not only out of religious fanaticism, but also because they suspected them of being the emperor's allies. The suspicion was actually frequently justified, especially during the lengthy holy war between Islam and Christianity, which made spiritual contacts, mutual understanding, and meaningful dialogue virtually impossible. For this reason, except in a very few cases, Byzantine Christianity was never able to make any missionary inroads among the Islamic invaders coming from the East.[9]

Missionary activity was quite successful, however, among the barbarians coming from the North—Mongols, Slavs, and Caucasians—who flooded imperial territories and eventually settled as the empire's northern neighbors. It is this missionary work which actually preserved the universal character of the Orthodox Church after the lapse of the non-Greek communities of the Middle East into Monophysitism and after the great schism with the West. After the ninth century particularly, Byzantine Christianity expanded spectacularly, extending its penetration to the Caspian Sea and the Arctic Ocean.[10]

The Byzantine mission to the Slavs is usually associated with what is called "Cyrillo–Methodian ideology" and is characterized by the translation of both Scripture and liturgy into the vernacular language of the newly converted nations by two brothers, Constantine-Cyril and Methodius, in the ninth century. In actual fact, however, Byzantine churchmen were not always consistent with the principles adopted by the first missionaries; historical evidence shows that enforced Hellenization and cultural integration were also practiced, especially when the empire succeeded in achieving direct political control over Slavic lands. Still the fundamental theological meaning of Christian mission, as expressed by Cyril (or "Constantine the philosopher," Cyril's secular name), was never challenged in principle:

> Since you have learned to hear, Slavic people,
> Hear the Word, for it came from God,
> The Word nourishing human souls,
> The Word strengthening heart and mind. . . .

Therefore St. Paul has taught:
"In offering my prayer to God,
I had rather speak five words
That all the brethren will understand
Than ten thousand words which are incomprehensible." [11]

Clearly, the author sees the proclamation of the Gospel as essential to the very nature of the Christian faith, which is a revelation of the eternal Word or Logos of God. The Word must be heard and understood; hence the necessity of a translation of Scripture and worship into the vernacular. This principle—expressed by the Prologue in terms which Martin Luther would not have disavowed—will remain the distinctive characteristic of Orthodox missions, at a time when the Christian West was opting for a unified but dead language—Latin—as the only channel for communicating the Word. Cyril and Methodius, during their mission to Moravia and their stay in Venice, had several discussions with Frankish missionaries who held the "heresy of the three languages," believing that the Gospel could be communicated only in the three languages used in Pilate's inscription on Jesus' cross: Hebrew, Greek, and Latin. By contrast, Cyril and Methodius stressed that, in the East, Slavs, as well as Armenians, Persians, Egyptians, Georgians, and Arabs, praised God in their own languages.[12]

The deliberate policy of translation implied a mission evolving into the rapid "indigenization" of the Church, which became an integral part of the various national cultures. Eventually, Byzantine Orthodox Christianity became deeply rooted in their lives, and neither foreign domination nor secular ideologies could easily uproot it. But indigenization also implied the existence of "national" churches, especially after the dismemberment of what Obolensky has called the "Byzantine Commonwealth." Modern nationalism further secularized the national self-consciousness of East European nations, damaging the sense of Christian catholicity among them.

Byzantine missionary methods and principles found their continuation in Orthodox Russia. Stephen of Perm (1340–1396), for example, is known as the apostle of the Zyrians, a Finnish tribe in northeastern Russia. Having learned Greek, Stephen translated the scriptures and the liturgy into the language of the Zyrians and became their bishop.[13] His example was followed until the twentieth century in the missionary expansion of the Russian Orthodox Church in Asia and even on the American continent, through Alaska.

3. ESCHATOLOGY

Eschatology can never really be considered a separate chapter of Christian theology, for it qualifies the character of theology as a whole. This is especially true of Byzantine Christian thought, as we have tried to show in the preceding chapters. Not only does it consider man's destiny—and the destiny of all of creation—as *oriented toward an end*; this orientation is the main characteristic of the sacramental doctrines, of its spirituality, and of its attitude toward the "world." Furthermore, following Gregory of Nyssa and Maximus the Confessor, it considers the ultimate end itself as a *dynamic* state of man and of the whole of creation: the goal of created existence is not, as Origen thought, a static contemplation of divine "essence," but a dynamic ascent of love, which never ends, because God's transcendent being is inexhaustible, and which, thus, always contains new things yet to be discovered (*novissima*) through the union of love.

The eschatological state, however, is not only a reality of the future but a *present experience*, accessible in Christ through the gifts of the Spirit. The Eucharistic canon of the liturgy of John Chrysostom commemorates the second coming of Christ together with events of the past—the cross, the grave, the Resurrection, and the Ascension. In the Eucharistic presence of the Lord, His forthcoming advent is already realized, and "time" is being transcended. Similarly, the entire tradition of Eastern monastic spirituality is based upon the premiss that *now,* in this life, Christians can experience the vision of God and the reality of "deification."

This strong emphasis on an "already realized" eschatology explains why Byzantine Christianity lacks a sense of direct responsibility for history as such. Or if it acknowledges such a responsibility, it tends to rely on such institutions as history itself may produce, particularly the Christian empire. The Christian state, and the Church as such, assume a responsibility for society as a whole, receiving guidance and inspiration from the Christian Gospel. But the dynamic "movement," which characterizes the "new humanity in Christ," and for which the Church is responsible, is not the movement of history but a mystical growth in God, known to the saints alone. The movement certainly occurs in the midst of history and may, to a degree, influence the historical process, but it does not belong to history essentially because it anticipates the end of history. It is, indeed, the "movement" of *nature,* and of the natural man, but *natural* humanity—humanity as originally conceived and created by God—presupposes communion with God, freedom from the world, lordship over creation and over history. It must, therefore, be independent from what the world understands as history.

Existing in history, the Church expects the second coming of Christ in power as the visible triumph of God in the world and the final transfiguration of the whole of creation. Man, as center and lord of creation, will then be restored to his original stature, which has been corrupted by sin and death; this restoration will imply the "resurrection of the flesh," because man is not only a "soul," but a psychosomatic whole, necessarily incomplete without his body. Finally, the second coming will also be a judgment, because the criterion of all righteousness—Christ Himself—will be present not "in faith" only, appealing for man's free response, but in full evidence and power.

These three essential meanings of the *parousia*—cosmic transfiguration, resurrection, and judgment—are not subjects of detailed speculation by Byzantine theologians; yet they stand at the very center of Byzantine liturgical experience.

The feast of the Transfiguration (August 6), one of the highlights of the Byzantine liturgical year, celebrates, in the "Taboric light," the eschatological anticipation of Christ's coming: "Today on Tabor in the manifestation of Thy Light, O Word, Thou unaltered Light from the Light of the unbegotten Father, we have seen the Father as Light and the Spirit as Light, guiding with light the whole of creation." [14] On Easter night, the eschatological dimension of the Resurrection is proclaimed repeatedly: "O Christ, the Passover great and most holy! O Wisdom, Word, and Power of God! Grant that we may more perfectly partake of Thee in the day which knows no night in Thy Kingdom." [15] The *parousia,* as judgment, appears frequently in Byzantine hymnology, particularly in the Lenten cycle. In this cycle, too, active love for one's neighbor is often emphasized by the hymnographers: "Having learned the commandments of the Lord, let us follow this polity: let us feed the hungry, let us give drink to the thirsty, let us clothe the naked, let us welcome strangers, let us visit the sick and the prisoners, so that the One who comes to judge the whole earth may tell us: come, O blessed of my Father, inherit the Kingdom which is prepared for you." [16]

The only subject on which Byzantine theologians were forced into more systematic and theoretical debates on eschatology was the medieval controversy on purgatory. The Latin doctrine that divine justice requires retribution for all sins committed, and that, whenever "satisfaction" could not be offered before death, justice would be accomplished through the temporary "fire of purgatory," was included in the Profession of Faith signed by emperor Michael VIII Paleologus and accepted at the Council of Lyons (1274).[17] The short-lived union of Lyons did not provoke much debate on the subject in Byzantium, but the question arose again in Florence and was debated for several weeks; the final decree on union, which Mark of Ephesus refused to sign, included a long definition on purgatory.[18]

The debate between Greeks and Latins, in which Mark was the main Greek spokesman, showed a radical difference of perspective. While the Latins took for granted their legalistic approach to divine justice—which, according to them, requires a retribution for every sinful act—the Greeks interpreted sin less in terms of the acts committed than in terms of a moral and spiritual disease which was to be healed by divine forbearance and love. The Latins also emphasized the idea of an individual judgment by God of each soul, a judgment which distributes the souls into three categories: the just, the wicked, and those in a middle category—who need to be "purified" by fire. The Greeks, meanwhile, without denying a particular judgment after death or agreeing on the existence of the three categories, maintained that neither the just nor the wicked will attain their *final* state of either bliss or condemnation before the last day. Both sides agreed that prayers for the departed are necessary and helpful, but Mark of Ephesus insisted that even the just need them; he referred, in particular, to the Eucharistic canon of Chrysostom's liturgy, which offers the "bloodless sacrifice" for "patriarchs, prophets, apostles, and every righteous spirit made perfect in faith," and even for the Virgin Mary herself. Obviously he understood the state of the blessed, not as a legal and static justification, but as a never-ending ascent, into which the entire communion of saints—the Church in heaven and the Church on earth—has been initiated in Christ.[19] In the communion of the Body of Christ, all members of the Church, living or dead, are interdependent and united by ties of love and mutual concern; thus, the prayers of the Church on earth and the intercession of the saints in heaven can effectively help all sinners, i.e., all men, to get closer to God. This communion of saints, however, is still in expectation of the ultimate fulfillment of the *parousia* and of the general resurrection, when a decisive, though mysterious, landmark will be reached for each individual destiny.

The Florentine debate on purgatory seems to have been largely improvised on the spot, and both sides used arguments from Scripture and tradition which do not always sound convincing. Still, the difference in the fundamental attitude toward salvation in Christ is easily discernible. Legalism, which applied to individual human destiny the Anselmian doctrine of "satisfaction," is the *ratio theologica* of the Latin doctrine on purgatory. For Mark of Ephesus, however, salvation is communion and "deification." On his way to God, the Christian does not stand alone; he is a member of Christ's Body. He can achieve this communion even now, before his death as well as afterward, and, in any case, he needs the prayer of the whole Body, at least until the end of time when Christ will be "all in all." Of course, such an understanding of salvation through communion excludes any legalistic view of the Church's pastoral and sacramental powers over either the living or the dead (the East will never have a doctrine of "indulgences"), or any precise description of the state of the departed souls before the general resurrection.

Except for the negative act of rejecting the Latin doctrine of purgatory implied in the canonization of Mark of Ephesus and in later doctrinal statements of Orthodox theologians, the Orthodox Church never entered the road of seeking exact doctrinal statements on the "beyond." A variety of popular beliefs, often sanctioned in hagiographic literature, exists in practice, but the Church itself, and especially its liturgy, limits itself to a fundamentally Christocentric eschatology: "You have died, and your life is hid with Christ in God. When Christ who is our life appears, then you also will appear with him in glory" (Col 3:3–4). Until that ultimate "appearance," the Body of Christ, held together with the bond of the Spirit, includes both the living and the dead, as symbolized on the paten during the liturgy, where particles of bread, commemorating those who repose in Christ and those who are still parts of the visible Christian community on earth, are all united in a single Eucharistic communion. For indeed, death, through the Resurrection, has lost its power over those who are "in Him." It cannot separate them either from God or from each other. This communion in Christ, indestructible by death, makes possible and necessary the continuous intercession of all the members of the Body for each other. Prayer *for* the departed, as well as intercession *by* the departed saints for the living, express a single and indivisible "communion of saints."

The ultimate fulfillment of humanity's destiny will consist, however, in a last judgment. The condemnation of Origenism by the Fifth Council (553) implies the very explicit rejection of the doctrine of *apocatastasis,* i.e., the idea that the whole of creation and all of humanity will ultimately be "restored" to their original state of bliss. Obviously, the basic reason why *apocatastasis* was deemed incompatible with the Christian understanding of man's ultimate destiny is that it implies a radical curtailment of human *freedom.* If Maximus the Confessor is right in defining freedom, or self-determination, as the very sign of the image of God in man,[20] it is obvious that this freedom is ultimate and that man cannot be forced into a union with God, even in virtue of such philosophical necessity as God's "goodness." At the ultimate confrontation with the Logos, on the last day, man will still have the option of rejecting Him and thus will go to "hell."

Man's freedom is not destroyed even by physical death; thus, there is the possibility of continuous change and mutual intercession. But it is precisely this freedom which implies responsibility and, therefore, the ultimate test of the last judgment, when—alone in the entire cosmic system, which will then experience its final transfiguration—man will still have the privilege of facing the eternal consequence of either his "yes" or his "no" to God.

NOTES

1. Henri Gregoire, *Byzantium: An Introduction to East Roman Civilization,* edd. N. H. Baynes and H. St. L. B. Moss (London: Oxford University Press, 1948), pp. 134–145.
2. *Mystical Theology,* p. 7.
3. See Chapter 11.
4. *Novella VI, Corpus juris civilis,* ed. Rudolfus Schoell (Berlin, 1928), III, 35–36. The basic study on the subject is Francis Dvornik, *Early Christian and Byzantine Political Philosophy: Origins and Background* (Washington: Dumbarton Oaks Studies [IX], 1966), in two volumes and containing exhaustive bibliography. See also J. Meyendorff, "Justinian, the Empire, and the Church," *Dumbarton Oaks Papers* 22 (1968), 45–60.
5. *The Festal Menaion,* p. 254.

6. *Acta patriarchatus Constantinopolitani*, edd. F. Miklosich and I. Müller (Vienna, 1862), pp. 188–192.

7. *Title 2, Jus graeco-romanum*, ed. Zepos (Athens, 1931), II, 241.

8. On this last aspect of Byzantine ideology, see D. J. Constantelos, *Byzantine Philanthropy and Social Welfare* (New Brunswick: Rutgers University Press, 1968).

9. See J. Meyendorff, "Byzantine Views of Islam," *Dumbarton Oaks Papers* 18 (1964), 115–132; and A. Khoury, *Les théologiens byzantins et l'Islam* (Louvain: Nauwelaerts, 1969).

10. For the history of these missions and their cultural consequences, see Francis Dvornik, *Byzantine Missions Among the Slavs* (New Brunswick: Rutgers University Press, 1970); and D. Obolensky, *The Byzantine Commonwealth: Eastern Europe, 500–1453* (London: Weidenfeld and Nicolson, 1971).

11. Trans. by Roman Jakobson in "St. Constantine's Prologue to the Gospel," *St. Vladimir's Seminary Quarterly* 7 (1963), No. 1, 17–18.

12. *Vita Constantini* 16, 7–8 in *Constantinus et Methodius Thessalonicenses. Fontes, Radovi Staroslovenskog Instituta* 4 (1960), 131.

13. On Stephen, see particularly George Fedotov, *The Russian Religious Mind* (Cambridge: Harvard University Press, 1966), II, 230–245.

14. *Exaposteilarion, The Festal Menaion*, p. 495.

15. Paschal canon, ode 9, *Pentekostarion*; this *troparion* is also used as a post-communion prayer in the Eucharistic liturgy.

16. Meat-fare Sunday, vespers, *Lite, Triodion*.

17. *Enchiridion Symbolorum*, ed. H. Denziger, No. 464.

18. *Ibid.*, No. 693.

19. See the two treatises of Mark on purgatory in L. Petit, "Documents relatifs au Concile de Florence. I: La question du Purgatoire à Ferrare," *Patrologia Orientalis* 15 (1920), No. 1, 39–60, 108–151. A Russian translation of these texts is given in Amvrosy, *Sviatoy Mark Efessky i Florentiiskaia Unia* (Jordanville, New York, 1963), 58–73, 118–150. J. Gill, *The Council of Florence* (Cambridge: Harvard University Press, 1959), pp. 119–125, offers a brief account of the controversy.

20. "Since man was created according to the image of the blessed and supra-essential deity, and since, on the other hand, the divine nature is free, it is obvious that man is free by nature, being the image of the deity" (*Disp. cum Pyrrho*; PG 91:304c).

CONCLUSION

Antinomies

To ATTEMPT A DESCRIPTION of Byzantine theology, using simultaneously the historical and the systematic methods, implies the obvious risk of provoking the dissatisfaction of both historians and systematic theologians. To the present author, however, the risk was worth taking because he fundamentally agrees with a recent statement by Jaroslav Pelikan about Christian doctrine: "Tradition without history has homogenized all the stages of development into one statically defined truth; history without tradition has produced a historicism that relativizes the development of Christian doctrine in such a way as to make the distinction between authentic growth and cancerous aberration seem completely arbitrary." [1]

In the case of Byzantine theology, Pelikan's methodological statement is particularly relevant, because of the internal characteristics of the Eastern Christian experience itself. Ever concerned with the truth and in principle excluding any relativism, Byzantine thought has avoided both conceptual rationalism and authoritarianism, which have always been components of "traditionalism" in the West. In its very conservatism, Byzantine theology relies on internal and experiential criteria, which, like life itself, imply change, but also fidelity to the past. Neither change nor conservatism, however, is an end in itself. A tradition which is reduced to the preservation of concepts and formulae excludes the progress of life and is insensible to the Christian virtue of hope: in their paschal hymns, and at each Eucharistic liturgy, the Byzantines never stopped hoping for "a more perfect communion" with God in the Kingdom to come. But this very progress for them was possible only if one would avoid the pitfalls of "novelties," inconsistent with the "apostolic" foundations of the faith, given once and for all in Scripture and the original *kerygma* of the eyewitnesses of Jesus.

Byzantine theology was neither systematically anti-conceptual nor anti-hierarchical. The conversion of Greek intellectuals to Christianity meant, after Origen, that philosophical concepts and the arguments of logic would be extensively used in expressing and developing Christian truths. Yet the sacramental understanding of the church implied the hierarchical structure, a continuity in the teaching office, and, finally, conciliar authority. Neither concepts nor hierarchy, however, were conceived as *sources* of the Christian experience itself, but only as means to safeguard it, to channel it in accordance with the original rule of faith, and to express it in such a way as to give it life and relevance in the changing and developing processes of history.

In order to preserve its identity, Byzantine theological thought had to experience several major crises: the recurring temptation of adopting the Hellenistic world-view of Origenism; the conflict with the Roman papacy on the nature of Church authority; the doctrinal controversy over the "energies" of God in the fourteenth century, and several others. Inevitably, the controversies led to formal attitudes and definitions, partly determined by polemics. A certain "freezing" of concepts and formulae was the inevitable result. However, even in their formal definitions, Byzantine theologians have generally succeeded in preserving a sense of inadequacy between the formulae and the content of the faith: the most obvious and positive truths of Christian experience were thus expressed in antinomies, i.e., in propositions which, in formal logic, are mutually exclusive without being irrational.

Thus, the Byzantine concerns on the doctrine of God, derived from the polemics of the Cappadocian Fathers against Eunomius and crystallized in fourteenth-century Palamism, affirms in God a real distinction between the Persons and the common "essence," just as it maintains that the same God is both transcendent (in the "essence") and immanent (in the "energies"). Similarly, while essentially unchangeable, God is affirmed as *becoming* the creator of the world in time through His "energy"; but since "energy" is uncreated—i.e., *is* God—changeability is seen as a real attribute of the divine. The philosophical antinomies required in this theology reflect a personalistic and dynamic understanding of God, a positive experience of the God of the Bible, inexpressible in Greek philosophical terms.

On the level of anthropology one finds equally antinomic concepts in Byzantine Christian thought. Man, while certainly a creature and, as such, *external* to God, is defined, in his very *nature,* as being fully himself only when he is in *communion* with God. This communion is not a static contemplation of God's "essence" (as Origen thought), but an eternal progress into the inexhaustible riches of divine life. This is precisely the reason why the doctrine of *theōsis*—i.e., the process through which, in Christ, man recovers his original relation to God and grows into God "from glory to glory"—is the central theme of Byzantine theology and of the Eastern Christian experience itself. Here again static concepts like "human nature" (i.e., that which is properly human) and "divine grace" (that which comes from God) can be used only antinomically: grace is seen as a part of nature itself.

Also, if one understands the ultimate destiny of man, and therefore also his "salvation," in terms of *theōsis*, or "deification," rather than as a justification from sin and guilt, the Church will necessarily be viewed primarily as a communion of free sons of God and only secondarily as an institution endowed with authority to govern and to judge. Again, it is impossible to define Byzantine ecclesiology without at least a partial recourse to antinomy, particularly in describing the relation between the "institution" and the "event," between the "Levite" and the "prophet," between the "hierarch" and the "saint." In the absence of any legal or infallible criterion of authority, with frequently reiterated statements that authority is not a source of truth but is itself dependent upon the faith of those who are called to exercise it, it was inevitable that the monastic community, as well as individual spiritual personalities, would occasionally compete with bishops and councils as spokesmen of the authentic tradition and as witnesses to the truth. In fact, this polarity was an integral part of the Church's life and did not necessarily lead to conflict: it only reflected the mystery of human freedom which was seen as the very gift of the Holy Spirit, bestowed upon every Christian at his baptism and making him a fully responsible member of Christ's Body. However, even then, the sacramental understanding of ecclesiology served as a guarantee against individualism and arbitrariness: responsibility could only be understood in this ecclesial and sacramental framework, which, in turn, was impossible without an identifiable ministry of bishops and priests.

These are the basic intuitions which determined the social and individual ethics of the Byzantine Christians. Actually, one can hardly find, in the entire religious literature of Byzantium, any systematic treatment of Christian ethics, or behavior, but rather innumerable examples of moral exegesis of Scripture, and ascetical treatises on prayer and spirituality. This implies that Byzantine ethics were eminently "theological ethics." The basic affirmation that *every* man, whether Christian or not, is created according to the image of God and therefore called to divine communion and "deification," was of course recognized, but no attempt was ever made to build "secular" ethics for man "in general." Byzantines were ready to find seeds of the divine Logos in the precepts of ancient philosophers or even occasionally among Moslem Arabs, but these were always understood as dynamically oriented toward the only true incarnated Logos, and were all to be fulfilled in Him.

The religious inheritance of Christian Byzantium has frequently defined itself in opposition to the West, and indeed its entire concept of God–man relationships is different from one which prevailed in post-Augustinian Latin Christianity. Contemporary man—searching for a God who would be not only transcendent but also existentially experienced and immanently present in man, and the gradual discovery of man as essentially open, developing, and growing—should be more receptive to the basic positions of Byzantine thought, which may then acquire an astonishingly contemporary relevance.

NOTE

1. Jaroslav Pelikan, *The Christian Tradition: A History of the Development of Doctrine* I. *The Emergence of the Catholic Tradition* (*100–600*) (Chicago: University of Chicago Press, 1971), p. 9.

Bibliography

This Bibliography provides the possibility of further reading. It indicates the books and articles which were used and which contain further bibliographical information. An almost exhaustive bibliography—until 1959—can be found in Hans-Georg Beck's *Kirche und theologische Literatur im byzantinischen Reich.*

Not all the books and articles referred to in the notes are included here. The general books, under Chapter 1, are not repeated, although these items are obviously relevant to the subject-matter of other chapters as well.

CHAPTER 1

Beck, Hans-Georg. *Kirche und theologische Literatur im byzantinischen Reich.* Munich: Beck, 1959.
> The most comprehensive reference book on Byzantine ecclesiastical thought and institutions; bibliographically very complete, except for literature in Slavic languages.

Gouillard, Jean. "Le Synodikon de l'Orthodoxie. Edition et commentaire," *Travaux et mémoires* II. Paris: Centre français d'études byzantines, 1967.
> A fundamental source for the history of theology in Byzantium after 843. The commentary touches on all major theological issues.

Jugie, Martin. *Theologia dogmatica Christianorum orientalium ab Ecclesia Catholica dissidentium.* I–V. Paris: Letouzey, 1926–1935.
> Monumental survey including many direct quotations and precious bibliographical references; criticizes Byzantine authors from a narrowly scholastic approach to theological problems.

Pelikan, Jaroslav. *The Christian Tradition: A History of the Development of Doctrine.* I. *The Emergence of the Catholic Tradition.* II. *The Spirit of Eastern Christendom (600–1700).* Chicago: University of Chicago Press, 1971, 1974.
> The most comprehensive history of ideas in the Christian East. Very perceptive and challenging.

Florovsky, Georges. *Vizantiyskie Ottsy V–VIII vekov* (The Byzantine Fathers of the Fifth to the Eighth Centuries). Paris: YMCA Press, 1933.
> Full of brilliant insights.

Lossky, Vladimir. *The Mystical Theology of the Eastern Church.* London: Clarke, 1957.
> Has become something of a classic for the understanding of God–man relations in the Christian East.

———. *Vision of God.* London: Faith Press, 1963.
> An historical treatment of the subject in Greek patristic thought.

CHAPTER 2

Grillmeier, Aloys. *Christ in Christian Tradition from the Apostolic Age to Chalcedon (451)*. New York: Sheed & Ward, 1965.
Meyendorff, John. *Christ in Eastern Christian Thought*. Washington: Corpus, 1969 (a translation of *Le Christ dans la théologie byzantine*. Paris: Cerf, 1969).
   A general review of Christological concepts after the Council of Chalcedon.
Elert, Werner. *Der Ausgang der altkirchlichen Christologie: eine Untersuchung über Theodor von Pharan und seine Zeit als Einführung in die alte Dogmengeschichte*. Berlin: Lutherisches Verlagshaus, 1957.
   Important for the understanding of Theopaschism and the so-called neo-Chalcedonian developments in the sixth century.
Rozemond, Keetie. *La Christologie de Saint Jean Damascène*. Ettal: Buchkunstverlag, 1959.
   A summary of Greek patristic Christology.
Moeller, Charles. "Le Chalcédonisme et le néo-chalcédonisme en orient de 451 à la fin du VIᵉ siècle," *Das Konzil von Chalkedon: Geschichte und Gegenwart* edd. A. Grillmeier and H. Bacht. 3 vols. Würzburg: Echter, 1951–1952. I, 637–720.
   An important article interpreting the mainstream of Byzantine Christology as a "Monophysite" betrayal of Chalcedon.
Oksiuk, M. "Teopaskhitskie spory" (The Controversies on Theopaschism), Kiev, Dukhovnaia Akademia, *Trudy* 1 (1913), 529–559.
   A counterpart to Moeller's view.

CHAPTER 3

Ostrogorsky, George. *Studien zur Geschichte des byzantinischen Bilderstreites*. Breslau, 1929; repr. Amsterdam: Hakkert, 1964.
   Basic historical study.
Grabar, André. *L'iconoclasme byzantin: dossier archéologique*. Paris, 1957.
   Important for the understanding of the cult of images, especially as it developed in the seventh century; the archaeological evidence gathered by the author provides numerous insights for the theologian.
Florovsky, Georges. "Origen, Eusebius and the Iconoclastic Controversy," *Church History* 19 (1950), 77–96.
   Establishes the Origenistic roots of some of the iconoclastic theology.
Alexander, P. J. *The Patriarch Nicephorus*. Oxford, 1958.
   The monograph on a major Orthodox theologian.
Kitzinger, Ernst. "The Cult of Images in the Age Before Iconoclasm," *Dumbarton Oaks Papers* 8 (1954), 83–150.
Anastos, Milton V. "The Argument for Iconoclasm as Presented by the Iconoclastic Council of 754," *Late Classical and Medieval Studies in Honor of A. M. Friend, Jr.* Princeton, 1955. Pp. 177–188.
Meyendorff, J. *Christ in Eastern Christian Thought*. Washington: Corpus, 1969. Pp. 132–148, 203–207.
   The link with Christology; the "describability" of God.

CHAPTER 4

Dobroklonsky, A. *Prepodobny Theodor, igumen Studiisky* (St. Theodore, Abbot of Studios). 2 vols. Odessa, 1913-1914.
  Basic monograph on the great monastic reformer.
Grossu, Nicholai. *Prepodobnyi Theodor Studit* (St. Theodore the Studite). Kiev, 1907.
Gardner, A. *Theodore of Studium, His Life and Times.* London, 1905.
Hergenröther, J. *Photius, Patriarch von Konstantinopel: sein Leben, seine Schriften und das griechische Schisma.* 3 vols. Regensburg, 1867-1869; repr. Darmstadt: Wissenschaftliche Buchgesellschaft, 1960.
  Still the only systematic survey of Photius' theology; very critical of the Greek "schismatics."
Dvornik, F. *The Photian Schism: History and Legend.* Cambridge: Harvard University Press, 1948.
  Historical rehabilitation of Photius by a Roman Catholic scholar.
Zervos, Chr. *Un philosophe néoplatonicien du XIᵉ siècle: Michel Psellos.* Paris, 1920.
Joannou, P. *Christliche Metaphysik in Byzanz. I. Die Illuminationslehre des Michael Psellos und Joannes Italos.* Studia Patristica et Byzantina, 3. Heft. Ettal, 1956.
Stephanou, P. E. *Jean Italos, philosophe et humaniste.* Orientalia Christiana Analecta, 134. Rome, 1949.
Uspensky, Theodor. *Ocherki po istorii Vizantiiskoy obrazovannosti* (Notes on the History of Byzantine Learning). St. Petersburg, 1891.
  Especially important for intellectual developments in the eleventh century.

CHAPTER 5

Dörries, Hermann. *Symeon von Mesopotamien: die Überlieferung der messalianischen "Makarios" Schriften.* Texte u. Untersuchungen, 55, 1. Leipzig, 1941.
  The most authoritative presentation of the "Messalian" theory about the writings of pseudo-Macarius.
Meyendorff, J. "Messalianism or Anti-Messalianism?—A Fresh Look at the 'Macarian' Problem," *Kyriakon: Festschrift Johannes Quasten* edd. P. Granfield and J. A. Jungmann. Münster: Aschendorff, 1970. II, 585-590.
  A survey of arguments against the "Messalian" theory.
Guillaumont, Antoine. *Les "Kephalaia Gnostica" d'Evagre le Pontique et l'histoire de l'Origénisme chez les Grecs et les Syriens.* Paris: du Seuil, 1962.
  The definitive study of Evagrius and his tradition.
Zarin, S. *Asketizm po pravoslavno-khristianskomu ucheniu* (Asceticism in Orthodox Christian Teaching). St. Petersburg, 1907.
  A major collection of patristic texts and their interpretation.
Minin, P. "Glavnyia napravleniia drevne-tserkovnoi mistiki" (The Main Orientations of Mysticism in the Ancient Church), *Bogoslovsky Vestnik* (December 1911) 823-838; (May 1913) 151-172; (June 1914) 304-326; (September 1914) 42-68.
  A short but very perceptive study of the "Evagrian" and "Macarian" traditions.

Völker, W. *Maximus Confessor als Meister des geistlichen Lebens.* Wiesbaden: Steiner, 1965.
  Maximus and the tradition of Origen and Gregory of Nyssa.
Meyendorff, J. *A Study of Gregory Palamas.* London: Faith Press, 1962.
  The original French edition (*Introduction à l'étude de Grégoire Palamas.* Paris: du Seuil, 1959) contains a full analysis of the published and unpublished writings of Palamas.

CHAPTER 6

Nikodim Milash, Bishop of Dalmatia. *Das Kirchenrecht der morgenländischen Kirche.* 2nd ed. Mostar, 1905.
  A classical textbook; there are translations of the Serbian original into several East European languages.
Pavlov, A. *Kurs tserkovnago prava* (A Course in Ecclesiastical Law). Moscow, 1902.
  One of the most comprehensive reference books.
Herman, E. "The Secular Church," *Cambridge Medieval History* IV, 2. Cambridge, 1967.
  A survey of Byzantine ecclesiastical organization.
Žužek, I. *Kormchaya Kniga: Studies on the Chief Code of the Russian Canon Law.* Orientalia Christiana Analecta. Rome, 1964.
  Contains much information on the history of Byzantine canon law, and a rich bibliography on the subject.
Kotsonis, H. *Provlēmata ekklēsiastikēs oikonomias* (Problems of Ecclesistical "Economy"). Athens, 1957.
  Deals with *oikonomia* mainly in reference to relations with non-Orthodox Christians; the author was Archbishop of Athens from 1967 to 1973.

CHAPTER 7

Meyendorff, J. *Orthodoxy and Catholicity.* New York: Sheed & Ward, 1965.
  Several essays on the ecclesiological background of the schism.
Sherrard, Philip. *The Greek East and the Latin West.* London: Oxford University Press, 1959.
  Discusses the theological nature of the schism, insisting particularly on the *Filioque* issue.
Jugie, Martin. *De processione Spiritus Sancti ex fontibus revelationis et secundum Orientales dissidentes.* Rome, 1936.
  The *Filioque* issue seen from a strict Thomistic viewpoint.
Dvornik, F. *The Legend of the Apostle Andrew and the Idea of Apostolicity in Byzantium.* Cambridge: Harvard University Press, 1958.
  Historical facts involving Eastern and Western ecclesiology gathered and brilliantly commented upon by a Roman Catholic historian.
Meyendorff, J.; Afanassieff, N.; Schmemann, A.; Koulomzine, N. *The Primacy of Peter in the Orthodox Church.* London: Faith Press, 1963.
  Contains an analysis of the Byzantine tradition on the succession of Peter.
Denzler, G. "Lignes fondamentales de l'ecclésiologie dans l'empire byzantin," *Concilium* 67 (1971), 57–68.

CHAPTER 8

Papadopoulos, S. G. *Hellēnikai metaphraseis thōmistikōn ergōn. Philothōmistai kai antithōmistai en Byzantiō* (Greek Translations of Thomistic Writings. Thomists and Anti-Thomists in Byzantium). Athens, 1967.
> Important critical survey.

Candal, E. *Nilus Cabasilas et theologia S. Thomae de processione Spiritus Sancti.* Studi e testi, 116. Vatican City, 1945.
> Examines the major source book of the Greek delegation at Florence.

Mercati, Giovanni. *Notizie di Procoro e Demetrio Cidone, Manuele Caleca e Theodoro Meliteniota ed altri appunti per la storia della teologia e della letteratura bizantina del secolo XIV.* Studi e testi, 56. Vatican City, 1931.
> The Byzantine Thomists in the fourteenth century.

Gill, J. *The Council of Florence.* Cambridge: Harvard University Press, 1959.
> The standard history of the council by a Roman Catholic historian.

Laurent, Venance, ed. *Les "Mémoires" du grand ecclésiarque de l'église de Constantinople, Sylvestre Syropoulos sur le Concile de Florence (1438-1439).* Publications de l'institut français d'études byzantines. Paris: Centre National de la Recherche Scientifique, 1971.
> First translation into a modern language of a basic source on the Council of Florence. The introduction and commentary contain a mine of information on theological issues.

Möhler, L. *Kardinal Bessarion als Theologe, Humanist und Staatsman.* I–III. Paderborn: Schöningh, 1923-1942.
> The monograph on Bessarion, with original sources.

Turner, C. J. G. "George-Gennadius Scholarius and the Union of Florence," *Journal of Theological Studies* 18 (1967), 83-103.
> The waverings of one of the greatest among the Greek theologians.

Ševčenko, I. "Intellectual Repercussions of the Council of Florence," *Church History* 24 (1955), 291-323.
> Important for the understanding of Byzantine mentality.

Amvrosy (Pogodin), Archimandrite. *Sviatoy Mark Efessky i Florentiiskaia Unia* (St. Mark of Ephesus and the Union of Florence). Jordanville, N.Y., 1963.

Mamone, K. "Markos ho Eugenikos. Bios kai ergon," *Theologia* 25 (1954), 377-404, 521-575.

Lot-Borodine, Myrrha. *Nicolas Cabasilas.* Paris: l'Orante, 1958.
> Cabasilas' theology of deification.

CHAPTER 9

The Festal Menaion. Mother Mary and K. Ware, trans. London: Faber & Faber, 1969.
> The Byzantine hymns for the major feasts, translated; useful introduction, explaining the structure of Byzantine offices.

Hapgood, I. F. *Service Book of the Holy Orthodox Catholic Apostolic Church.* New York: Association Press, 1922.
> Contains the English text of the liturgies and sacraments.

Brightman, F. E. *Liturgies Eastern and Western.* I: *Eastern Liturgies.* Oxford, 1896.
> A classic.

Wellesz, E. *A History of Byzantine Music and Hymnography.* 2nd ed. Oxford, 1961.
> Basic.

Schmemann, A. *Introduction to Liturgical Theology.* London: Faith Press, 1966.
> The development of Byzantine liturgical concepts, viewed by a contemporary Orthodox theologian.

Dalmais, H. I. *The Eastern Liturgies.* New York: Hawthorn, 1960.
> Useful introduction.

CHAPTER 10

Florovsky, Georges. "Tvar' i tvarnost'" (Creatures and Creatureliness), *Pravoslavnaia Mysl'* 1 (1927), 176–212.
> Comprehensive study of the patristic doctrine of creation; partial translation in "The Idea of Creation in Christian Philosophy," *Eastern Church Quarterly,* 8 (1949).

Epifanovich, S. L. *Prepodobnyi Maksim Ispovednik i vizantiiskoe bogoslovie* (Maximus the Confessor and Byzantine Theology). Kiev, 1915.
> Still the most comprehensive book on Maximus, relating his system to Byzantine theology as a whole; important for the understanding of Maximus' doctrine of the *logoi.*

Balthasar, H. Urs von. *Kosmische Liturgie. Das Weltbild Maximus des Bekenners.* 2nd ed. Einsiedeln, 1961.
> A pioneering study on Maximus; to be consulted in conjunction with Thunberg's *Microcosm and Mediator* (cited under Chapter 11).

Roques, René. *L'Univers dionysien. Structure hiérarchique du monde selon le pseudo-Denys.* Paris: Aubier, 1954.
> The most important book on the "hierarchies."

Meyendorff, J. "Note sur l'influence dionysienne en Orient," *Studia Patristica* II (Papers presented to the Second International Conference on Patristic Studies. Oxford, 1955). Texte u. Untersuchungen 64 (1957), 547–553.
> The limited influence of the Dionysian angelology among the Byzantines.

CHAPTER 11

Gross, Jules. *La divinisation du chrétien d'après les pères grecs: contribution historique à la doctrine de grâce.* Paris: Gabalda, 1938.

Lot-Borodine, Myrrha. *La déification de l'homme.* Paris: Cerf, 1969.
> Reprint of an important series of articles published in the *Revue d'Histoire des Religions,* 1932–1933.

Popov, I. V. "Ideia obozhenia v drevne-vostochnoi tserkvi" (The Idea of Deification in the Ancient Eastern Church), *Voprosy filosofii i psikhologii* 97 (1906), 165–213.
> Very important article.

Thunberg, Lars. *Microcosm and Mediator: The Theological Anthropology of Maximus the Confessor.* Lund: Gleerup, 1965.
> The most recent comprehensive study on Maximus, whose anthropological views were most influential among Byzantine theologians.

Bibliography 235

Burghardt, W. J. *The Image of God in Man According to Cyril of Alexandria.* Washington: Catholic University Press, 1957.
   The anthropological basis for the doctrine of deification.

Gaïth, J. *La conception de la liberté chez Grégoire de Nysse.* Paris: Vrin, 1953.
   Very important for the grace–freedom problem.

Ladner, G. B. "The Philosophical Anthropology of St. Gregory of Nyssa," *Dumbarton Oaks Papers* 12 (1958), 58–94.

Leys, R. *L'image de Dieu chez Saint Grégoire de Nysse.* Brussels and Paris, 1951.

Kiprian (Kern), Archimandrite. *Antropologia sv. Grigoria Palamy* (The Anthropology of St. Gregory Palamas). Paris: YMCA Press, 1950.
   Contains an original review of the entire patristic tradition.

Romanides, J. S. *To propatorikon hamartēma* (The Ancestral Sin). Athens, 1957.
   The contrast between the Greek and the Augustinian view on original sin.

Meyendorff, J. "*Eph ho* chez Cyrille d'Alexandrie et Theodoret," *Studia Patristica* IV. Texte u. Untersuchungen 79 (1961), 157–161.
   The crucial passage of Rm 5:12 as understood by the Greek Fathers.

Lossky, V. *On the Image and Likeness.* New York: St. Vladimir's Seminary Press, 1974.
   A very suggestive collection of studies on patristic anthropology, soteriology, and other theological subjects.

CHAPTER 12

Gordillo, M. *Mariologia Orientalis.* Orientalia Christiana Analecta, 141 (1954).
   Attempt to reconcile the Eastern and Western traditions by taking Western presuppositions for granted.

Mascall, E. L. ed. *The Mother of God: A Symposium.* London: Dacre Press, 1949.
   Important articles by V. Lossky and G. Florovsky.

Draguet, René. *Julien d'Halicarnasse et la controverse avec Sévère d'Antioche sur l'incorruptibilité du corps du Christ.* Louvain, 1924.
   The debate on Julianist "Aphthartodocetism" is important for the understanding of the anthropological dimension of Christology.

Dubarle, A. M. "L'ignorance du Christ chez S. Cyrille d'Alexandrie," *Ephemerides Theologicae Lovanienses* 16 (1939).
   On "ignorance by economy," a classical concept in Byzantine Christology.

CHAPTER 13

Galtier, Paul. *Le Saint-Esprit en nous d'après les pères grecs.* Analecta Gregoriana 37 (1946).
   Useful analytical survey of patristic texts.

Krivochéine, Basile. "The Most Enthusiastic Zealot: St. Symeon the New Theologian as Abbot and Spiritual Instructor," *Ostkirchliche Studien* 4 (1955), 108–128.
   The life in the Holy Spirit experienced by the great Byzantine mystic; one of several suggestive articles on Symeon by the editor of his writings.

Afanassieff, Nicolas. *Tserkov Dukha Sviatogo* (The Church of the Holy Spirit). Paris: YMCA Press, 1970.
   A study in ecclesiology by a modern Orthodox theologian, containing numerous insights for the understanding of Byzantine thought.

CHAPTER 14

Prestige, G. L. *God in Patristic Thought.* London: SPCK, 1952.
  The best introduction in English.
Régnon, Th. de. *Etudes de théologie positive sur la Sainte Trinité.* Troisième
  série, II (Théories grecques des processions divines). Paris, 1893.
  Basic work on the difference of the Greek and Augustinian models of Trinitarian
  thought.
Popov, I. V. *Lichnost' i uchenie blazhennago Avgustina* (Personality and Doc-
  trine of the Blessed Augustine). I. Sergiev Posad, 1917.
  A very important critical analysis of Augustine by a specialist in Eastern patristic
  thought; the second volume never appeared. Important for the understanding of
  Eastern approach to the Augustinian models of thought.
"Concerning the Holy Spirit," *Eastern Church Quarterly* 7 (1948); also published separately.
  A symposium on the *Filioque* question by Orthodox and Roman Catholic theologians.

CHAPTER 15

Raes, A. *Introductio in liturgiam orientalem.* Rome, 1947.
King, A. A. *The Rites of Eastern Christendom.* 2nd ed. Rome: Catholic Book
  Agency, 1947.
Schmemann, A. *Sacraments and Orthodoxy.* New York: Herder, 1966.
Cabasilas, Nicholas. *The Life in Christ.* Trans. C. J. de Catanzaro; Intro. B. Bob-
  rinskoy. New York: St. Vladimir's Seminary Press, 1974.
  First English translation of the famous *De vita in Christo.*

CHAPTER 16

Salaville, A. *An Introduction in the Study of Eastern Liturgies.* London: Sands,
  1938.
Bornaert, R. *Les commentaires byzantins de la divine liturgie du VIIe au XVe
  siècle.* Archives de L'Orient Chrétien 9. Paris: Institut français d'études byzantines, 1966.
  Text, French translation, and commentary. Important for the evolution of liturgical
  symbolism.
Kiprian (Kern), Archimandrite. *Evkharistiia* (The Eucharist). Paris: YMCA, 1947.
  Especially important for the question of the epiclesis.

CHAPTER 17

Michel, A. *Die Kaisermacht in der Ostkirche (843–1204).* Darmstadt: Gentner,
  1959.
  Important, but must be used together with Dvornik's *Political Philosophy.*
Alès, A. d'. "La question du purgatoire au concile de Florence en 1438," *Grego-
  rianum* 3 (1922), 9–50.
Jugie, M. "La question du purgatoire au concile de Ferrare–Florence," *Echos
  d'Orient* 20 (1929), 322–332.

Sergii (Stragorodsky). *Pravoslavnoe uchenie o spasenii* (The Orthodox Doctrine of Salvation). Sergiev Posad, 1894.
An authoritative patristic study, containing numerous references to Byzantine theologians, by a subsequent patriarch of Moscow; criticizes the "legalism" of Western thought.

ADDENDA

CHAPTER 1

Podskalsky, Gerhard. *Theologie und Philosophie in Byzanz: der Streit um die theologische Methodik in der spätbyzantinischen Geistesgeschichte (14./15. Jh.), seine systematischen Grundlagen und seine historische Entwicklung.* Munich: Beck, 1977.

CHAPTER 3

Schönborn, Christoph von. *L'icône du Christ: fondements théologiques élaborés entre le Ier et le IIe Concile de Nicée (325–787).* Fribourg, 1976.

CHAPTER 7

Haugh, Richard. *Photius and the Carolingians: The Trinitarian Controversy.* Belmont, Massachusetts: Nordland, 1975.
Meijer, Johann. *A Successful Council of Union: A Theological Analysis of the Photian Synod of 879–880.* Thessaloniki, 1975.

CHAPTER 14

Radovich, A. *To Mystērion tēs hagias Triados kato ton hagion Gregorion Palaman* (The Mystery of the Holy Trinity According to Saint Gregory Palamas). Thessaloniki, 1973.
Meyendorff, John. "The Holy Trinity in Palamite Theology," *Trinitarian Theology East and West.* Brookline, Massachusetts: Holy Cross Press, 1977. Pp. 25–43.

Index

DATE DUE